KU-794-964

DISPOSED OF
BY LIBRARY
HOUSE OF LORDS

COMMITTEE GOVERNANCE IN THE EUROPEAN UNION

MANCHESTER
UNIVERSITY PRESS

SERIES EDITOR *Emil Kirchner*

already published

Theory and reform in the European Union
DIMITRIS N. CHRYSSOCHOOU, MICHAEL J. TSINISIZELIS,
KOSTAS IFANTIS, STELIOS STAVRIDIS

Greece in a changing Europe
Between European integration and Balkan disintegration?
KEVIN FEATHERSTONE AND KOSTAS IFANTIS (EDS)

Turkey's relations with a changing Europe
MELTEM MÜFTÜLER-BAC

Righting wrongs in Eastern Europe
ISTVAN POGANY

Two tiers or two speeds?
The European security order and the enlargement of the European Union and Nato
JAMES SPERLING (ED.)

Recasting the European order
Security architectures and economic cooperation
JAMES SPERLING and EMIL KIRCHNER

forthcoming titles

The new Eastern Question
ANDREW COTTEY

The new Germany and migration in Europe
BARBARA MARSHALL

Democratic theory and the European Union
ALBERT WEALE

Thomas Christiansen & Emil Kirchner
EDITORS

COMMITTEE GOVERNANCE IN THE EUROPEAN UNION

MANCHESTER UNIVERSITY PRESS
Manchester and New York

distributed exclusively in the USA by St. Martin's Press

Copyright © Manchester University Press 2000

While copyright in the volume as a whole is vested in Manchester University Press, copyright in individual chapters belongs to their respective authors, and no chapter may be reproduced wholly or in part without the express permission in writing of both author and publisher

Published by Manchester University Press
Oxford Road, Manchester M13 9NR, UK
and Room 400, 175 Fifth Avenue, New York, NY 10010, USA
http.//www.man.ac.uk/mup

Distributed exclusively in the USA by
St. Martin's Press, Inc., 175 Fifth Avenue, New York, NY 10010, USA

Distributed exclusively in Canada by
UBC Press, University of British Columbia, 2029 West Mall,
Vancouver, BC, Canada V6T 1Z2

British Library Cataloguing-in-Publication Data
A catalogue record for this book is available from the British Library

Library of Congress Cataloging-in-Publication Data applied for

ISBN 0 7190 5552 0 *hardback*

First published 2000

07 06 05 04 03 02 01 00   10 9 8 7 6 5 4 3 2 1

Typeset in Minion with Lithos
by Northern Phototypesetting Co Ltd, Bolton
Printed in Great Britain
by Bookcraft (Bath) Ltd, Midsomer Norton

CONTENTS

FIGURES AND TABLES

Figures

Tables

Contributors

Thomas Christiansen is Jean Monnet Lecturer of European Studies in the Department of International Relations at the University of Wales, Aberystwyth

Rhys Dogan is Jean Monnet Scholar and Principal Lecturer in European Public Policy, Department of Politics, University of Plymouth, Devon

Andreas Faludi is Professor of Spatial Planning at the University of Nijmegen

Brendan Flynn is Lecturer in the Department for Political Science and Sociology at the National University of Ireland, Galway

Simon Hix is Lecturer in EU Politics and Policy in the Department of Government at the London School of Economics and Political Science

Emil Kirchner is Jean Monnet Professor of European Political Integration in the Department of Government at the University of Essex

Andreas Maurer is Lecturer in the Department of Political Science at the University of Cologne

Jürgen Mittag is Lecturer in the Department of Political Science at the University of Cologne

Anna Murphy is Jean Monnet Fellow at the Robert Schuman Centre, European University Institute, Florence

Ben Tonra is Lecturer of European Studies in the Department of International Relations at the University of Wales, Aberystwyth

Amy Verdun is Assistant Professor of European Studies in the Department of Political Science at the University of Victoria, BC

Bas Waterhout is Junior Research Fellow in the Catholic University of Nijmegen

Albert Weale is Professor of Government and Head of the Department at the University of Essex

Wolfgang Wessels is Jean Monnet Professor of European Integration Studies in the Department of Political Science at the University of Cologne

Wil Zonneveld is Research Associate at the Amsterdam Study Centre for the Metropolitan Environment and at the Research Institute OTB at Delft

${A}$CKNOWLEDGEMENTS

We gratefully acknowledge financial assistance from the British Council in Germany, which was instrumental in launching the research project leading to this publication. The grant facilitated a workshop that was held at the Zentrum für Europäische Rechtspolitik (ZERP) at the University of Bremen in April 1997. It provided an opportunity for authors to present their ideas on the role of committees and to generate a debate among academic experts and EU policy-makers. ZERP also contributed to the cost of this workshop, and we are indebted to Professor Dr Christian Joerges and to Dr Armin Höland for their intellectual input and organisational support. At the University of Essex, Ozgur Unal assisted with the editorial work, and we are grateful for the efficiency with which she completed the task. Finally, our thanks also go to Nicola Viinikka at Manchester University Press, whose support and encouragement helped to keep us on track and complete the manuscript (almost) on schedule.

Abbreviations

AME	Amsterdam Study Centre for the Metropolitan Environment
BSE	Bovine Spongiform Encephalopathy
CCP	Common Commercial Policy
CELEX	database of European law
CFSP	Common Foreign and Security Policy
CGCB	Committee of Governors of Central Banks
CoR	Committee of the Regions
COREPER	Committee of Permanent Representatives
COREU	network for telex-communication among EU Foreign Ministries
CSD	Committee on Spatial Development
DATAR	French Planning Agency
DG	Directorate General
EC	European Community
ECB	European Central Bank
ECJ	European Court of Justice
ECOFIN	Council of Economics and Finance Ministers
ECPR	European Consortium for Political Research
ECSC	European Coal and Steel Community
ECU	European Currency Unit
EDC	European Documentation Centre
EEB	European Environment Bureau
EEC	European Economic Community
EFC	Economic and Financial Committee
EIPA	European Institute of Public Administration
EMAS	Eco-management and Audit Scheme
EMI	European Monetary Institute
EMS	European Monetary System
EMU	Economic and Monetary Union
ENDS	Environmental Data Services
EP	European Parliament
EPA	US Environmental Protection Agency
EPC	European Political Co-operation
EPU	European Political Union
ERDF	European Regional Development Fund
ERM	Exchange Rate Mechanism
ESC	Economic and Social Committee
ESDP	European Spatial Development Perspective
ESPON	European Spatial Planning Observatory Network
EU	European Union
EURATOM	European Atomic Energy Community

GAC	General Affairs Council
GATT	General Agreement on Tariffs and Trade
GM(O)	Genetically Modified (Organism)
IGC	Intergovernmental Conference
IR	International Relations
ISA	International Studies Association
JHA	Justice and Home Affairs
MC	Monetary Committee
MECU	million ECUs
MEP	Member of the European Parliament
MERCOSUR	free trade area in Latin America
NES	New European Space
NGO	Non-governmental Organisation
OECD	Organisation for Economic Co-operation and Development
PHARE	EU aid programme for central and eastern Europe
PoCo	Political Committee
PSD	Pesticides Safety Directorate
QMV	Qualified Majority Vote
SEA	Single European Act
STOA	Science and Technology Office of Assessment
TEU	Treaty on European Union
WTO	World Trade Organisation
ZERP	Zentrum für Europäische Rechtspolitik

Thomas Christiansen & Emil Kirchner

Introduction

In the study of European integration, committees constitute a curious paradox: on the one hand, committees seem to be omnipresent at every stage in the decision-making process of the Union. On the other hand, committees have hardly been at the forefront of academic research, and their role in the integration process has – until recently – not been approached comprehensively. The obscure nature of much of what has become known as 'comitology' appears to have deflected any sustained effort at concentrating research efforts at this phenomenon, even though observers have been in agreement about its expansive nature and potential significance.

More recently, though, comitology has received greater attention. There is recognition that – though elusive and secretive – committees play too important a role in the integration process to be ignored. Perhaps the BSE crisis, in particular, with the limelight it placed on the Standing Committee of Veterinary Experts, has acted as a watershed in demonstrating the political importance of 'technical' committees. But also in other policy areas as well as in institutional analysis comitology has left its mark and consequently become the object of greater academic scrutiny (Pedler and Schäfer, 1996; Joerges and Neyer, 1997a; Joerges and Neyer, 1997b; Buitendijk and Van Schendelen, 1995; Bradley, 1997; Vos, 1997; Dogan, 1997; Wessels, 1998).

Together with the higher profile of committees in the 1990s, there has also been greater controversy. Especially normative issues have been frequently discussed: while some view committees in the EU as evidence for 're-nationalisation' of Community policies by the Member States, others regard comitology as an outgrowth of the 'technocratic' and 'unaccountable' Brussels machinery. Even this brief reference to one of the main debates about comitology in the 1990s shows that committees can be different things to different people, and they frequently are. The nature of the beast is difficult to define, in part because committees are so diverse in their powers, membership and procedures.

But beyond topicality and controversy, the role of committees is interesting and deserving of greater attention, because it has been such an essential and, in our view, inherent feature of the integration process. On the one hand, committee governance in the European Community/European Union (EC/EU) has a long history that it is worth revisiting. On the other hand, there is a close relationship between the key characteristics of committee governance and the nature of the integration process at large. Here we will first address the underlying institutional and conceptual issues, before turning to the historical evolution of committees in the European Union.

Committee governance and European integration

The pivotal role of committees in the EU's institutional structure is best understood by examining, in the first instance, the development of EU governance more generally. The key institutions of the Union – Commission, Parliament, Court and Council of Ministers – are well known. The legislative process which links them together involves, first, proposals by the Commission, second, co-operation or, depending on the subject-matter, co-decision between Council and Parliament, third, supervision of implementation by the Commission and fourth, adjudication of disputes by the European Court of Justice (ECJ). Policy-making across multiple institutions has engendered a particular kind of governance in the European Union. The different institutions all have their respective powers – and one might discuss the balance of powers between them – but no single institution is ultimately 'sovereign' or in control of the process. Essentially, power is shared between institutions, with a requirement to work together in order to achieve results.

The Commission, for example, has the authority to influence the course of integration through the timing, content and subject-matter of its legislative proposals. Particular periods in the Union's history, especially during the presidency of Jacques Delors, demonstrated the power the Commission can derive from its elevated role in agenda-setting and policy-framing. But we have also seen, at the end of Jacques Santer's reign, how the Commission is vulnerable in the face of opposition from Parliament and the national governments. And yet, while Parliament and Council share the decisional power in the Union, neither institution can actually be seen as 'ruling' the EU. Apart from the checks which one imposes on the other, their freedom to operate is limited, on the one hand, by the proposal put forward by the Commission and, on the other hand, by judicial control from the European Court of Justice. The Court, with its powers to interpret and reform – even to 'constitutionalise' – the treaties has played a powerful role in the European construction.

But while each institution has particular powers and responsibilities, it is only through co-operation between them that the EU can take decisions and make effective policies. During the 1980s, as the volume and the significance of

EU decision-making increased, the need for ongoing co-operation became evident through the growing number of 'inter-institutional agreements'. These became necessary as key decisions, in particular about the Union's budget, implied lengthy negotiations. Instead of returning every year to the conference table, Commission, Parliament and Council sought longer-terms solutions on these issues.

In the course of repeated treaty reforms, the policy process and the ensuing institutional dynamics have become ever more intricate. As a consequence, there has been a growing need for each institution to co-ordinate its actions with the others on a permanent basis. In the Commission, each Commissioner's *cabinet* includes a member responsible for relations with the Parliament, and the regular meetings of this group of advisers has become an important feature of policy co-ordination within the Commission. In addition, one ommissioner has designated responsibility for relations with the European Parliament.

While relations between EU institutions have become increasingly interdependent, there has also been growing need for co-operation between the national and the EU level. One reason for this development has been the increasing significance of implementation of EU policies. Since, in the course of establishing the Single Market, much of the European economy has been re-regulated at the European level, greater responsibility has fallen on Member States' administrations to implement European legislation. This has had dynamic effects at both the national and the European level: within Member States, national (and often also regional and local) authorities have had to familiarise themselves with the European regulation that they have had to implement. On the European level, the decision-making institutions, and the Commission in particular, had to design regulations for decentralised application, anticipating and overcoming difficulties in ensuring uniform implementation and compliance.

The result from these ripple effects of developments in the 1980s and 1990s has been the need for effective and continuous communication between policy-makers and scientific experts from the Member States, Commission and Council officials and Members of the European Parliament. The absence of any institution or set of interests having hierarchical control over the decision-making process is one of the reasons why committees have become such an important part of the EU's institutional machinery. The greater need for inter-institutional and inter-level co-ordination and co-operation requires fora in which policy ideas can be deliberated, policy-proposals discussed, and policy implementation monitored.

The mushrooming number of committees that have been set up for these purposes is explained by the increasingly technical and specialised nature of EU policy-making. As, during the 1980s and 1990s, EU regulation has moved into ever wider areas of economic and social life, a greater number of specialists from both national administrations and EU institutions has had to become involved in policy-making. Within Member States, EU policies have made greater demands on a wider range of political actors: more economic sectors, social groups and territorial levels have become affected by EU policies, and have subsequently been included in the making and implementation of EU policies. On the European level, the gradual extension of competences of the EU has not been matched by a comparable expansion of the EU's civil service, and as a result Commission and Parliament have come to rely more on advice from national policy-makers and independent scientific experts. One key meeting place for this greatly expanded community of policy-makers have been committees.

Committees and the EU policy-process

Recognising the important contribution that committees have made to the integration process from the start, we believe that a thorough and in-depth study of committees is now overdue. To that effect, we first need to address the characteristics of 'governance through committees' and deal with some of the definitional problems of this subject. In this respect it is important to point out at the start that the perspective adopted here includes both 'comitology committees' and those in a wider category of either treaty-based or ad hoc committees.

'Comitology' has become the accepted term for a narrowly defined set of committees within the EU's institutional structure. Essentially, a distinction is made here between advisory, management and regulatory committees. Made up of national officials, these comitology committees are charged with overseeing the work of the Commission in implementing EU policies (Docksey and Williams, 1994). In most areas, implementation is principally a competence of the Member States – the Commission's role under the Treaties is merely to ensure that Member States implement EU policies correctly. Frequently – and increasingly so – Member States have delegated implementory powers to the Commission. As this practice has expanded, Member States have sought to maintain overall control over the nature of implementation, and comitology has become the instrument of this control.

Based on practice originating from the 1960s and on legislation from the 1980s, comitology has now become a pervasive presence in the EU system. Rhys Dogan's statistics in Chapter 2 demonstrate the growth of comitology since the late 1980s. The growing need for co-ordinated implementation at the European level, the expansion of EU competences and the increasing functional specialisation of European administration have combined to create a dense network of intergovernmental bodies whose activity remains largely hidden from the public eye. Depending on the type of comitology – advisory, management or regulatory – the powers of these committees differ, but as a feature within the EU system they have achieved an authoritative presence.

As the power of comitology has become apparent, the struggle over their control has intensified. As the number of comitology committees increased significantly as part of the '1992' programme, Delors began a discursive offensive against a phenomenon which he regarded as an instance of 're-nationalisation' of European integration. At around the same time, the European Parliament started to consider ways of exercising greater control over the growth and responsibility of comitology – a quest charted in Chapter 3 by Simon Hix. Given the debates about this issue during the 1990s, it is fair to say that comitology has become a key arena in the development of inter-institutional relations in the EU.

Much of the discussion in this volume and elsewhere is concerned with these comitology structures. Given their formal place in the EU decision-making framework, they deserve indeed special attention. But beyond narrowly defined comitology structures, committee governance is a wider phenomenon in the EU. In attempting a typology of committees, one might start with the legal status of committees. Among the committees based on primary law one might distinguish between those which are formal institutions of the Union – such as the Economic and Social Committee (ESC) and the Committee of the Regions (CoR) – and the advisory and regulatory committees set up in specific policy areas – for example the K3 committee, the Monetary Committee in the area of monetary policy, and the Art. 113 Committee in the area of external trade. The latter two are discussed in Chapters 7 and 5 by Amy Verdun and Anna Murphy, respectively. Paradoxically, the elevated status that some committees have in the institutional framework of the Union does not at all match their actual decision-making powers. Both the ESC and the CoR, for example, have merely advisory functions (Morgan, 1991; Christiansen, 1996) whereas comitology committees may have extensive regulatory powers.

Another powerful committee is that of Member States' permanent representatives, known by its French acronym as COREPER. It is a committee that encapsulates the linkage which intergovernmental committees provide between national interest representation and EU policy-making. COREPER's members have a dual role (and possibly a split identity): on the one hand, the are the 'servants of their country', working as Member State ambassadors to implement a given European policy; on the other hand, they are part of the institutional structure of the Council of Ministers, and as such have a firm place within the decision-making structure in Brussels. The example of COREPER shows that multi-level governance in the EU crucially depends on committees to provide the hinge between the various levels.

COREPER is simply the tip of an iceberg. There is a second committee, made up of deputy representatives, which is known as COREPER I, whereas the meetings of the permanent representatives have come to be called COREPER II. The two committees have, over time, developed a way of dividing up their workload of preparing and managing the agenda of the various Councils of Ministers (Hayes-Renshaw and Wallace, 1996). Underneath them is a whole host of Council 'working groups', bringing together case officers from the Council Secretariat and Member State officials from ministries and the national representations (Beyers and Dierckx, 1998). In a sense, the committee character of these working groups is stronger than that of COREPER, which could be seen as a permanent part of the Council. The detailed expertise brought together in Council working groups, the shifting membership of individual committees and the affiliation of most of their members with institutions in the national capitals rather than in Brussels all combine to give them the particular identity of committee governance.

With the extension of Community competences and the growing number of sector-specific Councils, the number of working groups has increased exponentially – the result is a formidable parallel bureaucracy alongside the European Commission. But rather than being charged with developing policy proposals – the job of the Commission – or overseeing implementation – as is the role of comitology – Council working groups are in the business of managing the inter-governmental response to any policy proposal from the Commission.

In recent years, with the growing influence of the European Parliament, its members have also developed new strategies for inter-institutional bargaining. The Maastricht Treaty introduced a new committee charged specifically with the negotiations between Council and EP in cases where – under the new co-decision procedure – no immediate agreement on legislation could be reached. This new conciliation committee is composed of an equal number of Members of the European Parliamant (MEPs) and Member State representatives who will seek to find a compromise in those cases where the normal co-decision mechanism failed to bring a legislative proposal to a successful conclusion (Miller, 1995). The Conciliation Committee is thus the horizontal equivalent to COREPER – the hinge not between the national and the European level, but between the two legislative institutions on the Union.

We have already distinguished between the roles committees play in the implementation and decision-making phases of the EU's policy process. But committees are also a dominant feature in the process of agenda-setting that precedes the formal process of decision-making. Especially in areas that are not heavily regulated by Community law, committees have developed significant political power in shaping the agenda and ultimately the nature of EU policies in these areas. In such cases, the first role of committees is simply the co-ordination of national policies which have some bearing on EU policies, but which themselves fall not into the sphere of competence of the Union. We find that over time the significance of these committees increases, in particular as 'high politics' issues join more technical matters in the ambit of committee governance. By the time at which their role in the EU systems is formalised, these committees are the hub to opinion-formation and agenda-setting in the EU. As a matter of course, their impact on the final shape of policy will be very powerful indeed. The Monetary Committee and the Political Committee, bringing together key decision-makers from the national political systems in the field of monetary policy and foreign policy, respectively, are prime examples of this evolution. The latter is the subject of Ben Tonra's chapter (8).

In these cases we witness the role of committee governance in areas of policy-making, which are anything but 'low politics'. The Europeanisation of monetary policy and of foreign policy – charted by the significance of these committees – not only has major effects on the EU's relationship with its citizens and with the outside world. These processes also contribute significantly, though in different ways, to the development of a distinct political identity for the EU. Yet another contribution to that process is the development of the European Union as a political space. The economic and infra-structural foundations for this are being laid by the European Spatial Development Initiative, and the role of the Committee on Spatial Development in setting the agenda in this policy-area is the subject of Andreas Faludi's, Wil Zonneveld's and Bas Waterhout's chapter (6).

It will be apparent from this brief overview that committees constitute a widespread and important aspect of European governance. We have identified committee(-like) structures in all stages of the policy-process: agenda-setting, decision-making and implementation (see Figure 1). A further distinction can be drawn with respect to the membership of committees: in the decision-making stage; in particular, committees may be constituted predominantly of Member State representatives or of EU representatives. Finally, committees differ with respect to their powers: while some have a purely consultative or deliberative role, others are actively involved in decision-making. As we have seen, this is a distinction which is particularly important with respect to comitology committees.

The commonality of all these types of committees is that they bring together a diverse group of policy-makers under consensual, rather than adversarial, conditions. Unlike the more 'political' and potentially more divisive institutions

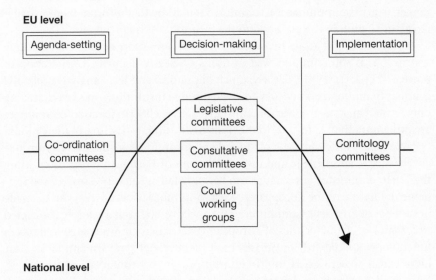

Figure 1 Committees in the EU policy process

– the Parliament, the Council and, increasingly, the college of Commissioners –
committees are characterised by the search for consensus rather than the resort
to voting or other majoritarian solutions. This is not to say that there will not be
differences of opinion or power politics within individual committees – indeed,
anything else would be come as a surprise. But even the presence of internal
divisions within committees will not normally detract from the search for solutions which are inclusive of the diversity of views, and which will be regarded as
legitimate by all participants. That is also why committees can be seen to provide the bridge between different institutions or levels of government.

We therefore take a broad view of the 'committee' phenomenon in the EU.
It is an approach guided by the recognition of underlying principles rather than
other, more formal, criteria. This inclusive definition seeks to establish that
'committees' are not just as an institutional feature within the European Union,
but an important contribution to its particular mode of governance. We call this
'committee governance', in recognition of the wider significance that it has for
the integration process.

Committees and supranational governance

In this introduction there is little space to offer more than a brief survey and a
tentative typology of the kind of committees which are at the heart of European
administration. As indicated, the individual chapters of this book deal with
cases of the various types of committees in more details. The picture that
emerges demonstrates the pervasiveness of committee governance in the EU's
administrative system. Committees are everywhere, and their responsibility
ranges from the minutiae of technical regulation to the fundamental issues
facing the Union in the present and the future.

Still, one might argue that committees are some sort of aberration from a
system that is sometimes viewed in terms of clearly delineated 'separation of
powers' (Lenaerts, 1991). Clearly, much of political and legal analysis of the EU
assumes that interaction occurs between discrete institutions and levels, leaving
only limited analytical space for committees. In such a perspective, committees
are little more than 'add-ons' to the basic institutional structure of the Union.

We take a different view of the role of committees in the EU. Committee
governance is an intrinsic and essential feature of European integration. More
than that, committee governance can be regarded as the expression of the fundamental nature of the European project. A number of arguments can be made
in support of this view. Committee governance can be seen as closely connected
to certain key characteristics of European governance: committee governance is
functionally specialised, comprises multiple levels of government, lacks clear
hierarchical structures, is multi-cultural, process-based and path-dependent.
We consider these to be defining characteristics of the European system, which
is why they deserved more detailed attention.

First, committee governance can be seen as the institutionalisation of collective rule which has been the hallmark of European integration – committees are an expression of, and a catalyst for, decision-making based on consensus and consultation in EU decision-making. Much more than occasional partisan votes in the Council of Ministers or in the European Parliament, committee governance sums up the need for agreement in the EU system. Crucially, collective decision-making in the EU coincides with the respect for the diversity of views. Committees will normally include a multiplicity of views and positions, not only in terms of Member State origin, but also with respect to the variety of vantage points and opinions that may be present within a particular policy community. But as we will see, there are important and interesting divergences from this – monetary policy is such a case in point.

This leads to the second point of interest: committees will usually consist of a diverse membership, something that not only implies different institutional and national positions on policy-proposals, but also a plurality of administrative cultures. Given the enormous volume of comitology – the substantial amounts of time which is spent by national officials in EU committees – this feeds into a two way process of cultural learning: on the one hand, committees provide the central institutions with an ability to observe at first hand, and from close range, the cultural diversity in European public administration; on the other hand, committees permit national officials to familiarise themselves with the nature of the EU's administrative system.

Cultural diversity confronts officials with different social norms, which might lead to conflicts when societal values are translated into policy. Risk regulation is such an area where disagreements could be expected. But on a more immediate level, there are substantial differences between Member States when it comes to the characteristics of public administration. Administrative secrecy or openness is one such issue that pitches Sweden against France, to name but two extreme examples. Bargaining-styles or policy styles in public administration, where the co-operative German mode might clash with the more conflictual British attitude, are another example.

Third, committees are creatures of another inherent characteristic of European integration: functional specialisation. Functional integration, or the 'Monnet method', has long been seen as the hallmark of this integration process. Just as attempts at explicitly 'political' integration – from the EDC/EPC plans in the 1950s to the 1984 Draft Treaty of European Union – have failed, so an indirect path based on functional integration – including the Single Market and the Euro – has been comparatively successful. Functionalism – David Mitrany's theory of integration – regarded the growth of political institutions as a response to the dictum 'form follows function' (Mitrany, 1943), and over the years many observers have seen European integration in this light (e.g. Pentland, 1973). This perspective may include committee governance, which in many instances can be regarded as the institutional 'form' necessitated by functional integration.

Fourth, an important issue is the lack of transparency in the EU system. Neither the EU as a whole, nor committee governance in particular, has been very transparent in their operation and decision-making. Despite succeeding in moving the integration process along, the 'Monnet method' has caused some tensions, namely between technocracy and democratic accountability (Wallace and Smith, 1995). Committees exemplify – and indeed personify – the reliance on technical expertise as well as the lack of transparency. Much more so than Commission or even Council, it is committee governance that actually makes it difficult for the public to scrutinise EU decision-making effectively. Their members are usually delegated to committees because of their intimate knowledge of one discrete aspect of EU legislation. With frequent meetings over often long periods of time, it is not unreasonable to expect a communal spirit to grow among the policy-makers involved – but it will be an expert community, not necessarily a political community. Improvements are on the way, but what remain in the public eye are technology and a perceived lack of responsiveness to citizen concerns.

Fifth, in recent years, an increasing number of authors has viewed the EU system along the lines of 'multi-level governance'- a system of decision-making in which various territorial levels form intermeshing network and require mutual co-operation in order to carry out joint tasks (Marks *et al.*, 1996). Two levels – the Member State and the European level are sufficient to make the argument, but often the examples for multi-level governance have been drawn from regional or structural policy. And it is with respect to this policy area that – under the heading of 'partnership' – intensive inter-level co-operation has been necessary.

In this multi-level governance system, an element of co-operation between tiers of government is essential and commonplace; committees provide the main linkage between policy-makers on these levels. Whereas decision-making occurs mainly on the EU level, with consultation and institutionalised representation from the affected regions and states, the agenda-setting and implementation aspect of European governance is regularly entrusted to advisory and management committees which contain members from the lower territorial tiers of government. In other words, multi-level governance and committee governance are closely linked.

A related question takes the multi-level governance issue one step further: the relationship between committees and 'non-hierarchical' or 'post-sovereign' governance, which is how some authors see the EU develop (Schmitter, 1992; MacCormick, 1993). One answer here lies in the fact that committees are not circumscribed by finality – the presence of an authority to which appeals can be made and whose rulings are final. Decisions, once agreed upon, may well become re-negotiable in the course of the integration process. As has been mentioned earlier, what is missing is clear hierarchy – the committees discussed here are not an exclusive part of the Commission, the Council or the Parliament. Instead, they are usually chaired by the Commission or by the Presidency, with neither being able to develop a leadership role in this respect.

These then are the parameters of non-hierarchical committee governance: the growth of a specific system of public administration in the EU which is at the same time closely connected to national and European institutions, but hardly subordinated to any of them. The result is not chaos, but a continuous process of bargaining, re-negotiation and re-constitution with a resultant mix of uncertainty and continuity.

Finally, we need to recognise that European integration is a process – an apparently obvious point, but one which has numerous effects on the EU's institutional structure. EU institutions – as creatures of this process – are subject to continuous change. In many instances, an element of tension is built into the system (e.g. Christiansen, 1997). The continuity and rigidity of institutional structures confronts the frequent need for adaptation, expansion or other changes required by changes in the climate of integration. Committees are also subject to the vagaries of frequent change and constant evolution that is part of the integration process. In fact, one can go one step further and see committees as the escape valve helping to reconcile these tensions.

The 'stop-and-go' mentality of the integration process at large is replicated at the committee level by the mixture between the stability of long-lasting committees and the uncertain and undefined evolution of others. The chapters by Faludi *et al.* (6) and by Ben Tonra (8) testify to this tension in the nature of committee governance: newly established committees, or those whose functions have been re-defined substantially, find the early years in their evolution difficult to negotiate. Yet, once established, their position is fairly entrenched, and further development usually extends their powers – a picture mirroring the path-dependency that has been identified for the integration process more generally.

Committee governance is less rigid than formal institutions, and therefore better able to adapt to changing circumstances. New committees are easily established if the integration process so requires, and the way in which their numbers have swelled in recent years is proof that this is in fact how Member States have viewed them. At the same time, committees are more stable than policy networks. Their work is based on explicit rules, for example on voting, and once they start operating, committees will develop their own *acquis*, which then provides the trajectory for further decision-making.

This list of parallels between committee governance and the wider integration process demonstrates that committees can be seen as a microcosm of European integration, containing the same qualities and pathologies. An in-depth study of committees is therefore useful not simply because of the importance of committee governance in the European Union, but also because of the linkages between the micro- and the macro-levels of integration. In this sense, committee governance can be seen as a microcosm also when it comes to the process-based nature of European integration.

Committee governance in comparative perspective

Committees may be pervasive in the system of supranational governance, but they are also generic features of modern political life. Above we alluded already to distinctions between various domestic political cultures when it comes to the accommodation of committee governance in the EU. In Chapter 3, Simon Hix takes this perspective one step further by comparing comitology to the US and German experience in delegating legislative oversight over executive action to committees. While there are obvious differences between national political systems, it is fair to say that many exhibit their own forms of committee governance.

Just as in the EU, the operation of such systems can be observed at any level. In systems where the consociational nature of politics leads to entrenched or even institutionalised coalition government, the outcome is little more than committee governance writ large. Contemporary Switzerland is one case in point: here a continuous coalition brings together the main political parties – the resultant collective rule of elites in bodies with limited transparency has been identified as 'government by committee' (Baylis, 1988). Italian politics before 1992 had similar characteristics.

But also in federal systems, where policy-makers from federal and from state levels need to co-ordinate policy as a matter of course, committees often perform vital functions. Thus, in the German federal system – where joint decision-making within a culture of co-operative federalism is the norm – hundreds of 'inter-ministerial committees' are charged with policy co-ordination. Such committees link various centres of decision-making horizontally (among the constituent states) and vertically (between state level and federal level), and their significance within Germany's public administration should not be underestimated (Hesse, 1987).

The US federal system relies less than the German one on joint decision-making, but the need for co-ordination between state and federal level remains. The committee charged with providing this linkage, the Advisory Commission on Intergovernmental Affairs, has had a purely consultative function, though other bodies have developed in its shadow (Kincaid, 1995). While German federalism requires extensive administrative co-operation, the American model places greater responsibility on legislative structures, as Hix explores in greater detail in Chapter 3.

But even in unitary states, the devolution of legislative or administrative competence requires inter-level co-operation, and committees inevitably take their place in the system. In the United Kingdom, for example, the proposal for a 'Joint Ministerial Committee' has been part of the process of establishing devolved parliaments in Scotland, Wales and Northern Ireland – an innovation in the British political system which has been likened to 'a gearbox which becomes central to the whole system', comparable to similar bodies in the Australian or German federal systems (*Economist*, 24 Oct. 1998).

The British system also provides numerous examples of the way in which committees or commissions are used in order to bridge the partisan divide in politics. One prominent case from the 1990s, the Nolan Committee, was set up in order to police parliamentary standards. What started out as a commission of inquiry later turned into a permanent institution that is now part and parcel of the British parliamentary system – an evolution which mirrors the nature of committee governance elsewhere. The Blair government also introduced a cabinet committee on constitutional reform comprising both Labour and Liberal Democrat MPs, even though the latter are not part of the government. Here we witness the way in which committees are used to facilitate political contacts – and to establish political practices – which are impossible within the framework of formal institutions.

The incidence of committee governance in a political system like that of the UK might be regarded as remarkable, given that it is generally seen as a paradigm case of divisive politics. One would expect committees to flourish in corporatist, consociational or federal-type systems, and the significance of committee governance in Germany, Switzerland or Austria bears this out. But the British case – like the French with its abundance of committees at the local, regional and national level – demonstrates that committees have their place in any democratic system of government. Whenever formal institutions appear as too rigid, the time frame of governmental activity is uncertain, political divisions need to be overcome and issues of technical complexity are at stake, committees provide the recurrent response.

As it happens, in the EU all these conditions are ever present. Issues of great technical complexity need to be regulated in a manner which respects diverging political interests and priorities, and the constant evolution of the system as a whole requires a flexible and open-ended institutional response. Committee governance is the way in which this circle is squared in the European Union. Looking at the functions performed by committees in national systems, and the functions that need to be performed in the EU system, it comes as little surprise that committee governance has developed into such an essential aspect of the integration process.

The genesis of committee governance

The development of EC Advisory or Consultative Committees, until the late 1970s, reflected the overall expansion of EC competencies and policy areas, though a few were created right from the start in the Treaties of the European Coal and Steel Community (ECSC) in 1952 and of the European Economic Community (EEC) in 1958 (ESC, 1980). Of the main ones coinciding with the start of the ECSC and EEC respectively were the ECSC Consultative Committee, the Economic and Social Committee, the Advisory Committee on Transport and the Article 113 Committee. Besides a number of committees that were created in the mid- to late 1950s in the coal and steel sector, the initial burst of committees, around thirty, occurred between 1962 and 1972 and accompanied the introduction of EU policies primarily in the sectors of agriculture, customs union, and social policy. For the majority of these committees their main task was either involvement in the implementation of established policies or participation in the framing of new policies, Among the latter was the Committee of Governors of the Central Banks (CGCB), and the Political Committee. Some committees were also engaged in the operation of structural funds.

Proposals for EU programmes in social, consumer and environmental policy, announced at the Paris Summit of 1972, resulted in the formation of a second wave of around eight committees between 1973 and 1977, relating essentially to matters in these two fields: committees were established to discuss Community actions in the areas of social problems in agriculture and in sea fishing; safety, hygiene and health protection at work; working conditions in coal and steel industries; and consumers' advice. The mid-1970s also saw the creation of another organisation form – independent agencies – which provided an alternative to committee governance: the European Centre for the Development of Vocational Training, and the European Foundation for the Improvement of Living and Working Conditions were established in 1975 in Berlin and in Dublin, respectively. The Administrative Boards of these two bodies comprise representatives of national governments, European Commission, employers' associations and trade unions, and have a managerial role. Unlike Advisory Committees, they do not deliver Opinions on proposed EU legislation, but have a novel power of co-decision making with the European Commission, in their annual programmes of work. But decentralised agencies remained a marginal presence in the Community system, until a burst of new agencies in the mid-1990s (Kreher, 1997).

The number of committees, on the other hand, continued to grow more steadily. The mid-1970s also saw the arrival of Advisory Committees on the harmonisation of legislation, e.g. the Advisory Committees on Foodstuffs, the Advisory Veterinary Committee, and the Advisory Committees on the Training of Doctors, Dentists and Nurses. Such committees were further examples – beyond the Economic and Social Committee – of institutionalised access for organised interests. In cases where the Commission was responsible for appointing members to Advisory Committees, involving two-thirds of committees until 1978, representatives were usually drawn from European umbrella organisations or professional organisations.

By contrast, in instances where the Council of Ministers was the appointing authority, the Advisory Committee generally consisted fully or in part of national organisations (who were usually, however, also members of European umbrella or professional organisations). With few exceptions these committees related to social policy in the broad sense. Among these were the Standing Committee on Employment, and the Advisory Committees on Social Security for Migrant Workers, the Free Movement of Workers and the European Social Fund. Other Advisory Committees falling under the jurisdiction of the Council of Ministers involved the Economic and Social Committee, the Advisory Committee on Transport, the Tripartite Conference, the ECSC Consultative Committee and the Article 113 Committee. Council appointed Advisory Committees consisted of combinations of representatives of national governments/administrations, employee's organisations, employers' organisations, agricultural associations, and consumers' organisations.

The most common form of Advisory Committees had representatives from the two sides of industry either alone or in combinations with other interest groups, such as agriculture, commerce, consumers, but did not include representatives from national governments or administrations. Among the Committees with a distinct feature were the Committees for the Training of Doctors and Nurses, in which Experts featured prominently: representing the (practising) professions concerned; university medical faculties; and relevant authorities in the Member States. Both Committees provided advice on the mutual recognition of diplomas for the professions.

Although one could speak of a high degree of institutionalised participation of interest groups through a large number of EU Advisory Committees (Kirchner and Schwaiger, 1981: 9), this did not mean that every interest group was represented on all these committees or that all interest groups were equally represented on individual ones. Nor did it say anything about the relative importance of some of these Advisory Committees or conferences. Certainly, the Economic and Social Committee, the Tripartite Conference on Employment and the Standing Committee on Employment performed more important roles, were composed of more high calibre representatives and had, if not direct Council of Ministers involvement, access to this institution. In contrast the majority of Advisory Committees only had access to the Commission. In the following, a brief description of the role and importance of the before mentioned three Committees will be provided.

The Standing Committee on Employment was created at the time of the first Tripartite Conference in 1970, in order to address employment issues. Member are not appointed in a personal capacity; the parties designate their representative at their own discretion, either for a specific period or depending on the subject to be dealt with, for specific meetings. In the terms of reference for this Committee stress was laid on the continuous dialogue, joint action and consultation between the Council and/or representatives of the governments of the Member States, the European Commission, and the two sides of industry. This definition of the Committee's task implied that no real power or decision or joint decision-making was conferred upon it. However, it gave participants an opportunity to play a role in both agenda setting and opinion formation of the Committee's proceedings.

Unlike the Standing Committee on Employment whose functions and working procedures were laid down by decision of the Council of Ministers in 1970, the Tripartite Conference itself worked on an informal basis. The first Conference, held in Luxembourg in April 1970 and officially entitled 'Conference on the problems of employment', was the result of concerted action by trade unions and employers' federations which were dissatisfied with the Community's social policy, especially in the field of employment. The Conference led to two concrete achievements: first, the creation of the above-mentioned Standing Committee on Employment, and, second, the acceptance of the idea of holding regular conferences between the two sides of industry, the Council of Ministers, Member States and the European Commission.

After the fifth Tripartite Conference in 1976, a further institutional element was added in the form of a Steering Group, whose task it was to follow up the previous conference and prepare for the following one. The Tripartite Conference can be seen as an effort to bring the social partners face to face with high-level EU and national decision-making authorities (Commission, Council, Member State Ministries) in a dialogue transcending the conventional forms of consultation, as exercised traditionally by Advisory Committees, including the Economic and Social Committee. Hence the aim was to involve more closely the two sides of industry in the shaping of economic and social policy, particularly in the employment field, of the EU. However, attempts by trade unions, and possibly the Commission, to use these conferences for the advancement of collective bargaining agreements at EU level were resisted by the employers' federations.

In contrast to the Tripartite Conferences or the Standing Committee on Employment, which tried to achieve a consensus of agreement between independent economic forces at EU level, and participate primarily in the shaping of EU policies, the ESC delivered (and still delivers) either requested Opinions or Opinions on own initiative, and hence took (takes) part in the EU's decision-making and legislative process. Its scope of activities or range of consultation are wide and involve economic, social and sector specific policies as well as institutional issues and questions of EU development. Members of the ESC are appointed in a personal capacity by the Council of Ministers and are not bound by instructions of those national socio-economic organisations to which they belong or are otherwise associated. They serve their four year term of office as representatives of the 'various categories of economic and social activity', as described in the Treaty of Rome. This does not necessarily mean that they act as a 'free agent'. Rather, because of their background, their expertise and their desire to exert pressure on behalf of their associations, ESC members can generally be looked upon as a kind of 'front-line post' for the organisations they come from.

The ESC, in its role as the spokesman of socio-economic interests, regards itself as the usual talking partner of the Council of Ministers, the European Commission and the European Parliament (Kirchner and Schwaiger, 1981: 38). However, the impact, according to figures drawn up by the ESC's secretariat were mixed, in that a large number of the Committee's Opinions were either not taken into consideration at all or only partly taken into consideration by the Council of Ministers (Kirchner and Schwaiger, 1981: 95).

The mushrooming of Advisory Committees led the ESC to take a critical look at this trend in its 1974 Opinion on the Place and Role of the ESC in the Institutional Machinery of the Communities in the Context of a Possible Evolution thereof. In it, the ESC expressed anxiety over possible encroachment by these Advisory Committees, and urged the European Commission and the Council of Ministers to consult it before setting up any further committees with either similar membership to that of the ESC or terms of reference which represent an amputation of its overall responsibility. Since then, the ESC has generally stuck to its critical line on the setting up of new Advisory Committees.

Paradoxically, what is today regarded as the sister organisation of the ESC, CoR, can trace its existence back to an advisory committee. As part of the reform of the structural funds in 1988, the Commission sought to involve local actors in the deliberation of policy, and a Consultative Committee of Local and Regional Authorities was created. Its 42 members were chosen by the European associations of local and regional governments, but meetings of the committee were infrequent and its membership highly diverse. The Maastricht Treaty changed much of that. The CoR now has 222 members which are appointed by national governments but in most cases chosen by the national associations of local and regional authorities. The impact of its opinions is debatable (McCarthy, 1997), but the symbolic significance of such a Committee in the EU system should not be underestimated.

The CoR has, in turn, created a number of sub-committees – called 'Commissions' – on subjects such as 'Regional Development', 'Spatial Planning', 'Urban Planning' and 'Land-Use Planning'. A special commission was charged with preparing the Committees opinion for the Intergovernmental Conference that negotiated the Amsterdam Treaty. Despite the arguably limited effectiveness of its role in the decision-making process, the CoR has proven to be a useful place for policy-learning and socialisation among sub-national actors in the Union. In contrast to the evolution of the ESC, whose star has been waning in line with negative integration and the increasing 'voluntarism' in industrial policy, the CoR – in tune with the growing interest in subsidiarity – has become the hub of regional interest representation in the EU.

In the 1980s, the Single European Act (SEA) Treaty had stimulated a second wave of committees. Many of these newly created, or in a few instances upgraded, committees had the task of assisting the European Commission in the implementation of the internal market programme, especially in the area of technical standards, public procurement, health and safety at work, environmental standards, and consumer protection. The Maastricht Treaty resulted in the formation of further committees, such as in the field of external relations, involving often Joint Committees, established in the framework of agreements on trade and economic co-operation between the EU and certain groups of countries.

Studying committee governance in the EU

The omnipresence of committee governance in the EU, its close linkage to the overall integration process and the diverse nature of the phenomenon pose numerous questions for analysis. These relate both to the internal dynamics of committees as well as to their relationship with the wider integration process. If, as we have argued, committees encapsulate the nature of European integration, then it is important to find out, in some detail, how they operate and what impact they have on the politics of the Union.

One obvious starting point is the theoretical positioning of committee governance: is it something which underpins the intergovernmental nature of the Union, given that in most instances committees are comprised of Member State representatives? Or, on the other hand, is it a sign for the increasing Europeanisation and bureaucratisation of all areas of policy-making, even those which are not formally part of EU competences? It is in the first instance a conceptual issue, raising questions about the way in which we approach the study of committees. The chapter by Jürgen Mittag, Andreas Maurer and Wolfgang Wessels (1) develops a way of relating the development of committee governance to the wider theoretical debate on European integration. Linking the main theoretical positions on European integration – functionalism, federalism, realism/intergovernmentalism and fusion theory – to various forms of administrative interaction, their model offers a mapping device for the study of the EU's committee system. This is succinctly expressed in a matrix, which locates committees along two scales: one side gauges the autonomy, or the subordination to politics, of public administration; the other side locates administration on a spectrum from national level to EU level dominance. They arrive at nine different categories of European administration which 'mix' these parameters in different ways.

Mittag, Maurer and Wessels conclude that administrative fusion – co-operation between national and European administrations who jointly share power and responsibilities – is the most suitable explanation for the growth of committee governance. But the significance and the nature of committees in the EU is diverse and the authors acknowledge that, beyond their own analysis of statistical data on the growth of comitology committees, a comprehensive answer to these questions requires further empirical analysis. Different chapters in this book respond to this call in their own ways.

Rhys Dogan's chapter (2), containing further, sectorally specific statistical data, confirms the fusion thesis: he concludes that 'elite concertation', the collusion of Member States and Commission to use comitology procedures, is one of the main causes for committee governance. Dogan sees this in the context of attempts to manipulate domestic political opposition. In all he identifies five causes of EU committee governance as the defence of institutional prerogatives, administrative and internal political convenience, pluralist competition and variable administrative adaptation in domestic systems – a typology which goes some way to explain the rise of committee governance. As we noted at the outset of this introduction, committees provide different functions to different actors. In his chapter (2), Dogan illustrates the reasons for this.

Elsewhere, a picture of conflicting evidence has been presented with respect to the working groups in the Council (Beyers and Dierckx, 1998). With respect to the wider issue of committee governance, it is impossible to advance simple generalisations. The number and types of committees are too great to permit an overall judgement of whether their impact on integration is intergovernmental rather than supranational. The only way of advancing our understanding of the effects of committee governance on the EU is to look at specific areas of EU policy-making and assessing the developments in some detail. In this respect, the case studies presented here help to shed further light on this complex issue.

Brendan Flynn in Chapter 4 on the role of committees in EU environmental policy-making demonstrates that committees of national and Council officials indeed serve to maintain an element of Member State control over areas that have been formally delegated to the Commission. In what has become an increasingly politicised area of dispute between Council and Parliament, the Commission has taken to the backstage. Given the only limited hold of the EP in the whole area of comitology, there is bound to be some slippage. One aspect of this question is that, even in a specific sector like that of environmental policy, the multitude of committees defies simple generalisation. Flynn argues that we need to look at the way in which individual committees are being constituted. In an area in which national interests intersect with commercial interests, there is concern over the way in which, under the cover of comitology, regulation has increasingly been replaced by voluntary agreements.

If environmental policy is an example of the re-nationalisation of EU policies through comitology, Tonra's chapter on the evolution of the Political Committee (PoCo) in the Common Foreign and Security Policy (CFSP) illuminates what might be the seen as the opposite effect: the 'hybridisation' of intergovernmental decision-making with an evolving Brussels-centred framework. The creation of a committee of senior officials from national foreign offices, its regular meetings in Brussels to discuss the co-ordination of national foreign policies and its insertion into the wider policy-process of the Union have contributed to the development of what is coming to be seen as a European 'foreign policy'. The proceedings of PoCo have been drawn into the COREPER framework and its wider, intermeshing network of committees. The result is a policy process that resonates increasingly with the 'Community method' rather than with the traditional, intergovernmental models of decision-making originally aspired to by Member States.

And while we can witness, in the examples provided by Flynn, the dissolution of institutional structures in the area of environmental policy, Tonra's chapter (8) demonstrates the increasing institutionalisation of foreign policy co-ordination. The latter process is one in which informal meetings among national officials first led to the setting up of formal committees and, after the ratification of the Amsterdam Treaty, to the creation of new institutions charged with the tasks of the committee. It is an experience resonant of developments in the area of monetary policy, where – as Verdun shows in Chapter 7 – both the Monetary Committee and the Committee of Central Bank Governors have been instrumental in laying the foundations for Economic and Monetary Union (EMU). As a result, the functions of the latter committee have been taken over by the European Central Bank.

Beyond the issue of intergovernmentalism vs. supranationalism in committee governance, all these cases also raise a related issue – the role of expert knowledge in the decision-making process. Committees are regularly regarded as technocratic, concerned with the minute details of policy proposals. This may well be true, but the investigations in this volume also show that this does not at all remove politics from the process. The proceedings of committee governance are highly political, whether or not the issue at stake is regarded as high or low politics. There are varying degrees of politicisation, though, and the politicisation of disagreements in committee is bound to compromise the weight of scientific arguments.

Still, it is worth asking whether the regular and frequent convening of experts does add a special quality to their interaction. Do experts who share knowledge of a highly technical nature – and who might find themselves frequently at odds with their political masters – develop a common set of values and, as a result, a sense of community? The analytical category of epistemic communities has been proposed for this kind of scenario on international politics (Haas, 1992), and has found increasing application also in the sphere of EU politics. The realm of committee governance is an obvious place to look for such communities.

Verdun (Chapter 7) identifies such a community in the area of monetary policy, an area in which policy-makers tend not only to be insulated from partisan political interest, but have also, over the past decades, developed a strong consensus based on neo-liberal economic theory. In the case of the environment – one of the original cases advanced by Haas – Flynn (Chapter 4) shows that while there might well be an epistemic community of environmental policy-makers in the EU, their effectiveness is compromised by the way in which commercial interests have become involved in the deliberations.

Faludi, Zonneveld and Waterhout, in Chapter 6, also show how the interaction of a group of policy-makers, in this case in the area of spatial development, relates to the process of competence transfer in the European Union: on the one hand, the informal negotiation process among policy-makers makes it possible to establish general principles and a sort of blueprint for co-operation in an area which is not yet within the domain of the Union. Actually transferring new competences to the Union is fraught with difficulties, with the Commission and the Parliament lobbying hard to move beyond agenda-setting, while national governments seek to maintain intergovernmental modes of decision-making. In the meanwhile, as the case of spatial development demonstrates, a substantial number of years may pass during which policy deliberation remains in the institutional limbo of informal, intergovernmental committees

Faludi's, Zonneveld's and Waterhout's chapter (6) also demonstrates another important point that the study of committee governance needs to address: the role of agency. Committees might well be the institutional backbone to epistemic communities, but the nature of their meetings might also facilitate leadership by individuals – and thus work against conceived notions of the power of Member States' influence. This is especially true in areas in which decision-making is consensual rather than based on voting. Monetary policy is a case in point: Verdun suggests that in this field the reputation of individuals stands alongside the size of their Member States and the weight of national currencies in explaining their influence within the committee. The concept of 'political leadership' has been applied to the upper echelons of the European Commission (Page and Wouters, 1994; Drake, 1995), but it is just as pertinent to look for its role in the study of committees.

Moving from the internal dynamics of committees to their position within the broader institutional framework of the Union brings the discussion to the democratic credentials of the committee governance. The general assumption here has been that the lack of transparency and the unelected membership of committees turn these into the enemy of democratic procedure. Most of the chapters here provide material to reinforce that view. Verdun, for example, in Chapter 7, challenges the secrecy of discussions in the Monetary Committee, whose membership she compares to an 'old boys' club'. But matters are not necessarily as clear-cut as they might seem. Flynn (Chapter 4) closes on the interesting point that committees might even help democratic oversight if and when they are constituted in a manner conductive of this aim.

One important aspect to the democratisation of committee governance clearly lies in the development of an entrenched involvement of the European Parliament (EP) in the creation and control of these committees. Hix, in Chapter 3, deals with this issue comprehensively, assessing the advances made by the EP in the 1990s, but also debating the limitations facing further extension of parliamentary powers. His conclusion is critical about the strategies adopted by MEPs – who tend to ignore the lessons that can be learned from domestic experiences – and of the disjointed nature in which parliamentary oversight is being extended. In response, Hix argues for a comprehensive review of the EP's powers of controlling comitology rather than a continuation of gradual changes to the current, imperfect system.

Accountability is also the theme of Albert Weale's normative considerations (Chapter 9) with which this volume closes. Weale develops three principles for the evaluation of committees: functional effectiveness, transparency and deliberative rationality. Looking at the overall picture of committee governance through these lenses, we see how an assessment of EU committees in these terms points to continuing problems. On the other hand, as Weale points out, a judgement of the working procedures of Union in terms of democratic theory ought not to neglect the complexities of modern government and the *sui generis* nature of the European Union. Committee governance is an outgrowth of an integration project which followed the 'Monnet method', but while 'integration by stealth' may be waning as the democratisation of the EU advances, the legacy of its working methods – including the reliance on expert committees – plays an important part in its legitimation.

Finally, in further broadening the perspective, one might consider the way in which committee governance not only encapsulates the nature of EU politics, but in fact exemplifies the essence of a novel administrative culture in Europe. Earlier we mentioned the diverging administrative cultures in the European Union, and the way in which these might lead individual Member States to respond differently to the EU committee governance system. We might close with the suggestion that committee governance, in providing the typical working environment for an increasing number of national officials and experts, is bound to develop into an administrative culture in its own right. In a number of the contributions here, the authors consider this question with regard to their specific policy-areas. Thus, Faludi, Zonneveld and Waterhout conclude that a European 'planning culture' is on the horizon, aided by the activities of the Committee on Spatial Development. The chapters by Tonra (8) and by Verdun (7) allow us to hypothesise the same for foreign and monetary policy, respectively.

But beyond the individual case studies here, committee governance raises the spectre of a new administrative culture for Europe. What has initially been restricted to the backrooms of Brussels might over time spill over into the administrative systems of the Member States. If there is a process of convergence in the public administration in the EU (Burnham and Maor, 1995), committee governance is the most likely transmission belt of such a transformation. All the more important is a critical enquiry into the institutional dynamics and democratic credentials of this form of governance. This is a task only recently taken up by political science. We hope the contributions to this volume help to place the study of committee governance firmly on the research agenda of European integration.

ANDREAS MAURER, JÜRGEN MITTAG
& WOLFGANG WESSELS

1

Theoretical perspectives on administrative interaction in the European Union

A once fully implemented bureaucracy belongs to the most difficult social constructions to destroy.

(Max Weber, Bureaucracy, in *Economics and Society*, Tubingen 1947, p. 668)

Introduction: administration in the European Union – a substantial feature in a growing multi-level system

The European Union (EU) is a political system in full evolution. It is undergoing fundamental changes in respect to its functional as well as to its geographical scope and organisational structure. Permanent institutional and procedural changes, the outcomes of the Treaty on European Union and the Amsterdam Treaty have provided the Union with additional rights and obligations. Many key issues – embodying vital political sensibility – have become subject matter for the European Union since the 1960s. Though many citizens take the increasing competencies and the significance of the Union for granted, serious concerns circulate about its transparency and democratic accountability particularly with regard to those acting inside the European bureaucracy. In general terms, administration plays a significant role in West European political systems as it is an elementary part in the functioning of modern governments and governance. Related to the European Union, public administration reveals special attention and arouses controversial debates. A major feature in this discourse are latent fears of an 'Archipel Brussels', an ever-growing swamp bearing a new political class of 'Eurocrats' (Spinelli 1996). Beyond this popular scenario, analysing the impact of public administration and civil servants on the governing process has a long and extremely varied academic tradition in Western Europe, evoking stimulating research results in the fields of law, economic and social sciences (e.g. Mayntz 1982). However, most of these contributions focus on the national level.

Though there has been a significant rise in studies about European policy-making, administration in the European context has so far received only limited recognition. Yet, one particular element of the Union's administrative infra-structure has found special attention in the last few years. Committees, which act on the comitology decision 87/373 of the Council, have become a serious matter of discussion (e.g. Bach 1992; Grams 1995; Van Schendelen 1996; Neyer 1997; Wessels 1998). The main controversy in the so-called 'comitology debate' centres around the extent that these comitology committees affect the process of imple-menting Community legislation and how they exercise influence through some kind of a 'government by committee' (e.g. Wheare 1979; Schäfer 1996).

Besides this debate, in more general terms public administration in the European context is still largely met with scepticism and indifference in acade-mic discourse. For three reasons much of the responsibility for this state of affairs lies in the theoretical and methodological framework. First, academics fre-quently tend to concentrate on the activities of a particular institution, a distinct policy-sector or a particular type of decision-making. Of course, differentiation across the spectrum of EU policy-making and a detailed analysis is a prerequi-site for understanding the Community system. Nevertheless, a wider and more dynamic view has to be considered as a necessary addition to such micro- or case-studies. A perspective, which takes into account the variety of interactions between different actors and embeds its findings in a broader context so that observations can be compared with other outcomes and overall developments, offers a substantial development. Second, research on European integration has difficulty devising empirical tests capable of demonstrating the relevance and impact of integration theories. Due to the lack of reliable data, clear empirical evidence is hard to reach.[1] The development of administrative committees is – because of their vague, discretionary, amorphous and constantly evolving char-acter – rather difficult to measure. However, in order to develop a progressive research programme, theories must devise hypotheses and test them against real data. Third, European integration theory is primarily affiliated with and com-pared to the nation-state. Methodological challenges stem from the widespread use of nation-state-like categories and the need to develop an analytical approach peculiar to administration in the European Union as a whole. Of course, one should have other western political systems in mind when touching upon administrative questions, but the sovereign state must not remain the single point of reference. With its current structure, the EU is neither compara-ble with national constitutional systems nor with international organisations or associations. Its autonomous development results from a process of growth and differentiation which has not yet reached a final stage and might not do so in the near future. Thus, research on European integration has to develop a more com-plex approach. We need coherent explanations for the mechanisms through which both national administrations and the European bureaucracy shape polit-ical outcomes. Using state-like instruments in its first pillar, the European Union has passed the boundary from horizontal cross-border co-operation to vertical policy-making in a dynamic multi-level system (Rometsch and Wessels 1996; Jachtenfuchs and Kohler-Koch 1996; Marks 1996). Such a new type of political system representing a new kind of polity requires theoretical approaches which reveal the mutual interplay of both levels (Siedentopf and Ziller 1988).

In order to accomplish these theoretical and methodological challenges, our conceptual approach to administration is based on a more general point of departure (Wessels 1998). We do not intend to scrutinise single administrative actors or the specific functions of committees in the various stages of the policy process. Instead, we try to take a closer look at the general dynamics of the EU's political system and organisational structure in total. Assuming that administrative interaction through and within committees should not be researched in the European sphere alone but also at the national level, we should take both perspectives into consideration. The phenomenon of administrative bodies as vital players in the European decision-making process should be regarded as a kind of simultaneous interaction of different institutional levels and several realms of European governance. It is essential to reflect on both supranational institutions and different governance 'circuits' and to some extent on sub-units of national governments, as regional powers. We have to go beyond those descriptions and categorisations which separate the legislative activity of the supranational institutions on the one hand, and the policy-implementation activity of national administrations on the other. Opening up the 'black box' of European legislation in our study means analysing the patterns of interaction between administrations and other actors in regard to what other allies and competitors are doing in the political sphere. 'Brussels' is thereby not an isolated arena but an integral part of the relationship between interlocking systems, non-governmental networks, governmental institutions and actors (Streeck and Schmitter 1991).

What does this mean in concrete terms for our study? As a first step, we will give a short survey on the development of administrative bodies in order to sketch a typology of committees in the EC process. Subsequently, we introduce in the second section a set of different models on administration and administrative interplay within the entire EU system. We distinguish between two analytical dimensions – national and European dominance in the production of binding European law on the one hand (vertical) and bureaucratic versus governmental supremacy on the other hand (horizontal). In this sense, it is not the stringent reproduction of a particular school of thought that matters, but general assumptions on the way administrations try to shape their environment. We combine this set of administrative models with 'macro-theories' on European integration, sketching the outlines of each. In a third step, the models and theoretical approaches are contrasted with empirical findings on historic and present administrative trends in the European Union. Some typical features of administrative interaction such as the civil servants involved in the EU policy process by means of various committees can be elaborated upon by this approach. Taking into account the results of this enquiry, the final part of our chapter deals with the 'multi-dimensional ways' of governance in Europe and its shortcomings.

Committees in the context of public administration and policy formulation

Committees 'shape policy and play a significant role in contributing to the formulation and adoption of binding rules' (Schäfer 1996). They can generally be defined as 'institutionalised groups of specialised and representative people' (Van Schendelen 1996). Committees may fulfil rule-interpreting, fund-approving or rule-setting functions (Schäfer 1996: 16). In other words, committees act both as decision-takers and decision-makers. Besides comitology committees, one may find in the EU context consultative committees, which are almost private, i.e. non-governmental as well as sectoral specialists and expert groups consisting mostly of national administrators or specialists nominated by the Member States surrounding the Commission. Administrators from the EU institutions, the Member States and third parties are joined in several Council infrastructure committees, COREPER, working groups and intergovernmental joint committees. The potential influence of committees differs largely: advisory committees of the Commission have a high potential for influence at the early pre-proposal stage of the EU's policy cycle. Unlike consultative committees, expert groups advise the Commission on the basis of the Member States' interest. In general, expert groups indicate the Member State's acceptance on a given issue. In this way, they act as 'early warning units' for the Commission: Will Member State 'X' and its administration be able to transpose the Directive within a given time period? Will the envisaged legal act have an effect on the administrative law of Member State 'Y'? The influence of the Council's working parties may be found at the stage of decision-making. According to van der Knaap, 90 per cent of EC legislation is 'adopted' at this stage (Knaap 1996).

If we put a particular emphasis on the comitology committees, they can briefly be defined as a number of miscellaneous committees in the process of implementing European legislation and policies. The comitology process historically originated from the delegation of Council's executive powers to the Commission in the early 1960s (Vos 1997). The Council's intention was to implement a number of Council regulations organising the agricultural market. Since this initiative the total number of these committees has grown eminently. Generally, the European Commission was responsible for implementing decisions adopted by the Council (Article 145). In 1987, the Single European Act (SEA) added a third indent to Article 145 of the EEC Treaty. The Council used this text as basis for adopting the already mentioned 'comitology' decision, determining three distinct procedures for the exertion of implementing powers conferred on the Commission: Advisory Committees counsel the Commission on matters of policy or technical issues. The Commission presents a draft proposal for an implementing act. The committee then delivers its opinion by simple majority. Finally, the Commission takes the opinion into account and adopts the measure in question. Management committees also have an advisory function. However, if the committee adopts a negative opinion on the Commission's draft, the Council may take a different decision by qualified majority. Under type A, the Commission may defer the application of the measure for one month. Under type B, the period of time is extended to three months. If the original legal act establishes a regulatory committee, the powers of the Commission are widely reduced: given that the committee is not willing to support the Commission's draft (and decides so by qualified majority), the Council may decide so within a three month period. If the Council takes no decision, two variants apply: under procedure A (*procédure du filet*), the Commission may adopt its measure unilaterally. Under procedure B (*procédure du contre-filet*), the Commission may adopt the measure when there is no simple majority in the Council against it. Consequently, procedure B of the regulatory committee can lead to a '*vide juridique*' i.e. secondary legislation, which cannot be implemented due to a missing measure required to apply it. Because of its right to finally choose the kind of implementing committee, the Council prefers management and regulatory committee procedures. Consequently, the different comitology committee formulas lead to the question of which kind of multi-level administration is emerging within the EU system: is the Commission's DG-administration dominating? Or the Member States? Who influences what, whom and in which way? Do committees act as an independent network of specialists or are they mirroring the Council's predominance in the EU's policy cycle?

Integration theories and models of administrative interaction: a heuristic overview

In order to illustrate the widespread assumptions and theoretical approaches in academic debates on administration, we need to pay special attention to a range of administrative models which may be deduced from theories on European integration.[2] These models are in some way heuristic and ideal archetypes and do not gain subsistence in this distinct manner. However, to classify the potential of administrative interaction we are interested in describing these focused models which might then prove helpful. Two different dimensions of participation in the multi-level system of the European Union can be distinguished: for an initial overview, these dimensions are figured in the following matrix (Figure 2). The first categorisation – described in the vertical axis – explains the relationship between the national and European level of the EU's policy process. In the model across the first line 'Dominance of national level', administrative interaction originating out of the EU's institutions is almost neglected. Yet, while supranational civil servants are not entirely excluded, they remain without any further influence. All core matters in the policy-making process depend solely on national actors while supranational actors are only engaged in some subordinated cases.

Axis I: Member States vs. EC/EU \ Axis II: Administration vs. government	Bureaucratic autonomy	Co-operation	Subordination of administration
Dominance of national level	1 Diplomatic administration — R	2 Functional co-operation — R/FUN	3 Intergovernmental monitoring — R
Sharing of power and responsibilities	4 Mega-bureaucracy — ERO	5 Administrative fusion — FUS/GOV	6 Co-operative administration — FUS
Dominance of EU-level	7 Supranational bureaucracy — R-FED	8 Supranational technocracy — NEO-FUN	9 Federal administration — FED

R = Realism; FUN = Functionalism; NEO-FUN = Neo-functionalism; ERO = Erosion; GOV = Governance; FED = Federalism; FUS = Fusion

Figure 2 Models of administrative interaction and integration theories

In contrast to this concept, across the lower line (dominance of the EU level) illustrates administrative archetypes incorporating comprehensive activities for supranational actors able to affect political outcomes. National actors remain important, but the making of substantial decisions has shifted to the European arena. A second dimension of the matrix – depicted in the horizontal axis – refers to the perennial tension between bureaucracy and government. Relating to administrative supremacy, the left column emphasises the influence of civil servants in preparation, adoption, implementation and control of binding legislative acts. These archetypes are characterised by a form of bureaucratic self-regulation. Pursuing an opposing view, the right column highlights the impact of governments, leaving administrative actors only limited choices. Both national civil servants and Commission administrators are merely carrying out the decisions of the political class having little ability and scope to present and defend proposals for political decisions. This matrix basically leads to the main question arising in several analyses of administration in the European Union: does the national or the EU-administration take a dominant role or is there any kind of administrative 'mixture' in which both levels work together?

Realism, diplomatic administration, functional co-operation and intergovernmental monitoring

Realists conceive the sovereign nation-state as the authoritative actor in cross-border interactions. Although various internal state actors participate in the making of political decisions, the nation-state acts as a sole player. According to this concept, the committees surrounding the EU's organisational set-up are products of a general strategy of national governments and administrations to exercise more influence in the Brussels sphere (Wessels 1990). The principal tasks of respective administrative committees is to restrain the supremacy of the Member States as 'masters of the treaty' (Bundesverfassungsgericht 1993). In particular, the Council's administrative infrastructure and the comitology committees are considered as an additional means for national administrations to control the Commission's activities, thus preventing the evolution towards an unrestrained *supranational bureaucracy*. Furthermore, national administrations are regarded as essential in maintaining the 'institutional balance'. From this perspective, committees show a persistent pattern of confrontation between national and EC administrations, intensifying the cleavage between the two levels. Following this school of thought, conflictual voting will occur frequently and the capacity of transferring responsibilities from the committee level to the Council, which is seen as the advocate of national interests, will be strengthened. Realist assumptions would also reveal conflicts between Member States in which zero sum games predominate. According to this logic, national administrations are to some extent ambiguous. They share a common interest in defending their status against 'intrusion' by the Commission, but they also endeavour to defend their interests to achieve particular individual objectives. The behavioural pattern is characterised by conflictual status and distributive bargaining (Scharpf

1988). Considering the various forms and procedures of comitology committees mentioned above, such an approach would anticipate a constant trend towards a typology which would guarantee national civil servants an extremely large influence. In relation to the question of legitimacy, committees would have a high rating on the scale since they are representatives of the holders of national sovereignty. Accordingly, realists would neglect the relevance or oppose the reality of *supranational administration*.

Following the model of *diplomatic administration*, binding European legislation is principally influenced by national administrations. Civil servants – regularly hailing from foreign ministries – prevent any attempts by supranational actors to gain influence. As a kind of autonomous bureaucracy, national administrators try both to emphasise the supremacy over the national politicians and to keep the frequency of political cross-border meetings restricted. Neither legislative outcomes nor spill-overs stem from the few cross-border activities. A different model of European administration which would fit into the realist conceptualisation of the integration process would be *intergovernmental monitoring*: referring to this model, national governments dominate the European arena and the administrative bodies. The sovereign nation-states co-ordinate their policies as is typical in inter-state relations under traditional international law. Cross-border interactions are shaped by national politicians, particularly by ministers of foreign affairs. The very few external contacts take place within intergovernmental conferences or Councils at the level of national ministers allowing governmental actors to remain sovereign to both external and internal political decisions. Finally, *functional co-operation* might also be interpreted with the theoretic tools offered by realism. Thus European policy output is shaped by national government–administration interactions, where co-operation between civil servants and government depends on the subject matter of European negotiations. Consequently, the Brussels based administration serves as a 'sherpa' for Member States' interests. Functional and technical requirements determine the number and depth of administrative interactions. Information inflow would depend on the performance of national administrations and governments.

Federalism and federal administration

Opposing the realist view, traditional federalists would understand committees as bodies primarily serving national interests, thus constituting a major obstacle to a proper federal institutional system which alone could guarantee efficient, effective and legitimate European policies. Concomitantly, committees would then be interpreted as fortifying institutions standing against the real – i.e. federalist inspired – European public interest. The demands of national administrations and national parliamentarians are rejected as a strategy against the real will of the European people and the path to a federal union (Schneider 1994). Moreover, inter-administrative bargaining within committees is considered an obstacle to solving the problems of the European Union and its Member

States. From this viewpoint the opposition of the European Parliament to the comitology committees goes beyond the quest for more power; it is in fact a key issue, in the constitutional organisation of the EU government. Consequently, federalist theories on European governance would suggest abolishing both the management and the regulatory committees. Following this school of thought, the model of European administration would be one with a European bureaucracy which clearly dominates national administrative bodies in each relevant field of European public policy, but which itself is dominated by a supranational government. Thus, the model of a *supranational bureaucracy* is – compared to realist views – considered as a kind of antagonist. Since federalism suggests a division of competencies between the different levels of policy-making (European – national – regional – local), co-operation between administrations would be modelled according to the subsidiarity principle. Moreover, federalism would assume a European Bureaucracy acting as a 'political promoter' which formulates far-reaching policy agendas, articulates ideals and brokers strategies for the deepening of the integration process.

Neo-functionalism and the supranational technocracy

Linked with (neo-)functional assessments (Mitrany 1966; Zellentin 1992), comitology committees would be considered as functional necessities, tackling technical problems together without the need for further reflection on their democratic legitimisation. From this perspective, one would expect comitology committees to be arenas where functional 'problem-solving' rather than political 'bargaining' (Scharpf 1988) would dominate the interaction style. Committees would be conceived as bodies of experts, where people with highly specialised technical knowledge in a certain area come together in order to shape secondary European legislation. The participants would not be interested in the exact legal form of their committee, but in agreements on the basis of common analysis. Distributive effects, vertically among the two levels, or horizontally between member countries, would clearly be subordinated to the best technical solution in the interest of the common good. Neo-functionalism generally explains the growth in number of committees and in the frequency of their meetings as product of spill-over processes (Schmitter 1996). According to this logic of an ever-growing extension of common policy-making, the actors would – as Ernst Haas put it – 'shift their loyalties, expectations and political activities towards a new centre whose institutions possess or demand jurisdiction over the pre-existing national states' (Haas 1968). Given this basic orientation, the neo-functionalist model of European administration would be characterised by the existence of relevant administrative interactions depending in its number and characteristics primarily on the functional scope of the Union. Cross-border contacts would be considered a necessary addition to the interstate bureaucracy. These interactions strengthen the proficiency of national administrations in finding adequate task-orientated solutions without lessening the conventional relationship to other interstate actors or distressing the relationship with the political leadership. The impact of supranational actors remains to some extent restricted: domestic political concerns dominate the convenience of national actors for supranational co-operation. Whereas the model of *functional co-operation* would suggest a dominance of the national level in European policy-making, the model of a *supranational technocracy* would tend to argue, that the European level, i.e. the European Commission and its Directorates General, would dominate the game of policy oriented administration. Similar to the model of *functional co-operation*, this kind of bureaucracy would not depend on a particular constitutional basis or on certain institutional arrangements which organise joint decision-making. The co-operation of national and European civil servants would not be undertaken for its own merits, but seen as a chance to find problem-orientated solutions at the European level. The technical requirements would determine the number and depth of administrative inter-actions. However, unlike *functional co-operation*, information inflow and the specific demands for implementing secondary European legislation would depend on the services of the Commission and only to a lesser extent on those of national administrations.

The erosion view and the model of a European mega-bureaucracy
In the view of the erosion school of thought,[3] bureaucratic expansion is the con-sequence of intense national and European administration's interactions, shap-ing together a multi-level *mega-bureaucracy*.[4] By pursuing a highly regulated multi-level game, bureaucrats from both the European and the national level would emphasise their autonomy against the political class by using their administrative experience (Weber 1959). As experts in complex administrative procedures, they would replace democratic policy-makers, thus constructing a conglomerate unmatched by parliamentary or judicial control – to which national administrations are normally subjected. The logic of 'bureaucracy membership' and the influence which the actors involved may wield would pro-duce a strong 'logic of committees'.[5] Participating civil servants betray their gov-ernments and populations alike. Thus, the individual citizen would be confronted with a multi-layered functional set-up which is unwilling to be loyal to or establish any solidarity with the public. By excluding others from their activities, mega-bureaucracies create an independent political space, which is different from the norms established by legislatures or elected governments. In this perspective, the model of mega-bureaucracy is not only the product of 'Eurocrats', but also of national administrations, leading both to enlarge their areas of influence in areas uncontrolled by others. The characteristic indicators of the *mega-bureaucracy* are largely explicable in terms of an unlimited coinci-dence of national and supranational administrative structures. Using their spe-cial bureaucratic abilities both civil servants of the Commission and states administrators would use administrative interactions to prevent any serious control. The disappearance of other actors leads to 'government by committee' with a low level of efficiency.

Governance, fusion theory and the models of horizontal and vertical fusion and mixed administration

In view of the late 1980s school of governance (Bulmer 1994; Caporaso 1996; Jachtenfuchs and Kohler-Koch 1996), administrative interaction might be regarded as one particular element within the complex multi-level game of the EU. The EU polity is seen as a 'post-sovereign, polycentric, incongruent' arrangement of authority which supersedes the limits of the nation-state (Schmitter 1996). Assuming a non-hierarchical decision-making process over-arching the geographical limits of the EU and its Member States beyond, comitology committees do not (intend to) move the EU in a certain direction or transform its basic character and organisation. Instead, they act as defenders of the status quo. From the perspective of this school of thought, committees matter as arenas of collective decision implementation, thus indicating a new historical stage for both administrations and for the state. As Kohler-Koch puts it, if 'good governance' contributes to a 'decrease in the unilateral steering by government, and hence an increase in the self-governance of networks', committees could be taken as a significant indicator of this phenomenon (Kohler-Koch 1996).

Fusion theory (Wessels 1992) regards committees as indicators of a permanent process by which national governments and administrations, as well as other public and private actors increasingly combine and share resources from several levels. Committees are the manifestation of growing Europeanisation in national administrations. From this view, committees in general and comitology committees in particular are significant. As the European Court of Justice has described it: if powers 'fall partly into the competencies of the Community and in part within that of the Member States it is essential to ensure close co-operation between the Member States and the Community institutions'.[6] Thus, committees with national and European civil servants are examples and the main driving force behind the merging of public instruments. They are to some extent a product of the increasing competition for access and influence in the EU policy cycle. We could distinguish between the model of *horizontal and vertical fusion* and the model of *co-operative administration*, which differ mainly with regard to the level of influence of administrative bodies against governments. The Fusion model would help us to design interrelated processes of Europeanisation on the level between the Member States and EC/EU institutions on the one hand and on the level between national and European administrative bodies on the other. As in the case of the new Economic and Financial Committee (EFC), both Europeanised levels of interaction (Commission and European Central Bank (ECB) on the EC level and Member States representatives at the national level) meet in a special committee which co-ordinates views and opinions of Member State and EC/EU administrations on a given set of issues (Article 114 [ex-Article 109c] EC Treaty). Fusion theory would expect that committees like the EFC would act neither as the 'watch dogs' of national governments charged with controlling the ECB or the European Commission nor as forums for more intergovernmental negotiations. In opposition to both views, committees would behave as specialised bodies for joint action. Consequently specific interaction styles within committees – horizontally between its members and other committees (e.g. between the EFC and the Council of Economics and Finance Ministers (ECOFIN) working groups or the EC Employment committee) and vertically between its members and other specialised Member States institutions/committees – are to be expected: 'a constructive team spirit, a confidential club atmosphere, an effective collegiality will dominate over strict interpretation of legal texts and formal rules' (Hanny and Wessels 1999). Unlike horizontal/vertical fusion, *co-operative administration* would be more oriented towards, and more dependent upon the level of Member States' governments. A good example could be the new CFSP planning and early warning unit established by the Treaty of Amsterdam, where the members (from the Member States and the Commission) will act under the auspices of the Council's Secretary General and in the interest of the 'joint strategic decisions' to be formulated by the European Council.

Growth and differentiation in EU administration: empirical trends

Due to the absence of any central data base providing comprehensive and reliable statistical material, clear empirical evidence about administrative interactions within the European Union can only be obtained to a limited extent. Neither from the perspective of the EU institutions nor from the Member States level are we able to give more than a rough estimate which might differ from other calculations. Nevertheless, little existing information can be used to focus on some statistical trends which might illustrate the organic and evolutionary development within the inter-institutional framework of the EU as a whole, and its administrative bodies in particular. In order to give a first impression of political and administrative tendencies of the entire EU system, we analyse the comitology network in a broader perspective. Proceeding from some overall 'macropolitical' trends we can determine a number of tendencies in the administration and management of the EU system.[7] Of course, the findings of such a general exercise might be objected to for their vagueness. However, compared with more detailed and 'policy field' specific based data, these findings might serve as a basis for such an undertaking.

Concentrating on the development of the EC/EU's policy agenda between 1952 (ECSC Treaty) and 1997 (Amsterdam Treaty), we observe an extension of responsibilities leading to an extensively enlarged scope of action. The total number of Treaty articles dealing with decision-making rules in specific policy areas has considerably grown from 64 (EEC Treaty 1957) to 195 (Amsterdam Treaty).[8] Committees are both a product and a tool of the European policy-making process. Consequently, the EC/EU legislative output, i.e. the sum of binding decisions adopted either by the Council of Ministers and – since 1

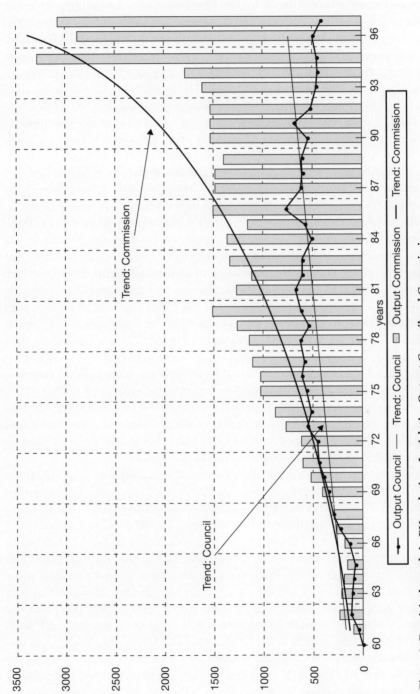

Figure 3 Empirical trends in EU evolution: Legislative Output Council and Commission
Source: Annual Reports of the Council and CELEX database.

November 1993 – of the European Parliament and the Council (acting under the co-decision procedure) or by the European Commission gives an initial impression about the potential for European administration by committees. Thus, we have to sketch out a general assessment on the EC/EU's legislative output from the 1960s onwards (Figure 3). From the original EEC Treaty to the Treaty of Amsterdam, the EC/EU has received an expanding number of competencies in an increasing set of policy fields. The legislative output of the Council (and the European Parliament) has increased from 10 acts in 1960 up to 575 in 1975 and 546 in 1993. Though there was a slight fall to 484 in 1996 the production of secondary EC legislation stagnates on a high level, exposing a linear growth. Until 1997, the Council had passed a high number of secondary binding legislation with more than 16,000 regulations, directives, decisions and recommendations in the meaning of Article 249 EC Treaty (Amsterdam Treaty version). If we concentrate our evaluation only on those acts, where the European Commission adopts powers pursuant to the implementation of EC legislation, we have another – even more plain – proof of the growth in EC legislation. Hence, the number of implementation measures has risen from just 6 in 1960 up to 2461 in 1994, presenting an exponential trend. These numbers depend on the CELEX European law database of the Commission, covering only those acts which have to be published in the *Official Journal of the European Communities*. According to the annual reports of the Commission the number is much higher: in 1994, the Commission adopted 7034 acts, including 3064 regulations, 3635 decisions, 33 directives, 26 recommendations and 263 opinions. Thus it can be concluded that the nature of the EU's political system is characterised by a growth in binding secondary legislation.

In order to successfully reconcile the management of growing responsibilities with the demands for participation of the different socio-political actors involved, the institutional framework has been altered and supplemented by newly established institutions and administrative bodies.

Institutional growth leads to institutional specialisation: since 1958, the number of the European Commission's Directorates General (DGs) has grown from 9 to 24 in 1995 (in fact, DG I is split into three different DGs: DG I – Commercial Policy and Relations with North America, the Far East, Australia and New Zealand; DG IA – Europe and NIS, External Policy and CFSP; and DG IB – Southern Mediterranean, Middle and Near East, Latin America, South and Southeast Asia and North–South Cooperation). Institutional partiality at the EC level also leads to a broader involvement of national administrations in coping with the daily business of the Euro-polity. Today, nearly every national ministry sends representatives to Brussels both to Council meetings and meetings of its working groups under COREPER I and II as well as to the Commission's expert and comitology committees. Summarising the various bodies for 1995 we can list roughly 270 working groups, approximately 400 comitology committees and at least 600 expert groups and ad hoc advisory committees for the Commission – altogether the administrative infrastructure includes at least

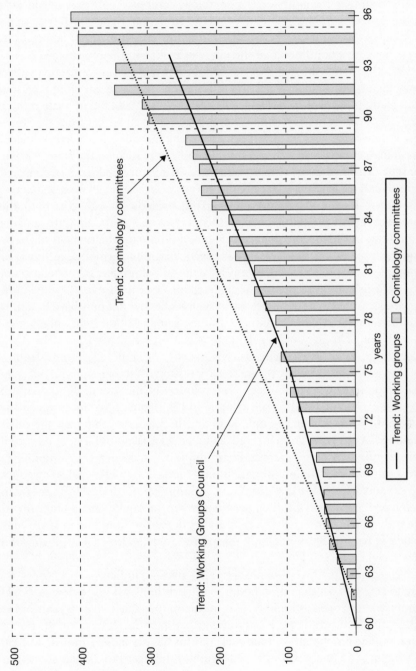

Figure 4 Empirical trends in EU evolution: number of Working Groups Council and comitology committees

Source: Annual Reports of the Council, general budget of the Community and CELEX database.

around 1,300 bodies. Again, we observe a remarkable growth during the development of the EU as well as a linear trend (Figure 4).

According to the policy cycle, comitology committees are precisely located in the implementation phase. Due to the different rights conferred upon national civil servants in the comitology committees it is rather laborious to assess the concrete influence of these bodies in shaping European law. Nevertheless, it can safely be said that the comitology network is confronted with a growing number of policy fields and thus in some way is decisive for preparing, taking and implementing the concrete 'appearance' of the EU in relation to its 'User-Community'. However, the overall picture which we get from the comitology network embodies divergent specimens but also convergent patterns. The concrete impact of each committees' indicators such as: the issue at stake, the type or character of a given policy area (regulatory, redistributive or programmatic), the legal basis (specifying the type of legislation allowed, the Council's voting rules and the decision-making procedures with regard to the European Parliament, the Council, the Economic and Social Committee and the Committee of the Regions) or the origin of a dominant chairperson might be more relevant. Some committees may have the right to harmonise technical or economic standards, others may only have the task of revising the appendices of original legislation. This should be analysed on a case to case basis.

To assess the overall importance of such bodies, we not only have to scrutinise the number of these bodies but also the number of their formal sessions. Though not all bodies hold regular meetings, their frequency is, in some cases, rather high. Whereas the general development of comitology committee frequency can be illustrated by the increase of sessions of the agricultural management and regulatory committees, the evolution of the overall EU committee network can be pictured by an increase in the frequency of meetings in the Council of Ministers on the one hand and its working groups on the other (Figure 5). As we know from the well documented agricultural sector, many civil servants meet weekly on average. For example, the management committee of the Common Organisations of Agricultural Markets for Sugar held 50 meetings in 1995 and delivered 161 opinions on the Commission's drafts.[9] With regard to several undocumented informal meetings, it becomes quite clear that the intensity with which some civil servants deal with European affairs in their daily agenda is remarkable – not only during the mid-1990s but with a constant growth since the 1980s.

As regards the number of civil servants involved in European business, we have to take into consideration both the Brussels level and the various national administration levels. If we first concentrate on the higher civil servants of the supranational institutions, we observe a constant increase from the 1960s onwards. The number of A-grade civil servants has expanded from 982 in 1960 to 2,565 in 1975 and 6,950 in 1997 (Figure 6). In regard to individual institutions the European Parliament has the highest growth-rate followed by the European Commission. This growth echoes the development of the European

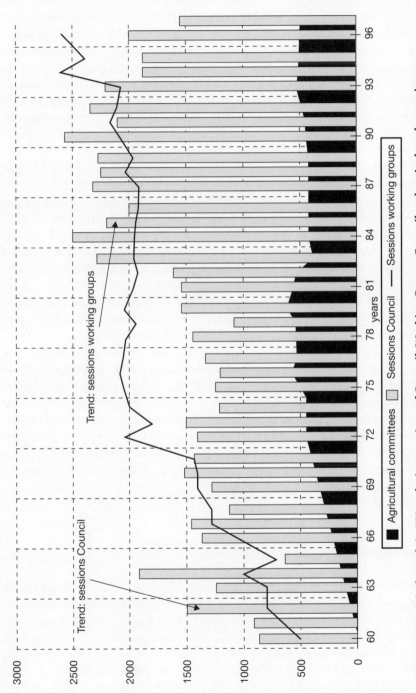

Figure 5 Empirical trends in EU evolution: sessions of Council, Working Groups Council and agricultural committees
Source: Annual Reports of the Council and Commission.

Parliament in the EU's institutional system.[10] From national budgetary statistics we get some more information about the tendencies at the European level. If we compare the growth in the number of higher civil servants in the Federal Republic of Germany with that of civil servants at the European level, we observe that the European level has increased over proportionally.[11] Nevertheless, the involvement of national actors in the European arena is still growing. Due to the 'dictation' in Brussels and, moreover, the considerable challenges to national administrations, the organisation of national governments orientates itself more and more to the requirements of the European arena. European Affairs are increasingly conceived of as a matter to be dealt with in every ministry affected by the activities of the EC/EU. If functional growth leads to institutional growth, differentiation, specialisation and administrative fragmentation in the Member States, co-ordination becomes a crucial element for efficient and effective policy-making. Both qualitative analysis and empirical data illustrate a more elaborate co-ordination in the Member States (Rometsch and Wessels 1996; Pappas 1994; Mény *et al.* 1996). Approximately 25 per cent of all higher civil servants of the German government are directly involved in miscellaneous types of EU policy-making and at various levels. These interaction patterns involve many levels of the national administrative hierarchy. For instance, in the case of the Federal Republic of Germany around 500 civil servants from the 'Länder' administrations are increasingly involved in EC/EU Council negotiations dealing with education, culture, research, justice and home affairs.

National and European administrations and governments are not alone in the Brussels sphere. To illustrate the quantitative growth in the various forms of interest representation, lobby groups and Non-governmental Organisations (NGOs) are a remarkable example. The number of listed groups had increased to approximately 2,000 interest group representations in Brussels by 1996.[12] These actors play an increasingly significant role, both in respective political systems of Western Europe and at the European level and in shaping the preparation taking and implementing of binding legal acts. National and supranational administrations are forced to take these actors into consideration either as competitors or partners.

Conclusions: the models revisited

Our overview indicates that from the original EEC Treaty to the Treaty on the European Union many core issues of public policy have become subject to supranational decision-making procedures. Like policy fields and decision-making norms, institutions have been further developed or newly introduced in order to cope with the functional scope of the EC/EU. Like the Parliament, the Council and the Commission, committees are the result of both functionalist institution-building and bargaining. They are part of the EC/EU's institutional structure and do not purely and simply constitute a neutral arena, but structure

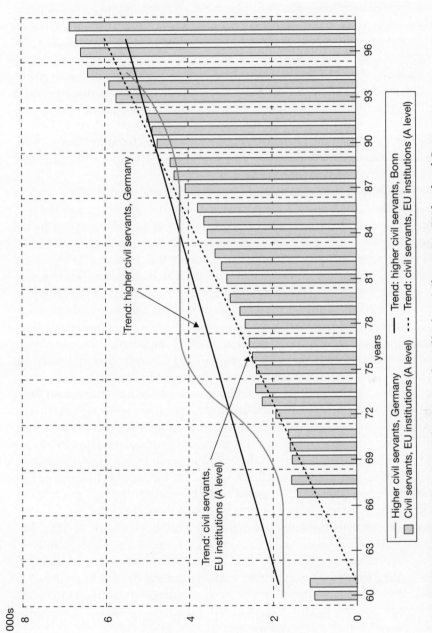

Figure 6 Empirical trends in EU evolution: number of higher civil servants, EU level and Germany

Source: Annual Reports of the Commission, Budgetary Reports, Germany.

the policy processes according to a variety of norms, rules and procedures. Thus, analysing committees in an unfixed but moving environment means scrutinising the various interactions between European and national governmental actors as well as bureaucratic ones, companies, non-profit and private interest representatives. If any dominant factor is to be made responsible for the popular fears of the 'bureaucratisation' in Brussels, it is the specific constellation of a de-nationalised public authority and the impact of the various multi-level arenas acting therein. Consequently, the patterns of administrative interaction cannot only be analysed as a search for consensus between a limited and stable number of actors. Not only should the well-known kinds of formal bargaining or other asymmetric dependency relationships be examined minutely, but also the exchange of resources on the basis of equality and mutuality. Due to their particular character, administrative interactions have to be investigated beyond the formal structures of the EC/EU policy cycle.

If we compare the explanatory power of the different models of administrative interaction, the empirical validity test does not paint a clear unequivocal picture. Certainly it can be concluded that committees in the EC/EU system are no artificial creation, not a typical development of purely accidental factors, nor merely a bureaucratic plot to keep, or even extend, their influence. Whereas the Member States acting in the Council of Ministers dominate the creation of comitology committees – as realism would suggest – the business of policy implementation through comitology is clearly shaped by the European Commission – an argument fitting more into a federalist conceptualisation of federal administration. Indeed, according to van der Knaap (1996), the Commission gets its own way in 99 per cent of all cases. However, the EC/EU's committee system is not characterised by a tendency whereby the different bodies are being replaced by pure Community institutions. The realist concept of diplomatic administration hardly corresponds to our empirical findings. Committee members in the Council's sub-units or acting in the European Commission's committee network may feel a certain type of 'togetherness'. But given the Commission's power to dominate the implementation game on the one hand, and the powers of the Council in establishing committees, as well as the power of the Member States to nominate their representatives and the power of the European Parliament to scrutinise the comitology system at least to a certain extent on the other hand, the image of independent diplomats shaping the preparation and implementation of EC law without the Commission is rather misleading. Of course, if we focus exclusively on the committee networks in the field of justice and home affairs established prior to the Maastricht Treaty (within the Schengen and the TREVI regime), we would have to acknowledge a certain trend of intergovernmental monitoring combined with some kind of governmentally monitored diplomatic administration between the early 1980s and the post-Maastricht era.

However, since Maastricht came into effect, the TREVI committee structure of the third pillar has shifted towards functional co-operation with a predominance of the national level at all stages of the policy process.[13] Some of the indicators may suggest neo-functionalism as the most appropriate tool for investigating the committee network in the field of EC legislation. The evolution of the Council's and the Commission's legislative output (Figure 3) in comparison to the increase of comitology committees (Figure 4) suggests the concept of administrative interaction as a supranational technocracy is in process. However, qualitative studies on national administrations and their interaction within the EU do not indicate subsequent shifts of loyalty from the nation-state towards the EU committee system as neo-functionalism would suggest. The concept of a multi-level mega-bureaucracy would imply growing complexity and a lack of transparency, hence administrative interaction networks that are impossible to control either by the European Parliament or by the national parliaments of the Member States. However, this concept ignores that the control capacities of the European Parliament, especially with regard to the comitology system, have been developed. This is not to say that Parliament's demands regarding the accountability of the comitology network have been fulfilled. But especially in those cases of post-Maastricht secondary legislation, where the co-decision procedure applies, the European Parliament is able to influence the choice and to control the operation of comitology procedures.[14]

Our interpretation of the empirical data leads to a characterisation of both the committee system and administrative interaction that is taking place following the concepts of horizontal and vertical fusion and co-operative administration. The growth rates of Council working group meetings (Figure 4), in the number of civil servants (Figure 6), in the frequency of comitology meetings in the field of agriculture and of the expenditure on comitology meetings, indicate a process of institutional and personal mobilisation within an unfixed and concentric political system, in which national administrations are shifting their attention towards Brussels. The challenges of a Commission providing the operational rules of comitology, the claims of a Parliament pressing COREPER into 'pre-conciliation' meetings for codecision and the demands of interest groups offering advice and bringing in 'transnational' expertise spill back into national administrative systems. Moreover, national civil servants are increasingly confronted with different administrative cultures and interaction styles. Consequently, mobilisation leads to some kind of Europeanisation of institutions and staff.

Thus, we need further research into the administrative interaction process. Special attention should be given to the question, if the emerging networks are changing the hierarchical institutional system or if they are leading to some kind of non-hierarchical governance. In other words, we propose a closer look at the real application of the committee rules by the different actors concerned. The lack of democratic accountability and transparency seems to constitute one of the most serious problems for the EC/EU committee network. Consequently, new insights on the level of secrecy, on the public acceptance of discretionary policy-making, and on the interaction between parliamentary committee structures on the one hand and administrative bodies taking ultimately binding decisions on the other should be considered. Intergovernmental and EC/EU institutional inputs into the committee system should be investigated in a comparative way: we need to know more about interests, ideas and political cleavages which occur during Treaty reforms, in order to evaluate the basic perceptions on the European Union and the daily integration process of the actors involved. Finally, incremental change in administrative structures due to the EC/EU and its committee system would be a challenging exercise for both comparative analysis and integration theory building.

Notes

1   The first empirical material was compiled by the Institut für Europäische Politik (1986) and by Falke (1996), Wessels (1998).
2   The following model is adopted from Wessels (1996).
3   For explanation of these terms see Delbrück (1987) and Scharpf (1991).
4   For explanation of terms see Wessels (1996), or expressly for the comitology committees, a 'comitocratie', Fabien (1995).
5   For the terms in this context see van Schendelen (1996).
6   European Court of Justice (1994): Rs. 1/94 (World Trade Organisation) Summary.
7   For such an approach see Wessels (1998).
8   Numbers for every Treaty: EEC Treaty 1957: 64; EEC Treaty after the Single European Act: 86; Maastricht Treaty: 152; Amsterdam Treaty: 195. We have counted every Treaty article and Indent which describes a specific decision-making procedure.
9   For current developments see the latest Annual Reports of Commission and for an overall picture up to 1995 Falke (1996, pp. 139–40).
10   Having been originally conceived as a consultative body with very limited powers in European decision-making, the European Parliament has gained more and more legislative powers. Hence, the share of Parliament's participation in the production of binding secondary legislation (defined as the sum of consultation, assent, co-operation and codecision procedures) raised between 1987 and 1997 from 28.6 to 53.5 per cent.
11   For tendencies in other European countries see Rometsch and Wessels (1996).
12   For the statistical data see Wessels (1997a).
13   Article 100d ECT in combination with Article K.4 Treaty on European Union (TEU) established the so-called K.4 Committee bringing together Senior Officials from the Member States in order to assist the Council and COREPER in the preparatory phase of measures in the field of justice and home affairs. The TREVI-system is thus being replaced by the K.4 Committee structure with 3 steering groups and 19 working groups. Unlike in the TREVI system, the European Commission is now fully associated in the work of the K.4 Committee.
14   See the contribution of Simon Hix in this volume, Blumann (1996), Bradley (1997) and Maurer (1999, 1999a).

2

A cross-sectoral view of comitology
Incidence, issues and implications

Introduction: the need for a global view

The debate over committees within the EU system of governance tends to reflect a bias towards either sectoral analysis or institutional architecture. Indeed, the contributions to this volume themselves indicate this structural tendency: clear patterns emerge at the sectoral level, and constitutional issues can be extrapolated from the general nature of the phenomenon, but it is difficult to obtain a global view of the overall trends and patterns of committee activity. This chapter seeks to address this problem through an examination of the extent and political significance of implementation committees: the infamous comitology procedure. It provides aggregate and cross-sectoral statistical data on the incidence of committees of national experts in the implementation of EU legislation. It also suggests an incipient typology of committee utilisation which provides a basis for more general considerations of the broader patterns of governance within the EU.

The essence of the committee problem within the EU system lies in the dynamic environment of contemporary governance. The Member States have endured a vast array of ideological, institutional, administrative and technological changes since the late 1970s (Müller and Wright, 1994). The stresses of globalisation, the imperatives of trade liberalisation, the associated processes of privatisation and marketisation have transformed the nature of domestic governance (Majone, 1994; McGowan and Wallace, 1996). These tensions have necessarily affected the EU, itself a part of the policy establishment subject to the processes of domestic administrative reform (Sun and Pelkmans, 1995). This chapter contextualises comitology within these broader transformations in the EU system of governance. It contends that the patterns of comitology – itself a division of administrative power between the EU and the Member States – reflects a complex matrix of national interests derived from the uneven process of administrative reform within the Member States (Wright, 1992).

Comitology reveals a deeply problematical picture of power relations in the EU. Whilst it represents the allocation of significant administrative powers, there appears to be no reliable pattern to that allocation (Pollack, 1995). Sometimes the Council grants control of implementation to the Commission, on other occasions it does not. Equally curious is the observation that the Commission and the EP also demonstrate complex comitology preferences. There are no obvious variables which serve to predict the preferences likely to be expressed by any of the legislative institutions. It is this irregularity and complexity of comitology preferment which suggests an explanation based on more profound dimensions of the EU system. This chapter investigates these deeper processes which appear ultimately to derive from the broad sweep of economic globalisation.

The hidden procedure

Unlike almost every other dimension of EU activity, comitology has received little attention beyond the aficionados of the Commission and EP (Bradley, 1992; 1997; Pedler and Schäfer, 1996; Dogan, 1997). A partial explanation of this lies in the lack of unambiguous data on the phenomenon itself. In fact, the actual incidence of comitology is extremely difficult to calculate, due to a number of characteristics of the establishment process. Committees of national experts have been involved in the implementation activity since the earliest days of the EU. Indeed, the EP first complained of the system of implementation associated with comitology in 1962 (European Parliament, 1962). However, despite the very useful codification of comitology procedures in 1987 (Council, 1987a), the ad hoc nature of its evolution means that comitology has been expressed in a variety of ways, and that a constellation of committees has been established with powers and constitutions which are only loosely similar, nor has the Commission been systematic in its efforts to apply the new version of powers to committees established prior to 1987. A further difficulty derives from the process by which implementation mechanisms are embedded in new legislation from areas of established EU activity, such as agriculture. It is common practice to indicate that implementation will be in line with procedures adopted in prior legislation (inherited comitology), but without indicating the form of implementation so implied. This problem is exacerbated by the habit of unconsolidated amendment legislation, whereby determination of the form of implementation to be used in new or amended legislation requires a paper chase through many other pieces of previous legislation and legislative amendments. In short, the empirical realities of comitology are opaque.

There is also an insurmountable difficulty in linking individual comitology procedures to the actual committees which exercise the relevant implementation power. Although reference is commonly made to the powers of established committees, such as the Standing Veterinary Committee, this represents a distortion of the legal position. There are two issues which need to be clarified. In the first instance, powers of implementation are not normally given to established committees, the legislation merely indicates that the Commission shall be assisted by a committee composed of representatives of the Member States: it is most uncommon for legislation to name a particular committee to exercise the relevant powers (Council, 1993f). Second, implementation procedures are specific to individual sections of EU legislation, and various activities authorised by a single piece of legislation may be subject to different implementation arrangements involving different committees of national experts (Council, 1994a). Thus, it is not possible either to identify what committee is likely to exercise the implementation function in relation to an individual piece of legislation, nor to identify the legislation for which an individual committee is responsible.

A final problem associated with the empirical analysis of comitology procedures relates to the multi-sectoral nature of a considerable proportion of EU legislation. For instance, legislation relating to research and technological development in the fisheries industry, needs to be coded under four headings: fisheries, industry, research and technological development (Council, 1991c). Whilst this is a second-order methodological problem, it does inform the overall status of the sectoral results obtained through statistical coding of the comitology-bearing legislation. It, also, necessarily informs the nature of the political debate over individual pieces of legislation: different Member States may well nominate different line departments for the negotiation of legislation with implications for more than one sector.

These problems notwithstanding, it has been possible to construct a database of the incidence of comitology between July 1987 (the commencement of the codified version of comitology procedures) and July 1995 (the end date of the relevant research) (Dogan, 1997). It is important to note, however, that detailed material on the type of procedure endorsed by the individual institutions is only currently available for new comitology procedures. Whilst aggregate figures will be presented for inherited comitology procedures, the data-base does not currently provide a full breakdown of the institutional preferences expressed in relation to these procedures. The empirical tables provided indicate aggregate comitology figures for all legislation adopted by the Council over the period of the census (new and inherited procedures), whereas those tables outlining institutional preferences relate only to legislation with new comitology procedures enacted during the relevant period. This data is based on the comitology procedures proposed by the Commission in legislative proposals, the opinions adopted by the EP in relation to those proposals and the actual procedures adopted by the Council in the final legislation. It should be noted that the tables distinguish between comitology-bearing legislation (Tables 1 and 2), and comitology procedures (Tables 3, 4 and 5).

Table 1 Incidence of legislation implemented by comitology procedures (new and inherited)

	All legislation	Legislation with new comitology procedures	Legislation with inherited comitology procedures	Legislation with comitology procedures
1987/88	551	12	71	83 (15.1)[a]
1988/89	703	35	88	123 (17.5)
1989/90	595	40	90	130 (21.8)
1990/91	594	43	67	110 (18.5)
1991/92	659	73	71	144 (21.9)
1992/93	530	45	76	121 (22.8)
1993/94	475	29	73	102 (21.5)
1994/95	494	43	52	95 (19.2)
Total	4601	320	588	908 (19.7)

Note: [a] % figures are given in parentheses.

Table 2 Incidence of comitology procedures (new and inherited) by category of legislation

	All ECU legislation	All ECU legislation with comitology	All legislation under consultation procedure[a]	All legislation under consultation procedure[a] with comitology	All legislation under co-op. or co-decision procedures	All legislation under co-op. or co-decision procedures with comitology
1987/88	44	19 (43.2)[b]	517	77 (14.9)	34	6 (17.7)
1988/89	71	39 (54.9)	649	95 (14.6)	54	28 (51.9)
1989/90	44	30 (68.2)	535	103 (19.3)	60	27 (45.0)
1990/91	55	31 (56.4)	527	83 (15.8)	67	27 (40.3)
1991/92	70	62 (88.6)	615	110 (17.9)	44	34 (77.3)
1992/93	45	30 (66.7)	477	88 (18.5)	53	31 (58.6)
1993/94	31	23 (74.2)	431	81 (18.8)	44	19 (43.2)
1994/95	53	38 (71.7)	461	68 (14.8)	33	21 (63.6)
Total	413	272 (65.9)	4212	705 (16.7)	389	193 (49.6)

Note: [a] Includes legislation enacted by majority vote under the Article 113 procedure from 1/1/93. This excludes EP from the legislative process and cannot be classified as co-operation or co-decision. [b] % figures are given in parentheses.

Table 3 Institutional comitology preferences: new comitology procedures granting the Commission executive autonomy

	Commission	European Parliament	Council of Ministers
1987/88	13 (46.2)[a]	10 (90.9)	5 (35.7)
1988/89	35 (85.4)	35 (87.5)	23 (56.1)
1989/90	32 (69.6)	32 (72.7)	24 (50.0)
1990/91	22 (44.9)	34 (70.8)	13 (26.0)
1991/92	59 (73.8)	59 (77.6)	30 (36.6)
1992/93	37 (82.2)	35 (87.5)	11 (21.6)
1993/94	32 (91.4)	29 (90.6)	17 (44.7)
1994/95	29 (61.7)	36 (87.5)	11 (23.4)
Total	252 (70.8)	270 (81.3)	134 (36.1)

Note: [a] % figures are given in parentheses.

Table 4 Longitudinal institutional comitology preferences: new comitology procedures granting the Commission executive autonomy in expenditure-related legislation

	Commission	European Parliament	Council of Ministers
1987/88	4 (57.1)[a]	7 (100.0)	4 (57.1)
1988/89	17 (89.5)	18 (94.7)	13 (68.4)
1989/90	17 (85.0)	17 (85.0)	12 (60.0)
1990/91	8 (57.1)	13 (92.9)	6 (42.9)
1991/92	23 (74.2)	25 (80.6)	14 (45.2)
1992/93	4 (66.7)	4 (66.7)	2 (33.3)
1993/94	9 (90.0)	10 (100.0)	5 (50.0)
1994/95	14 (66.7)	21 (100.0)	4 (19.0)
Total	96 (75.0)	115 (89.83)	60 (46.9)

Note: [a] % figures are given in parentheses.

Table 5 Longitudinal institutional comitology preferences: Commission autonomy by sector

Sector		1987/88	1988/89	1989/90	1990/91	1991/92	1992/93	1993/94	1994/95
Industry	CEC	2 (22.2)ᵃ	27 (87.1)	22 (66.7)	11 (36.7)	42 (76.4)	25 (80.6)	24 (96.0)	17 (63.0)
	EP	6 (85.7)	26 (83.9)	22 (71.0)	18 (60.0)	44 (81.5)	25 (86.2)	22 (95.7)	23 (85.2)
	CM	1 (10.0)	17 (54.8)	17 (51.5)	6 (20.0)	21 (37.5)	9 (27.3)	12 (46.2)	5 (18.5)
Expenditure	CEC	4 (57.1)	17 (89.5)	17 (85.0)	8 (57.1)	23 (74.2)	4 (66.7)	9 (90.0)	14 (66.7)
	EP	7 (100.0)	18 (94.7)	17 (85.0)	13 (92.9)	25 (80.6)	4 (66.7)	10 (100.0)	21 (100.0)
	CM	4 (57.1)	13 (68.4)	12 (60.0)	6 (42.9)	14 (45.2)	2 (33.3)	5 (50.0)	4 (19.0)
Agriculture	CEC	3 (50.0)	5 (100.0)	4 (30.8)	5 (35.7)	15 (75.0)	10 (90.9)	5 (83.3)	2 (33.3)
	EP	3 (75.0)	5 (100.0)	4 (36.4)	7 (50.0)	17 (85.0)	8 (88.9)	4 (66.7)	3 (75.0)
	CM	3 (42.9)	4 (80.0)	3 (21.4)	0 (0.0)	7 (33.3)	0 (0.0)	4 (66.7)	2 (33.3)
Technology	CEC	0 (0.0)	14 (93.3)	9 (100.0)	2 (33.3)	6 (50.0)	1 (50.0)	6 (100.0)	8 (50.0)
	EP	4 (100.0)	14 (93.3)	9 (100.0)	6 (100.0)	8 (66.7)	1 (50.0)	6 (100.0)	16 (100.0)
	CM	0 (0.0)	12 (80.0)	6 (66.7)	2 (33.3)	3 (25.0)	0 (0.0)	1 (16.7)	0 (0.0)
Research	CEC	1 (25.0)	12 (92.3)	7 (100.0)	2 (33.3)	6 (50.0)	1 (50.0)	5 (100.0)	8 (50.0)
	EP	4 (100.0)	12 (92.3)	7 (100.0)	6 (100.0)	8 (66.7)	1 (50.0)	5 (100.0)	16 (100.0)
	CM	0 (0.0)	10 (76.9)	5 (71.4)	2 (33.3)	3 (25.0)	0 (0.0)	2 (40.0)	0 (0.0)
Environment	CEC	nc	3 (100.0)	4 (100.0)	6 (66.7)	10 (71.4)	5 (83.3)	5 (100.0)	4 (57.1)
	EP	nc	2 (66.7)	4 (100.0)	7 (77.8)	10 (71.4)	5 (83.3)	4 (100.0)	4 (57.1)
	CM	0	2 (66.7)	2 (50.0)	2 (22.2)	6 (42.9)	1 (16.7)	3 (60.0)	1 (14.3)
Food	CEC	0	9 (75.0)	3 (100.0)	6 (66.7)	2 (40.0)	7 (87.5)	4 (100.0)	2 (40.0)
	EP	0	10 (83.3)	3 (100.0)	6 (66.7)	3 (75.0)	7 (87.5)	4 (100.0)	3 (75.0)
	CM	0	2 (16.7)	3 (75.0)	1 (11.1)	2 (40.0)	1 (12.5)	1 (20.0)	1 (20.0)
Social policy	CEC	3 (75.0)	6 (100.0)	7 (77.8)	2 (66.7)	6 (85.7)	5 (83.3)	6 (100.0)	8 (88.9)
	EP	4 (100.0)	6 (100.0)	7 (77.8)	2 (66.7)	6 (85.7)	5 (83.3)	5 (100.0)	9 (100.0)
	CM	3 (75.0)	6 (100.0)	8 (88.9)	2 (100.0)	5 (71.4)	4 (66.7)	5 (83.3)	4 (44.4)
Education	CEC	2 (66.7)	5 (100.0)	5 (71.4)	1 (100.0)	5 (83.3)	5 (83.3)	5 (100.0)	8 (88.9)
	EP	3 (100.0)	5 (100.0)	5 (71.4)	1 (100.0)	5 (83.3)	5 (83.3)	4 (100.0)	9 (100.0)
	CM	2 (66.7)	5 (100.0)	6 (85.7)	1 (100.0)	3 (50.0)	4 (66.7)	5 (100.0)	4 (44.4)
Health	CEC	0	0 (0.0)	7 (100.0)	2 (40.0)	2 (22.2)	6 (66.7)	1 (100.0)	2 (66.7)
	EP	0	0 (0.0)	7 (100.0)	2 (40.0)	3 (42.9)	8 (88.9)	1 (100.0)	2 (66.7)
	CM	0	0 (0.0)	6 (75.0)	1 (20.0)	0 (0.0)	2 (18.2)	0 (0.0)	0 (0.0)
Employment	CEC	1 (100.0)	5 (100.0)	5 (71.4)	1 (100.0)	6 (85.7)	6 (85.7)	6 (100.0)	6 (85.7)
	EP	1 (100.0)	5 (100.0)	5 (71.4)	1 (100.0)	5 (83.3)	6 (85.7)	5 (100.0)	7 (100.0)
	CM	1 (100.0)	5 (100.0)	6 (85.7)	1 (100.0)	4 (57.1)	5 (71.4)	6 (100.0)	2 (28.6)

Sector																
Veterinary	CEC	0	nc[a]	nc	(0.0)	6	(12.5)	1	(16.7)	2	7	(75.0)	1	(100.0)	nc	nc
	EP	0	nc	nc	(0.0)	7	(25.0)	2	(20.0)	2	5	(87.5)	1	(100.0)	nc	nc
	CM	0	nc	(100.0)	0	(0.0)	0	(0.0)	0	0	(0.0)	0	(0.0)	nc	(50.0)
Trade	CEC	nc	nc	nc	(0.0)	4	(20.0)	1	(50.0)	1	3	(80.0)	2	(75.0)	6	(50.0)
	EP	nc	nc	nc	(0.0)	3	(25.0)	1	(50.0)	1	2	(100.0)	0	(0.0)	6	(100.0)
	CM	nc	nc	(0.0)	2	(0.0)	2	(50.0)	0	1	(40.0)	2	(12.5)	3	(25.0)	
Statistics	CEC	1	4	(100.0)	nc	2	(100.0)	2	(66.7)	5	7	(100.0)	4	(80.0)	6	(85.7)
	EP	1	4	(100.0)	nc	2	(100.0)	3	(100.0)	3	6	(100.0)	3	(75.0)	5	(100.0)
	CM	1	3	(75.0)	nc	0	(0.0)	0	(0.0)	4	0	(80.0)	1	(20.0)	3	(42.9)
Telecoms	CEC	0	(0.0)	1	(50.0)	2	(100.0)	1	(16.7)	6	6	(75.0)	6	(100.0)	2	(40.0)
	EP	3	(100.0)	1	(50.0)	2	(100.0)	4	(66.7)	6	6	(75.0)	6	(100.0)	5	(100.0)
	CM	0	(0.0)	1	(50.0)	1	(50.0)	2	(33.3)	3	3	(37.5)	2	(33.3)	1	(20.0)
Transport	CEC	0	(0.0)	nc	1	(33.3)	3	(50.0)	8	1	(88.9)	2	(50.0)	3	(75.0)	
	EP	1	(100.0)	nc	1	(33.3)	4	(66.7)	9	1	(100.0)	2	(50.0)	3	(75.0)	
	CM	0	(0.0)	nc	0	(0.0)	2	(33.3)	2	1	(22.2)	0	(25.0)	0	(0.0)	
Safety	CEC	1	(100.0)	1	(50.0)	4	(100.0)	0	(0.0)	4	4	(57.1)	3	(66.7)	1	(50.0)
	EP	1	(100.0)	1	(50.0)	4	(100.0)	0	(0.0)	4	5	(57.1)	3	(100.0)	1	(50.0)
	CM	0	(0.0)	1	(50.0)	2	(40.0)	0	(0.0)	2	1	(28.6)	2	(16.7)	2	(50.0)
Develop. Aid	CEC	nc	1	(50.0)	2	(50.0)	3	(60.0)	3	2	(42.9)	0	(0.0)	2	(50.0)	
	EP	nc	2	(100.0)	2	(50.0)	4	(100.0)	3	2	(42.9)	1	(100.0)	3	(75.0)	
	CM	nc	0	(0.0)	2	(50.0)	1	(20.0)	0	2	(0.0)	0	(0.0)	1	(25.0)	
Customs	CEC	nc	nc	nc	(0.0)	1	(50.0)	2	3	(100.0)	1	(100.0)	2	(25.0)		
	EP	nc	nc	nc	(0.0)	1	(50.0)	1	3	(100.0)	nc	nc	3	(100.0)		
	CM	nc	nc	nc	(0.0)	0	(0.0)	0	2	(0.0)	1	(33.3)	0	(33.3)		
Fisheries	CEC	nc	nc	nc	3	(75.0)	3	4	(60.0)	2	(100.0)	0	(0.0)			
	EP	nc	nc	nc	4	(100.0)	4	3	(80.0)	1	(100.0)	1	(100.0)			
	CM	nc	nc	nc	0	(0.0)	3	2	(50.0)	2	(50.0)	0	(0.0)			
Energy	CEC	nc	3	(100.0)	1	(100.0)	1	3	(100.0)	3	(100.0)	2	(100.0)			
	EP	nc	3	(100.0)	1	(100.0)	1	3	(100.0)	3	(100.0)	2	(100.0)			
	CM	nc	3	(100.0)	2	(66.7)	1	3	(100.0)	2	(50.0)	0	(66.7)			
Regional policy	CEC	2	(100.0)	3	(100.0)	nc	2	(100.0)	2	3	(100.0)	4	(100.0)	4	(100.0)	
	EP	2	(100.0)	3	(100.0)	nc	2	(100.0)	2	3	(100.0)	4	nc	4	(100.0)	
	CM	2	(100.0)	3	(100.0)	nc	1	(50.0)	2	3	(100.0)	4	nc	4	(100.0)	
Industrial adjustment	CEC	1	(100.0)	3	(100.0)	nc	nc	1	1	(100.0)	1	(100.0)	5	(100.0)		
	EP	1	(100.0)	3	(100.0)	nc	nc	1	1	(100.0)	1	(100.0)	4	(100.0)		
	CM	1	(100.0)	3	(100.0)	nc	nc	1	0	(50.0)	0	(0.0)	5	(0.0)		
Competition	CEC	nc	nc	4	(100.0)	1	2	(100.0)	2	(100.0)	nc	nc				
	EP	nc	nc	4	(100.0)	1	2	(100.0)	2	(100.0)	nc	nc				
	CM	nc	nc	3	(75.0)	1	2	(100.0)	2	(100.0)	nc	nc				

Notes: [a] % figures are given in parentheses. 'nc' indicates no cases of new comitology recorded in relevant sector during reporting period.

Incidence of comitology

It is apparent that comitology has become a significant mechanism for the implementation of EU legislation. The aggregate figures indicate that it was utilised in approximately 20 per cent of all Council legislation between July 1987 and July 1995 (Table 1). The rate of application was relatively stable throughout this period, although it is possible to identify a slight longitudinal trend toward the increased use of the procedures. Thus, comitology is an important, but by no means ubiquitous aspect of EU governance. However, it is apparent that certain categories of legislation are much more likely to be implemented through the comitology procedures: over 65 per cent of expenditure-related legislation is implemented in this manner, whereas approximately 50 per cent of legislation approved under majority voting procedures were found to include comitology procedures (Table 2). There was also a degree of consistency in the positions adopted by the EU institutions in relation to the various types of comitology procedure. In general terms, the Commission and EP tended to favour Procedures I and IIa which enable the Commission to exercise the implementation power without direct intervention by the Council (executive autonomy), whereas the Council generally favoured the more restrictive Procedures IIb, IIIa and IIIb which facilitate Council involvement in implementation decisions (executive dependency) (Table 3).

Whilst these figures tend to support the traditional view of European politics as a contest between the EU institutions and the Member States, closer examination of the aggregate patterns of comitology preferment reveals a more complex picture. In the first instance, the preparedness of the Commission to deny itself executive autonomy in nearly 30 per cent of the relevant cases cannot be dismissed as a mere anomaly of the negotiation process (Tables 4 and 5): it is not that the Commission eventually accepts such procedures as a result of negotiation, rather, that it includes them in legislative proposals. Likewise, the preparedness of the Council to grant executive autonomy in 36 per cent of cases cannot be regarded as mere largesse. This ambiguity is further evidenced by the rate at which the Council allows the Commission executive autonomy over financial legislation. Whilst it is true that high levels of comitology can be found in expenditure-related legislation, it is also the case that the Council was significantly more relaxed about the grant of full powers of implementation to the Commission on financial matters, than it was in relation to any other category of legislation. Indeed, it did so in nearly 47 per cent of the relevant cases (Table 4).

This emergent complexity is reinforced by analysis of sectoral patterns of comitology. The longitudinal comitology preferences expressed by the legislative institutions are outlined in Table 5. There were substantial differences between the comitology preferences expressed by the legislative institutions (broad consensus over the Commission's executive autonomy was apparent in only a small number of sectors, notably Competition, Industrial Adjustment,

and Regional Policy). The EP generally preferred to grant the Commission executive autonomy (81 per cent of cases), the Commission itself showed a similar
preference (71 per cent of cases), whereas the Council generally preferred to
retain control over implementation decisions (36 per cent of cases). In addition,
the institutions only rarely adopted consistent preferment within individual
sectors or over time. Thus, the Council completely denied executive autonomy
only in the Veterinary sector, whilst the Commission and EP demanded it consistently in only four sectors (Energy, Regional Policy, Industrial Adjustment
and Competition). With relatively few exceptions all institutions tended to
endorse a much greater range of comitology procedures than might be expected.
Whilst it is possible to identify clusters of preference within sectors, the intra-
sector diversity of institutional comitology preferences suggests that they reflect
specific imperatives associated with individual legislative events.

The aggregate pattern of comitology produces ambiguous outcomes. The
use of comitology is significant, but by no means ubiquitous: it occurs in only
one-fifth of legislation. Whilst the use of the procedure is greater than average

Table 6 Institutional comitology preferences: all new procedures

		I	IIa	IIb	IIIa	IIIb	No committee	Misc.	Total
1987/88	CEC	1 (7.7)ᵃ	3 (23.1)	1 (7.7)	4 (30.8)	2 (15.4)	2 (15.4)	0	13
	EP	1 (9.1)	7 (63.6)	1 (9.1)	0	0	2 (18.2)	0	11
	CM	2 (14.3)	3 (21.4)	0	4 (28.6)	5 (35.7)	0	0	14
1988/89	CEC	23 (56.1)	6 (14.6)	1 (2.4)	5 (12.2)	0	6 (14.6)	0	41
	EP	24 (58.5)	6 (14.6)	0	5 (12.2)	0	5 (12.2)	1 (2.4)	41
	CM	18 (43.9)	5 (12.2)	2 (4.9)	14 (34.1)	2 (4.9)	0	0	41
1989/90	CEC	25 (54.3)	3 (6.5)	2 (4.3)	10 (21.7)	2 (4.3)	4 (8.7)	0	46
	EP	26 (56.5)	2 (4.3)	4 (8.7)	8 (17.4)	0	4 (8.7)	2 (4.3)	46
	CM	18 (37.5)	6 (12.5)	5 (10.4)	12 (25.0)	7 (14.6)	0	0	48
1990/91	CEC	18 (35.3)	3 (5.9)	2 (3.9)	26 (51.0)	0	2 (3.9)	0	51
	EP	22 (43.1)	11 (21.6)	4 (7.8)	11 (21.6)	0	2 (3.9)	1 (2.0)	51
	CM	7 (14.0)	6 (12.0)	5 (10.0)	22 (44.0)	10 (20.0)	0	0	50
1991/92	CEC	38 (45.2)	10 (11.9)	4 (4.8)	18 (21.4)	0	14 (16.7)	0	84
	EP	39 (45.9)	12 (14.1)	7 (8.2)	11 (12.9)	0	11 (12.9)	5 (5.9)	85
	CM	19 (23.2)	11 (13.4)	8 (9.8)	25 (30.5)	19 (23.2)	0	0	82
1992/93	CEC	30 (61.2)	4 (8.2)	1 (2.0)	7 (14.3)	0	5 (10.2)	2 (4.1)	49
	EP	30 (62.5)	3 (6.3)	2 (4.2)	3 (6.3)	0	4 (8.3)	6 (12.5)	48
	CM	7 (13.7)	4 (7.8)	7 (13.7)	19 (37.3)	14 (27.5)	0	0	51
1993/94	CEC	17 (47.2)	6 (16.7)	2 (5.6)	1 (2.8)	0	10 (27.8)	0	36
	EP	18 (48.6)	2 (5.4)	2 (5.4)	1 (2.7)	0	10 (27.0)	4 (10.8)	37
	CM	8 (21.1)	9 (23.7)	3 (7.9)	10 (26.3)	8 (21.1)	0	0	38
1994/95	CEC	25 (51.0)	4 (8.2)	6 (12.2)	12 (24.5)	0	2 (4.1)	0	49
	EP	34 (69.4)	2 (4.1)	1 (2.0)	4 (8.2)	0	2 (4.1)	6 (12.2)	49
	CM	7 (14.9)	4 (8.5)	8 (17.0)	26 (55.3)	2 (4.3)	0	0	47
Total	CEC	177 (48.0)	39 (10.6)	19 (5.1)	83 (22.5)	4 (1.1)	45 (12.2)	2 (0.5)	369
	EP	194 (52.7)	45 (12.2)	21 (5.7)	43 (11.7)	0	40 (10.9)	25 (6.8)	368
	CM	86 (23.2)	48 (12.9)	38 (10.2)	132 (35.6)	67 (18.1)	0	0	371

Note: ᵃ % figures are given in parentheses.

in expenditure-related legislation, and legislation agreed under majority voting, there does not appear to be any correlation between high incidence of comitology, and low levels of Commission autonomy (a full breakdown of institutional comitology preferences by type of proceure is provided in Table 6). Finally, there are very complex patterns of comitology preferment at the sectoral level. These suggest an issue-by-issue approach to implementation, rather than any global policy towards the type of implementation appropriate to particular sectors. Overall, then, comitology appears as a rather low-key administrative issue with a seemingly strong functional basis.

The political ambiguity of the comitology procedures

Despite the almost continuous complaints raised by the Commission and the EP about the use of restrictive comitology procedures documented in the chapter by Simon Hix, there are certain characteristics of the overall empirical record which help to explain the apparent ambiguity found in institutional comitology preferences. In the first instance, Procedure IIIa – the restrictive procedure most commonly endorsed by the Commission and the EP – actually offers significant political resources to the Commission in the implementation of controversial legislation. There is evidence which suggests that Commission control is actually enhanced by this seemingly restrictive procedure. Second, comitology is a relatively minor issue within the context of the pluralist process of legislative negotiation, and there are considerable incentives for the Commission (and even the EP) to pre-empt the comitology preferences of the Council in order to secure adoption of EU legislation. Third, institutional comitology preferences are vulnerable to pluralist intervention where sensitive political interests are at risk in comitology-bearing legislation. The preferences produced by this process are by definition issue-specific, and help to explain the diverse pattern of preferment within sectors. Finally, the implementation responsibility attracts political costs, as well as benefits, and there are political issues surrounding the location of the decision-maker within the broader EU system which appear to influence the type of comitology applied to certain categories of legislation.

Whilst it is appropriate to classify the seven comitology procedures in terms of the degree of autonomy they offer to the Commission,[1] the form of Council intervention enshrined in Procedure III differs from that under Procedure IIb. Whereas Procedure IIb requires the Commission to communicate the disputed implementation measures to the Council, Procedures IIIa and IIIb compel the Commission to submit to the Council 'a proposal relating to the measures to be taken' (Council, 1987a). In addition, whilst Procedure IIb allows the Council, acting by qualified majority, to take a *different* decision within the prescribed time limit, Procedure III merely states that the Council should act on the proposal by qualified majority. These distinctions effectively mean that measures referred under Procedure IIb are considered under special voting mechanisms established by Council Decision 87/373/EEC, which allow the Council to *modify* Commission measures by a qualified majority, whereas Procedure III operates under the voting procedures established by Article 148 (2) of the EU Treaty and, thereby, requires unanimity for the modification of Commission proposals. Furthermore, under Procedure IIIa, if there is neither sufficient support for acceptance of the proposal by qualified majority, nor unanimous support for an alternative decision, the Council is unable to act and the proposal may be adopted by the Commission on the expiration of the relevant time limit. Thus, whilst Procedure IIIa is certainly restrictive in that it denies the Commission executive autonomy and excludes the EP from the implementation process, it potentially places the Commission in a uniquely strong position.

Indeed, a highly controversial comitology decision under the Genetically Modified Organisms Directive (90/220/EEC) provides a perfect example of the Commission's capabilities under this procedure (Council, 1990a). In this instance, a series of complex political responses to the proposed market approval of a transgenic maize sponsored by France, but requiring Commission authorisation, led the relevant committee to prevent ratification of the Commission measure which was referred to the Council under Procedure IIIa.

> At the Environment Council of 25 and 26 June 1996, though thirteen of the national delegations indicated that they did not approve the Commission's proposal (and one abstained), the Council was unable to come to any contrary decision. The qualified majority necessary to adopt the Commission's proposal ... was clearly lacking; any amendment of the Commission's proposal would have required unanimity, which France, having already come out in favour of the market authorisation, was able to block. In these circumstances, the decisional power reverted to the Commission. (Bradley, 1999: 212–13)

What makes this case particularly interesting is the vociferous outcry against the Commission's position. In addition to the opposition met in the Council, the EP passed two resolutions condemning the authorisations (European Parliament, 1996 and 1997), and a major furore was raised by environmental and consumer groups throughout the EU. Nevertheless, the Commission proceeded to adopt the authorising decision on 23 January 1997 (Commission, 1997).

The official denigration of restrictive comitology by the Commission and the EP notwithstanding (Commission, 1991; European Parliament, 1991a), a study of the role played by comitology in the process of legislative negotiation reveals a degree of sanguinity in practice. There is substantial evidence that comitology is actually a fairly minor consideration in the day-to-day thrust of EU politics. In the first instance, the institutions have endorsed particular types of committee procedure merely to ensure administrative continuity with established patterns of consultation in individual sectors (Council, 1987b, 1990b and 1990e). Second, the primary concern of the Commission and the EP is the expansion of EU competence and responsibility; it follows that when confronted by a choice between comitologically restricted EU legislation and no EU legislation, it is entirely appropriate for these institutions to forbear on the question of implementation. Indeed, there is evidence that the Commission and EP actually pre-empt the likely response of the Council to the implementation of individual pieces of legislation by offering restrictive comitology as a part of the initial compromise (Council, 1993d and 1994b). There are much more important issues at risk in the legislative process than comitology.

Indeed, it is clear that comitology forms only one element in a range of resources traded within the legislative process (Commission, 1990). The EU system offers a variety of options for every aspect of the legislative process: there can be negotiation over the appropriate treaty basis and, thereby, the appropriate legislative and voting procedures; the form of the legislative instrument (Directive, Regulation or Decision) and, hence, the locus of daily implementation (Commission or National Administrations); the nature of litigation and the rigour of likely enforcement (direct effect, implied direct effect or indirect effect) (Burley and Mattli, 1993: 6; Mazey and Richardson, 1993). These are administrative/legal distinctions which can have a significant impact on the outcome of EU policies and feed into the pluralist legislative process. Interests which seek weak EU activity prefer the use of treaty articles which prescribe the Consultation Procedure, because it facilitates the blockage of undesirable legislation; alternatively, when faced with irresistible political demands for legislation, unanimity allows unavoidable legislation to be weakened by restrictive comitology (Council, 1993e). Indeed, national implementation offers a range of regulatory structures which are likely to afford opportunities for avoidance, particularly when national discretion concerns the definition of target areas and groups (Council, 1991e). This is also the case in relation to the form of enforcement – citizens, pressure or interest groups are more likely to launch prosecutions than Member States, or the Commission which must temper its own prosecution policy against a multitude of other political considerations (Ludlow, 1991). For example, it would have been politically difficult for the Commission to launch a high-profile prosecution against the British government for failure adequately to implement water quality Directives against newly privatised utilities during the prolonged agony of the Maastricht ratification debate.

Comitology falls into this category of negotiable procedural resource. Thus, permissive comitology procedures which grant autonomy to the Commission privilege interests which seek rigorous implementation, whereas restrictive comitology which facilitates Council intervention generally favours interests wishing to maintain a level of potential control over the implementation process.

The reality of EU politics involves a market in procedures, and the implications they have for outcomes. The price of legislative completion may be that legislation takes the form of a Directive instead of a Regulation, or that a Regulation can only be secured through restrictive comitology (Council, 1992b).

The extent to which implementation emerges as a key issue within legislative negotiation depends on the specific impact of individual proposals on mobilised interests: private, as well as public. These actors have no inherent attitude to comitology, but focus on likely outcomes associated with the political opportunity structures generated by a variety of institutional procedures. However, the full panoply of interest intermediation will only be activated when circumstances demand. This issue-specificity of pluralist intervention helps to explain the chequered pattern of comitology preferment within individual sectors.

Finally, it is apparent that comitology reflects a concern over the locus of decision-making. Whilst there is an established literature on the respective impact of Commission versus national implementation – who has the power to make discretionary implementation decisions – this has tended to concentrate on the advantages or disadvantages of social dumping and regulatory cheating for particular Member States on certain issues (Pollack, 1995; Majone, 1993). There are, of course, many instances where the Council has acted to reduce the Commission's executive freedom by imposing restrictive comitology. These obviously support the notion that the Member States are prepared to use comitology to maintain national control. However, they also indicate a concern about the administrative location of the implementation function. It is possible to identify several cases where the Council has imposed different comitology procedures within a single piece of legislation, and sub-divided implementation between separate comitology procedures (Council, 1993b and 1993c). The detailed motives of the Member States are not always open to investigation, particularly in the case of such arcane procedures as comitology. However, it is possible that the Member States may have a more sophisticated agenda than a desire merely to maintain control. Where the Council has sub-divided the implementation function, it has usually introduced an element of Council involvement by imposing Procedures IIa (Council, 1993b), IIIa or IIIb (Council, 1993c). Whilst such impositions may appear to strengthen national control, this may be more apparent than real. Procedures IIa and IIIa offer only partial relief to the Member States and Procedure IIIa can actually benefit the Commission, as occurred in the transgenic maize case detailed above. Whilst the limited literature on comitology did not highlight the ambiguity of Procedure IIIa until transgenic maize, it has long been acknowledged by practitioners and was raised with this author by officials in the United Kingdom Cabinet Office as early as 1992. Why, then, would the Member States bother to impose Procedure IIa or IIIa, if this does not substantially improve their power capabilities *vis-à-vis* the Commission? The answer may lie in transformations at the domestic level, whereby governments and elites occasionally find themselves obliged to endorse fiscal, and associated regulatory, policies which are potentially or actually unpopular. In such situations, governments may feel obliged to be seen to negotiate some degree of national control over policy implementation, but be delighted for the Commission to emerge as the wicked martinet during the actual implementation process. This 'scapegoat' hypothesis remains to be demonstrated, however the following analysis of the broader issues associated with administrative adaptation within the EU suggests that it may offer a useful focus for further research.

Comitology and the emerging patterns of EU governance

Comitology represents a body of administrative structures through which the EU system processes political demands. These structures are distinguished by the degree of control and responsibility exercised by the constituent polities of the system: the EU and national institutions. In this sense, comitology can be seen as part of the general process of institutional and administrative innovation and development observed at the national level (Wright, 1992). It represents an example of governmental adaptation. The particular configuration of control and responsibility apportioned between the EU and the Member States through comitology can, therefore, be placed in the context of associated developments within contemporary governance.

Such an approach to comitology is required by the extraordinary complexity and apparent inconsistency revealed by analysis of aggregate patterns of comitology activity and preferment. A traditional interpretation of institutional, national and sectoral interests would predict very clear patterns of actor preference with regard to comitology procedures: it would view comitology as a competition between EU and national control (Tranholm-Mikkelsen, 1991; Grieco, 1988). According to this debate, the Commission and EP should seek procedures which enhance EU control, the Council should prefer procedures which maintain national control, and individual social and industrial actors should prefer procedures which reflect desired outcomes associated with either EU or national control. In the event, a detailed examination of the pattern and politics of comitology preferment fails to support these rather simplistic interpretations of political interest within the EU system. In fact, the Commission, the EP, the Council, social and industrial actors all adopt positions which definitively contradict these traditional assumptions. The Commission regularly proposes committee procedures which prejudice its powers of implementation and these are occasionally endorsed by the EP, similarly the Council often approves implementation procedures which concentrate power in the Commission, and lobby groups demonstrate an issue-specific, rather than sector-specific, approach to implementation mechanisms. These unexpected policy preferences, and the conditions under which they arise, provide useful insights into the changing structure of EU governance.

To the extent that recent revolutions in public administration can be traced to the broad pressures of globalisation (Cerny, 1996), the location of comitology within the process of administrative adaptation provides the beginning of an explanation for the strange and unexpected pattern of comitology preferment. When the EU system considers individual instances of comitology (micro-instances of governmental structure), it actually addresses an almost unique combination of political and functional variables which reflect the momentary circumstances surrounding administrative adaptation in fifteen, distinctive political systems (Wright, 1994). There are three dimensions to this process. In the first instance, all Member States need to address problems generated by globalisation (expenditure constraint, trade and market liberalisation, corporate transnationality and mobility) (Strange, 1996): this forms the agenda of the implementation event. Second, EU polities have developed a variety of policy instruments through which potential solutions can be delivered (corporatisation, privatisation, marketisation and de-regulation) (Majone, 1994): this informs the debate over implementation. Finally, these problems and policy instruments interface with individual Member States differentially. The Member States have varying regulatory cultures, they have reached different points in the process of administrative reform, and they are subject to distinctive political pressures (Wilkes, 1996): this generates the dynamic and particular interests expressed in comitology preferences.

A further insight into comitology preferences may be found in the dual ideological nature of the Single Market Programme: long the dominant legislative project of the EU. Whilst a vast literature documents the desirability of increased competitiveness and the virtues of market economic ideology, only gradually have commentators begun to identify the governmental ideology associated with this approach to economic management (Müller and Wright, 1994; Majone, 1994; McGowan and Wallace, 1996; Schmidt, 1996). The emphasis on European competitiveness and non-discrimination inherent in the Single Market Programme requires governmental structures and processes which challenge the traditional notion of the interventionist state. It generates legal obligations, such as open public procurement (Council, 1992a), the transparency of public enterprise finance (Council, 1990c), common systems of prudential supervision (Council, 1989a and 1991d), common health and safety standards in food, agriculture, industry (Council, 1990d, 1991a and 1989b). These are all required in order to set up the single market, but they also have significant implications for the political economy of public policy management. This legislation establishes governmental processes, as well as economic policy instruments, which share a common politico-institutional ideology, essentially derived from the American experience of anti-trust regulation (Hancher and Moran, 1989). Only a modest portion of EU legislation (9 per cent during the period of the comitology research outlined above) seeks to address public policy concerns through the expenditure of financial resources (Table 2): the vast majority of these initiatives are regulatory in nature. They involve the determination of rules of the game, together with the establishment of rule modification and compliance procedures and, crucially they are directed with equal force to governmental, as well as private, actors.

This regulatory dimension of EU legislation is increasingly delivered through processes which include the comitology procedure, and embraces many issues which are politically fraught for national governments. It is at this point, that the 'scapegoat' hypothesis introduced above may be clarified. There is an emergent consensus among national and European elites that economic growth must be achieved through monetarist policies based on industrial specialisation, trade liberalisation and fiscal prudence. This consensus lies at the heart of the Single Market Programme and European Economic and Monetary Union (EMU). However, several Member States are confronted by enormous domestic political obstacles to the realisation of these policy goals. The trauma of the French, Italian and Belgian struggle to meet the EMU convergence criteria are testimony to these difficulties: France has struggled to control public sector unions, Italy has faced perennial difficulties in the modernisation and reduction of the public sector itself, and all Member States face occasional problems in confronting entrenched domestic interests threatened by this public policy paradigm (Schmidt, 1996).

This broad public policy context further contributes to the interpretation of institutional comitology preferences. If, for example, the Member States wish to increase competition in publicly owned utilities, they may well confront substantial opposition from the relevant, domestic, trade unions and management constituencies. There may be pressing reasons why, even a socialist, government would wish to reform such a sector: to reduce the investment burden, or to improve industrial efficiency (Majone, 1994). However, such a government may well wish to avoid direct responsibility for the relevant decisions, and may very possibly need to be seen to oppose such reforms. Under these circumstances, it is enormously useful for implementation of detailed reforms to fall squarely on the Commission, although the success of the reform process may require close and private consultation between the publicly outraged national government (essential for domestic political consumption), and the Commission. This would be a situation where Procedure I offers distinct advantages: the Commission bears the odium of responsibility for unpopular implementation decisions, the Member States can claim to oppose the reforms, but the Commission and Member States nevertheless remain able, privately, to co-ordinate the implementation process. It is not possible to prove from the comitology research that this is the nature of the political deals associated with certain comitology procedures, but it represents a useful hypothesis for explaining why the Member States appear to be relaxed about the transfer of politically sensitive implementation powers to the Commission via Procedure I (Council, 1990c and 1992a).

It is apparent that the various inconsistencies evident in the broad, cross-sectoral pattern of institutional comitology preferences raise intriguing questions about the nature of power in the EU. The research outlined in this chapter isolates five variables which appear to motivate institutional action in relation to comitology: defence of institutional prerogatives (the default position);

administrative and internal political convenience (maintain established patterns of consultation, keep the awkward members of the Council happy); pluralist competition (policy outcomes are highly issue-specific and associated with complex compromises); variable administrative adaptation (the Member States experience the demand for structural reform at different rates in different sectors); and, elite concertation (the Member States and Commission collude to use comitology procedures to manipulate domestic political opposition). Each of these causal imperatives are politically credible and supported by the general pattern of comitology. They also help to explain the obviously complex pattern of institutional comitology preferences. However, they are based on aggregate level analysis and the test of this typology must lie in detailed sectoral case studies, such as those provided in the other chapters of this volume.

Notes

1 There are few instances of Procedures IVa and IVb, and they were not included in the database.

SIMON HIX

3

Parliamentary oversight of executive power
What role for the European Parliament in comitology?

Introduction: executive rule-making and the 'decline of parliaments'

Across the democratic world, the use of executive rule-making powers to make public policy has increased dramatically. In post-industrial, high-tech and globally interdependent societies, governments have needed to respond quickly to changing market circumstances, new scientific findings, global forces, and new public demands. Also, as the task of regulating the production and supply of goods and services in the market has become more technical, the adoption of primary and secondary legislation via the traditional parliamentary route has been increasingly impractical. Parliaments consequently prefer to pass 'framework laws', delegating the responsibility to governments to 'fill the gaps' or even act as surrogate legislators. Furthermore, part of this process has been driven by the replacement of 'redistribution' by 'regulation' as the dominant instrument of modern government. Parliaments have been willing to delegate regulatory powers to independent agencies to protect policy outputs from electoral majorities and promote government in the long-term 'public interest'.

The story has been much the same at the European level as at the nation level in Europe (esp. Majone, 1994). To regulate the single market and implement EU legislation and policies, the European Commission adopts over 6000 executive instruments a year. But, the Commission is not alone in enacting these rules. As in several other federal-type systems, specialists from the administrations of the Member State governments participate directly in the adoption of executive instruments through the 'comitology' system.

The result, so many authors claim, is a 'decline of parliaments' as the power of executives has increased at both the national and European levels (e.g. Norton, 1990; Olsen and Mezey, 1991). The 'separation of powers' principle asserts that passing laws is the responsibility of legislative assemblies, whereas executives are responsible for the implementation and administration of law.

However, direct rule-making by governments occupies a grey area between legislation and execution. Secondary rules are necessary instruments for the implementation of primary legislation. In the classic hierarchy of legal norms, 'framework' legislation sets 'basic principles' and secondary rules are simply technical interpretations of these principles. However, where government instruments address high-profile issues, such as public health, or have significant indirect re-distributive implications, such as many competition policy decisions, the line between execution and legislation is compromised. The problem for parliaments is that there are powerful incentives for governments to cross this line: to reduce the risk of legislative defeat in the pursuit of policy goals, or re-election, or services for particular societal constituencies.

As other legislatures have criticised this growth of executive rule-making power, the European Parliament (EP) has been highly critical of the comitology system. Given the weakness of parliaments in other systems (where they used to be strong), one might assume that there is little hope for the EP to secure a role in the oversight of the comitology system (in a system where the parliament has traditionally been weak). Nevertheless, the 'decline of parliaments' thesis masks a more subtle picture. Parliaments do not need to participate in the adoption of secondary instruments to limit the discretion of executives. Legislatures have designed rules and procedures to limit executive discretion in the use of secondary instruments (esp. Carey and Shugart, 1998). Moreover, in the EU system, through the reforms of the Maastricht and Amsterdam Treaties, the EP has secured a central role in the legislative process of the EU. Indeed, in contrast with many other legislatures, the EP is often able to enforce its policy objectives on the holders of executive power (Garrett, 1995; Tsebelis and Money, 1997).

So, what should be the role of the EP in the comitology system? To address this question, section two elaborates a 'comparative approach', through a review of general theories of legislative control and a discussion of parliamentary oversight in the United States and Germany. Section three then looks at the evolution of the EP's strategy towards comitology, and analyses how this fits with the generalisable theoretical and empirical knowledge. Finally, section four draws the arguments together in a tentative conclusion.

A comparative approach to parliamentary oversight of executive rule-making

A growing number of scholars use a 'comparative approach' to understand how the EU political system works (Hix, 1994; Risse-Kappen, 1996). This approach operates on two levels. First, at a theoretical level, the EU can be analysed using generalisable (cross-systemic) models and concepts about particular elements of the political process. In our case, these are theories of legislative control of executive discretion. Second, at an empirical level, the EU can be compared with other political systems. In our case, the EU is compared with the United States and Germany.

Theoretical level: principals' strategies to control agents' discretion

A common theoretical framework for conceptualising the relationships between legislators and executives is 'principal–agent' analysis. In this approach, legislators (the principals) delegate powers to executive office-holders (the agents). This framework was originally developed to analyse the relationship between the US Congress and the US federal bureaucracy. However, a similar relationship exists between the legislature of the EU (the EP or the Council) and the EU executive (the Commission and the national governments) (Pollack, 1997).

In principal–agent analysis opinions are divided over whether agents are beyond-control once power is delegated, or whether principals remain in control (Weingast and Moran, 1983; Epstein and O'Halloran, 1998). On one side of the debate, principals face the problem of 'executive discretion', or the ability of an agent to pursue policy outcomes that are different from the policies originally envisaged by the principals when the responsibilities were first delegated. This phenomenon is illustrated in Figure 7.

In Figure 7, legislators A, B and C agree on policy position X, and decide that the policy should be implemented using direct instruments by the executive. However, if the ideal policy position of the executive is different from the intended goal of the legislators, the executive will try to enact a policy closer to its ideal point than the intended goal, at position Y for example. If the legislators must agree by majority, they will be unable to over-turn this executive strategy if two legislators (A and C in this example) are closer to the executive's implementation position (Y) than the original legislative agreement (X).

On the other hand, knowing that this will happen, legislators can design restrictions on executive discretion. Legislatures can use institutional and

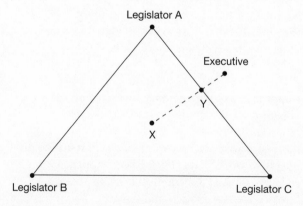

Figure 7 Executive discretion from intended legislation
Source: Adapted from McCubbins *et al.* 1989.

budgetary mechanisms to limit discretion (esp. Moe, 1989; Kiewiet and McCubbins, 1991). For example, rules could be used to specify who are the constituents of an agent's actions, how an agent must act before reaching a decision (such as listening to both sides of the debate), the relations between the agent and other administrative and political officials, and how deliberations and decisions are to be made public. Similarly, legislators can alter the size of agency budgets to punish agents who veer too far from the intended legislation and award agencies who supply policy outcomes close to the intended legislative goal.

The result of these controls is a restriction of the ability of an agent to move from the original policy intention. This is illustrated in Figure 8. As in Figure 7, the legislators agree on a policy goal X and that the policy should be implemented using direct instruments by the executive. However, to constrain the ability of the executive to achieve a policy outcome different from their intention, they include in a separate statute (or in legislation delegating the responsibility) a set of procedures defining how exactly the executive shall go about its job. The result is some drift towards the executive's ideal point, but only to Z instead of Y.

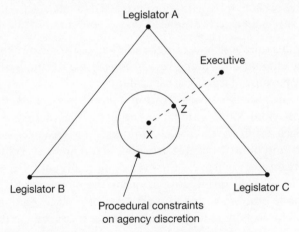

Figure 8 Procedural constraints on executive discretion
Source: Adapted from Epstein and O'Halloran 1999.

In sum, certain institutional configurations give more control by legislatures over executive agents than others (esp. McCubbins, 1985; Horn, 1995). In other words, if the EP has the power to choose institutions, it can design a set of procedures to limit the discretion of national governments and the Commission in the operation of the comitology system. However, before turning to the EU, we shall investigate how these theoretical issues operate in practice in several leading representative democracies.

Empirical level: parliamentary oversight in the United States and Germany

In both presidential and parliamentary systems, governments have increased their use of executive instruments. In the US (presidential) these are called 'orders' or 'regulations' and in Germany (parliamentary) they are '*Rechtsverordnungen*'. Also, the operation of legislative control over the exercise of these instruments has developed in similar ways in presidential and parliamentary systems (esp. Haibach, 1997).

In the United States, until the 1980s, proposed implementing measures by the US federal government had to be transmitted to the Congress, and could be enacted only if neither the Senate nor the House of Representatives rejected them during the two following sessions. To facilitate legislative oversight under this procedure, the US Congress adopted Section 136 of the Legislative Reorganisation Act of 1946:

> To assist the Congress in appraising the administration of the laws and in developing such amendments or related legislation as it may deem necessary, each standing committee of the Senate and the House of Representatives shall exercise continuous watchfulness of the execution by the administrative agencies concerned of any laws, the subject matter of which is within the jurisdiction of such committee; and, for that purpose, shall study all pertinent reports and data submitted to the Congress by the agencies in the executive branch of the Government.

Authorised by this rule, both houses of the US Congress voted on a regular basis to increase the amount of staff and resources available to congressional committees for the purpose of legislative oversight.

However, this system has been far from unproblematic. First, the conventional wisdom about Congressional oversight is that despite more staff, increased budgets for Congressional committees, more resources for information collection, and more detailed instructions about how to scrutinise executive rules, 'these measures fail to close or even significantly narrow any perceived oversight gap in either its quantitative or qualitative dimensions' (Ogul, 1997: 207–8). The basic problem is that in most areas of executive action there are little incentives for legislators to get involved. Most issues are too technical or too trivial to bother spending enough resources to enable a legislator to be able to effectively scrutinise a legislative decision. Also, the committee staff members who do have significant interests tend to develop close, long-term relationships with the agencies and end up serving more as an information channel between the executive and the congressional committee than active investigators: as agents of the executive instead of the political principals.

Second, in 1983 the US Supreme Court annulled the veto power of Congress. The case arose as a result of a veto by the House of Representatives of a decision by the Department of Justice's Immigration and Naturalisation Service to suspend the deportation of an individual under the Immigration and Nationality Act.[1] The Supreme Court ruled that the veto breached the principle of the separation of powers:

> Congress made a deliberate choice to delegate to the executive Branch ... the authority to allow deportable aliens to remain in this country in specific circum-

stances ... Congress must abide by its delegation of authority until that delegation is legislatively altered or revoked.

In other words, the US Congress can only over-rule an executive instrument through the introduction and adoption of new legislation under the existing legislative procedures.

Nevertheless, the US Congress has been able to limit executive discretion through other means. Most significantly, an alternative to the costly 'police patrol' method of oversight, where congressional committees scrutinise every piece of legislation, is the 'fire alarm' method (esp. McCubbins and Schwartz, 1984). This involves assuming that an executive instrument is fine until a congressional committee is notified by a private or public interest group to the contrary. This passes on the costs of monitoring to the private interests who are the subjects of the executive's actions, and who possess relevant expertise and information that would be costly for legislators to obtain. As a result, if an executive agency is doing an ineffectual job, is punishing a particular interest, or is captured by a particular interest, private groups will inform the legislators concerned and seek to overturn the executive actions.

In Germany, the committees of the *Bundestag* and *Bundesrat* are among the most highly developed of the parliamentary systems. Part of this is because of the specific role of the German parliament in the German federal system, and particularly in the oversight of the implementation of federal legislation. According to Article 80(2) of the German *Grundgesetz* (Basic Law), virtually all executive instruments require the consent of the *Bundesrat*. The *Bundesrat* is composed of the executives of the German federal states, in the same way that the national governments are represented in the Council in the EU system – which suggests that the EU comitology committees (composed of representatives of national administrations) are the functional equivalent of *Bundesrat* committees.

Furthermore, the *Bundesrat* is directly involved in the post-legislative implementation stage because of the 'co-operative federal' (also called 'executive federal') structure of the German system. In such a system, a large number of policy competences are 'shared' between the higher and lower levels of government. And in these policy competences, the executives of the lower level participate directly in the making of legislation at the higher level, and the lower and higher executives are jointly responsible for the implementation of legislation (Frowein, 1986; Bulmer, 1989). As a result, direct participation of the *Länder* governments in executive action via the *Bundestag* ensures certain policy efficiencies. First, the *Bundesrat* oversight system allows the transposition of federal legislation into practice in the *Länder* to be monitored collectively. Second, it ensures continuity between the actions of the *Länder* governments as legislators and executors.

As a result, for the EP, the role of the *Bundestag* vis-à-vis the *Bundesrat* is instructive. Because of the *Bundesrat's* powers under Article 80 of the *Grundge-*

setz, the *Bundestag* has assumed similar powers of prior consultation, non-objection and even consent. However, this practice was challenged before the *Bundesverfassungsgericht* (Federal Constitutional Court). In its ruling on the case, the German Court gave the *Bundestag* more freedom to veto legislation than the US Supreme Court gave the US Congress, but nonetheless restricted the *Bundestag's* oversight rights. The court ruled that:

> Authorisations for the adoption of regulations which are dependent on the consent of the *Bundestag* do not contribute to a clear separation of the responsibilities of the executive and the legislature. From the fact that Art. 80(1) *Grundegesetz* does not expressly allow them, it does, however, not follow that they are unlawful … Because the regulations to be made can be of considerable economic and political importance it is justified if the legislature reserves for itself a right to participation.[2]

In practice, the Court argued that the executive can enact direct instruments without having to wait for approval by the *Bundestag*, but in areas of 'considerable importance' the *Bundestag* can subsequently exercise a veto.

Finally, the ability of the legislature to influence the executive also depends on the process of selecting and de-selecting the holders of executive office. In presidential systems, the executive is elected independently of the legislature, but (as in the US case) the individual members of the President's cabinet are subject to a vote of approval by the committees of the legislature (the Senate in the US case). The legislature consequently has an initial veto power over ministerial appointments. In parliamentary systems, in contrast, the executive derives its authority from winning a majority of seats in parliamentary elections. In theory, the legislature can then withdraw support for the government as a whole, and in some systems pass a 'vote of no-confidence' in an individual member of the cabinet. In practice, however, the 'fusion' of the executive and a legislative majority allows the government to use 'party whips' to dominate the parliament and prevent a withdrawal of legislative support for the government or an individual minister. Nevertheless, the procedural norm of 'ministerial responsibility' in both systems enables the legislature to hold individual members of the executive accountable for actions by a ministry or agency for which they are responsible. *A priori* veto and *a posteriom* vote-of-no-confidence are blunt instruments. But they are both cheap and effective mechanisms for keeping the executive in-check.

The European Parliament and the comitology system

The comitology system

The comitology system was established by a Council Decision in July 1987.[3] The Decision established three sets of committees – advisory, management and regulatory committees – and a set of rules governing their operation. Table 7 shows how this system works. Under the advisory committee procedure (Procedure I),

Table 7 How comitology works

Procedure	Operation of the procedure
Advisory committees	
Procedure I	The Commission must take the 'utmost account' of the committee's opinion, but the Commission is free to enact the measures regardless of their opinion.
Management committees	The Commission can enact the measures *unless the committee opposes* the measures by Qualified Majority Vote (QMV), in which case the matter is referred to the Council, and either:
Procedure IIa	the Commission *may enact the measures* unless the Council rejects or modifies them by QMV within one month; or
Procedure IIb	the Commission *must defer enactment of the measures* until the Council either rejects or modifies them by QMV, or fails to act within three months.
Regulatory committees	The Commission can enact the measures *only if the committee supports* the measures by QMV, otherwise the matter is referred to the Council, and in a set time period either:
Procedure IIIa	('net') the Council can reject the measures by *QMV* or modify them by unanimity, but the Commission can enact the measures if the Council approves them by QMV or fails to act; or
Procedure IIIb	('safety net') the Council can reject the measures by *simple majority* or modify them by unanimity, but the Commission can enact the measures if the Council approves them by simple majority or fails to act.
Safeguard measures	The Commission must notify the Council of the proposed safeguard measures before acting, after which, either:
Procedure IVa	the Council may reject or modify the measures by *QMV*, but the *Commission can enact the measures if the Council fails to act* in a set time period; or
Procedure IVb	the Council may confirm, amend or reject the measures by *simple majority*, and *the measures are deemed revoked if the Council fails to act* in a set time period.

Note: QMV is a system of voting where (a) the votes of the Member State are weighted according to their size (10 for Germany, France, Italy, UK; 8 for Spain, 5 for Belgium, Greece, the Netherlands and Portugal; 4 for Austria and Sweden; 3 for Denmark, Ireland and Finland; and 2 for Luxembourg), and (b) 62 out of the 87 total votes is required for a motion to be carried.

Source: Adapted from Steunenberg *et al.* (1996), Docksey and Williams (1997) and Dogan (1997).

the Commission has the greatest degree of freedom. The Commission must simple take 'utmost account' of the opinion of the national experts, and can simply ignore their advice without any Council or governmental recourse (although the committee can record its opposition to a proposed measure in the committees minutes). This procedure is used in most areas of EU competition policy, such as Commission decisions on mergers and state aids to industry.

The management committee procedures are mostly used for the Common Agricultural Policy. The main management committee procedure (Procedure IIa) is much like the US system before the 1983 Supreme Court ruling and the role of the *Bundestag* in the German system, where the executive can enact measures unless they are overturned by the legislature. The more restrictive version of the procedure (Procedure IIb), where decisions must be deferred until approved by the Council, is mostly used on non-agricultural issues, such as the implementation of the PHARE programme of aid to central and eastern Europe.

The regulatory committee procedures were developed by the Council in the late 1960s to cover areas outside agriculture where the member governments wanted more control over the Commission than under the advisory or management committee procedures (Docksey and Williams, 1997: 136–7). These procedures are used in such areas as customs legislation, veterinary and plant health, and food. The more restrictive variant (Procedure IIIb), the so-called 'safety-net' (or '*contre-filet*'), is usually used in the sensitive area of veterinary health, as in the decision to impose a European-wide ban on beef exports from Britain during the BSE crisis.

Finally, the Commission can take 'safeguard measures' to protect the interests of the EU or individual Member States, for which the Council most give prior approval. These procedures (Procedure IVa and IVb) are usually used for issues under the common commercial policy, as in the signing of association agreements with non-EU states.

Development of the EP's position on comitology: from Plumb–Delors to Aglietta

The EP has been highly critical of this system. The EP's objections are essentially two-fold (esp. Corbett, 1994; Corbett *et al.*, 1995: 251–17; Bradley, 1997):

1   because the Commission is accountable to the EP, any procedure that gives executive power to the Council instead of the Commission undermines the ability of the EP to hold the EU executive accountable; and
2   the EP should have equal rights with the Council to review, approve and veto proposed implementation measures in those areas were it shares legislative authority with the Council.

The EP has pursued several strategies to enforce these objections, including internal organisational reform to enable its committees to scrutinise the comitology system more effectively, disruption of the EU legislative process to prevent the use of the comitology procedures that the EP opposes, negotiation with the Council and the Commission to secure inter-institutional agreement on the reform of comitology, and use of the budgetary procedure to restrict the budgets of certain types of comitology committees.

A basic problem for the EP has been a lack of information about the existence and operation of the various committees. As a result, in 1988 the President of the EP, Lord Plumb, and the President of the Commission, Jacques Delors, signed an agreement which gave the EP access to certain information. Under the so-called Plumb–Delors procedure, the Commission would send most draft implementing measures to the EP at the same time that they were submitted to the relevant committee of national experts. The EP reformed its internal rules to enable the relevant EP committee to receive and issue an opinion on the draft measure. On one occasion, the consumer protection committee of the EP was able to use this procedure to pressure the Commission to alter its proposed implementing measures (in the case of infant-formula milk).

However, in general the procedure was not very effective. First, the EP was excluded from reviewing routine management documents and issues that were considered 'urgent' or 'secret' by either the Commission or the national governments. Second, the Commission was not obliged to inform the EP of the exact timetable for the adoption of the decision. Third, the Commission was not obliged to take account of the EP's opinion on any of the proposed implementation measures.

The EP consequently supplemented this post-legislative oversight procedure with a strategy to secure the use of favourable comitology procedures in the adoption of legislation. This was set out in the Roumeliotis Report in 1990:[4]

> (1) in the first reading [of a legislative proposal], the EP should systematically delete any provisions for procedure IIIa or IIIb and replace it with procedure IIa or IIb, or, for proposals relating to the internal market (under Article 100A of the Treaty) replace it with procedure I; and
> (2) in the second reading, the EP should continue to oppose any provisions in a Council common position for procedure IIb, but IIIa could be accepted exceptionally, as a compromise, except for proposals concerning the internal market, where IIb should be the maximum acceptable position.

These guidelines were followed by the EP committees scrutinising legislative proposals. However, certain EP committees, particularly the environment and consumer protection committees, were reluctant to allow a free hand to the Commission and saw the Council as a possible break on Commission discretion. Also, because of the weak role of the EP in the legislative procedure, the Council was able to overturn most of the EP amendments that undermined the executive powers of the Council.

The introduction of the co-decision procedure in the Maastricht Treaty, which strengthened the EP *vis-à-vis* the Council in the adoption of certain pieces of legislation, gave a new incentive for the EP on the comitology issue. First, the co-decision procedure created a new cause for complaint. The EP argued that when measures for the implementation of legislation adopted under the co-decision procedure are referred by a comitology committee back to the Council, they should also be referred back to the EP, as the other chamber that adopted the initial legislation. The EP made this proposal to the Commission in 1993 (De Giovanni Report).[5] But, the Council refused to accept the EP's interpretation, arguing that co-decision legislation are acts of the Council and not of the Council and the EP.

Second, the co-decision procedure gave the EP new powers to force the use of the comitology procedures that it prefers. The EP exercised this power in July 1994, when it vetoed the Directive on the application of open networks provision (ONP) to voice telephony, on the grounds that the Council had refused to accept the EP's proposal to use the advisory committee procedure (I) instead of the restrictive variant of the regulatory committee procedure (IIIb) to implement the Directive. With this precedent, the EP threatened to block a whole series of draft Directives.

Under this pressure, in autumn of 1994 the Council and the Commission negotiated an inter-institutional agreement on comitology with the EP – known as the 'Modus Vivendi'. The Modus Vivendi formalised and strengthened the Plumb–Delors agreement as follows:

1   the EP would receive all draft implementation measures and the proposed timetable for their scrutiny in comitology and enactment by the Commission;
2   the Commission was obliged to 'take account to the greatest extent possible' of the opinions of the EP and to inform the EP on the progress of the measures through comitology; and
3   where a matter is referred to the Council as a result of a committee decision, the relevant EP committee would be briefed by the Commission, the Council could only adopt a measure having informed the EP and given it a reasonable deadline to deliver an opinion, and if the EP issued a negative opinion, the Council would attempt to 'find a solution'.

The inter-institutional agreement also provided that the 1996 Intergovernmental Conference (IGC) on the reform of the Maastricht Treaty would look closely at the issue of comitology.

In the meantime, the EP sought to use its budgetary powers to influence the comitology system (Bradley, 1997: 241–3). As early as 1983, the EP had cut the budgets of the committees to force the Commission to reduce the number of committees. This strategy was revived following the Modus Vivendi agreement. In adopting the 1995 budget, the EP transferred 90 per cent of the expenditure of the comitology committees to the reserve section of the budget, and demanded a list of all committee procedures used in 1994. The Commission duly issued a highly detailed report of almost 2000 pages, and the EP agreed to release 40 per cent of the funds in February 1995 and the rest in July. However, the EP was not completely satisfied with the information provided by the

Commission, arguing that the information was insufficient to allow the EP committees to see whether any of the comitology committees had acted beyond their mandate.

As a result, the EP repeated the strategy in the adoption of the 1996 budget, by withholding 50 per cent of the committees' budgets. The Commission refused to comply with all of the EP's 'demands', such as the supply of the minutes of all the meetings, and the EP consequently refused to release the rest of the budget. Nevertheless, a compromise was reached in September 1996 between the Chair of the EP's budgets committee, Detlev Samland MEP, and the Secretary General of the Commission, David Williamson. Under this so-called Samland–Williamson agreement, the Commission will supply the EP with the full agendas of management and regulatory committees in 'good time in advance of committee discussions'. Also, the Commission agreed to allow representatives of the EP and its committees attend the discussion of certain items in management and regulatory committees, upon the written request of the EP. As a result of the agreement, the EP agreed to defer any further inter-institutional bargaining until the outcome of the Intergovernmental Conference (IGC).

Upon completion of the IGC, the Amsterdam Treaty was adopted in June 1997. The Treaty extended the co-decision procedure to most areas of legislation relating to the regulation of the single market, reformed the procedure to further strengthen the power of the EP *vis-à-vis* the Council, and formally introduced the provision that acts adopted under the procedure are of both the Council and the EP. However, in the IGC the Member States failed to reach an agreement on the reform of comitology. As a result, in June 1997 the European Council invited the Commission to prepare a reform of the 1987 Council Decision on comitology.[6]

The EP immediately set about drafting its own proposals for the reform of the Council Decision. In March 1998 the EP Committee on Institutional Affairs examined the 'Second Working Document on Comitology', written by Maria Adelaide Aglietta MEP,[7] and in May 1998 the Rules Committee issued a Draft Opinion on Comitology, written by Richard Corbett MEP.[8] The Aglietta Working Document set out a four main EP proposals:

1 *'full compliance with the legislative procedure'*, through a clearer definition of legislative and executive actions, where 'general principles' are the exclusive preserve of the legislature, 'substantive provisions' may be legislative and executive (but when they amend or supplement general principles they are legislative), and 'implementing provisions' are the exclusive preserve of the executive;

2 *'effective control by Parliament over implementing provisions'*, where within a certain time limit the EP can amend or withdraw an implementing measure if there is a breach of the delegation procedures or if the substance of an implementing measure is legislative;

3   '*simplification of the committee system*', through the abolition of all manage-
    ment and regulatory committees (leaving only the advisory committees and
    the safeguard measures); and
4   '*transparency*', through 'regular and timely' information by the Commis-
    sion on comitology, including committee composition, the legal basis of
    references, updates of committee work, reports on committee decisions,
    publication of committee minutes and votes, and a register of interests of
    committee members.

To enable the EP to undertake this full-blown oversight, Aglietta proposed substantial new resources to the EP's committees and the establishment of an ad hoc
body of 15 MEPs, with the specific task of monitoring the implementation of a
piece of legislation. In other words, this body would be similar to the EP 'conciliation delegations' that negotiate with the Council in the adoption of legislation under the co-decision procedure. In addition, Corbett proposed a reform
of the EP Rules of Procedure to allow an EP committee to refer a comitology
issue to the full EP plenary, to allow the EP as a whole to vote on a proposed
implementing measure with which an EP committee is unsatisfied.

Consequently, the development from the Plumb–Delors agreement and the
Roumeliotis Report to the use of the budgetary powers in 1995 and 1996 and
the Aglietta Working Document is substantial. The EP has become more
refined in its demands for information and in its use of the budgetary
procedures to secure the information it seeks. More importantly, the
EP has developed a more sophisticated attitude towards the Commission.
The EP has consistently objected to the use of the management and regulatory
committee procedures, on the grounds that they undermine the executive
powers of the Commission. However, in its latest proposals, the aim is to
strengthen the EP's powers of oversight of the Commission as well as of the
Member State governments.

Implications of Parliament's demands
In generalisable political science terms, the latest EP demands amount to the
following:

1   a redefinition of the boundary between executive and legislative authority,
    such that executive authority is restricted to purely implementing measures;
2   a removal of certain executive powers of the Member State governments;
3   on implementation issues arising from bicameral legislation, equal powers
    with the Member State governments if (a) an issue is referred back for
    review at ministerial level by the governments or (b) new legislation is
    required;
4   rights to receive all draft instruments well in advance of their proposed
    adoption and full details of the implementation timetable; and
5   the right to veto executive instruments before they are implemented.

However, from the above theoretical and empirical analysis, there are problems with each of these demands.

First, the boundaries between legislative and executive acts are not as clear-cut as the EP suggests. As can be expected of a parliament, the EP is eager to restrict executive acts to implementing measures and regulations with only minor political salience. However, lessons from other systems suggest that this is unsustainable. As in the US, the Commission has legal grounds to claim that once power is delegated by the Council and the EP, the EP does not have the right to interfere. But above all, it is not in the long-term interests of EU citizens that the EP be involved in the day-to-day adoption of regulations. A central purpose of the delegation of regulatory law-making to an independent agency (such as the Commission) is to protect the rule-making from special interests and particular electoral majorities (esp. Majone, 1996). In other words, for precisely the same reason one would not want the EP to decide the level of interest rates set by the European Central Bank (ECB), the EP should not be allowed to approve regulatory decisions of the Commission, especially if they are high-profile decisions (such as competition policy rulings).

The EP should be arguing for a separation of 'political' and 'regulatory' responsibilities of the Commission, for example with the establishment of DG VI as an independent 'European Cartel Office'. In such a separation, the political executive (the College of Commissioners) would draw its legitimacy either from a parliamentary majority (via an EP right to censure the Commission as a whole) or from a direct election of the Commission President (Laver *et al.*, 1995). In addition, the political executive would be accountable via the principle of 'ministerial responsibility'. For example, the EP could argue for the right to censure individual members of the Commission. The regulatory agencies, in contrast, would draw their legitimacy primarily from their performance (the supply of 'pareto-efficient' policies). However, regulatory accountability can also be achieved through involvement of the EP in the appointment of the head of the agency, and in public justification of regulatory decisions.

Second, the removal of executive powers from the Member State governments is both unrealistic and undesirable in the EU system. In the adoption and implementation of single market legislation, the EU is an executive-federal system. In the transposition of EU legislation into domestic law, and in the regulation of the market by national agencies, the Member State governments are already a central part of the executive authority of the EU. The Commission does not possess the legal, administrative or fiscal means to implement EU legislation alone. The effective operation of EU 'government' consequently requires co-operation and collusion between the Commission and the national governments' administrations. Moreover, involvement of the national governments, who are the only office-holders with citizen support, is essential for the legitimacy of EU government. Instead of arguing for a separation of executive and legislative powers between the Commission and the Council, the EP should accept that the EU has a 'dual executive'. This would allow the EP to seek parliamentary oversight (together with the national parliaments) of *both* the Commission and the national governments. The result would be that management (and even regulatory) committees should be kept, and the EP should seek the same rights of oversight of these procedures as of advisory committee procedures.

Third, directly linked to this issue, the EP should not necessarily have the right to participate along-side the Council when any issue is referred back from comitology. In areas where delegation was originally made under the co-decision procedure, the EP should argue for the same rights as the Council on the approval/veto of implementing measures that redefine general legislative principles or when new legislation is required to update or complete existing acts. However, certain issues are referred to the Council that are purely executive. If the EP accepts the principle of a 'dual executive' in the EU, it should accept that on these issues the Council should be allowed to act alone, with certain rights of EP consultation and scrutiny. The problem, of course, will be to design comitology procedures under which such distinctions can be made.

Fourth, the demand to scrutinise and approve all executive instruments will be extremely costly for the EP. By demanding to receive all draft instruments in enough time to allow the EP to veto those it does not like, the EP has argued for a classic 'police patrol' oversight mechanism. Lessons from other legislatures (particularly the US Congress) suggest that this will be a huge drain on the EP's financial and staffing resources. Moreover, the marginal returns on each additional resource allocated to this task will decline to almost zero. And, within the limited budget of the EP, these resources will inevitably have to be taken from the more important job of scrutinising and amending legislation (also, this task will be under pressure as a result of the extension of the co-decision procedure to many new areas of EU legislation by the Amsterdam Treaty).

There are, however, alternative strategies. First, the EP could use 'fire alarm' oversight techniques. For example, on the receipt of draft executive instruments, the EP could post them on the EP's web-site and invite private interests to respond. This would pass on the costs of information collection to the private sector, and to actors with more expertise and direct interest in the proposed course of action. Second, in the event of serious mismanagement by the EU executive, the EP could restrict the comitology budgets (as it has done already) and even censure the Commissioner involved. Both of these strategies would achieve the same results as 'police patrol' oversight, but at much less cost.

Fifth, and finally, the right to veto executive instruments before they are implemented is highly unrealistic and probably undesirable. As we have seen, neither the US Congress nor the *Bundesrat* enjoy this right. For both practical and political reasons, it is more common for legislatures to reserve the right to challenge executive actions after they have been undertaken (ex-post). Only once executive actions have had time to take effect, and the subject parties have had time to air their views (such as launch private legal challenges), can a legislature challenge the executive with the full support of an electoral majority. Moreover, this final demand is a 'maximalist strategy' which harks back to the days (in the early 1980s) when the EP was an arch-federalising and largely irrelevant institution. It does not befit the modern EP, which is a powerful legislative chamber that has shown maturity and restraint in actions under the co-operation, co-decision and budgetary procedures.

Conclusion: towards parliamentary control of EU governance?

With the reforms of the Maastricht and Amsterdam Treaties, the structure of the EU legislature has begun to take shape: where the EP is an equal partner with the Council in the adoption of legislation governing the single market. In stark contrast, the structure of legislative–executive relations in the emerging system of EU governance is less settled. The comitology system is a classic example of this situation. Comitology committees have been the 'dual-executive' pistons driving the EU engine since the birth of the Common Market. Yet the role of the EP in comitology remains unresolved.

When thinking about this issue, we can thankfully draw on what political science already knows about parliamentary oversight of executive power. At a theoretical level, once implementing and regulatory powers have been delegated to an executive agent, we can assume that the agent will have the desire and the ability to move from the intended goals of the principals. Nevertheless, with this knowledge, principals can design procedures and incentive-structures to limit the degree of discretion, which will curtail the need to use expensive ex post oversight mechanisms. In other words, the EP should seek to design *a priori* rules to limit the need for ex post oversight; either within legislation or through general rules relating to the appointment of executive office-holders and the transparency of executive decisions.

These observations are confirmed at an empirical level. For example, in both the United States and Germany, constitutional courts have restricted the role of the legislature to the *a priori* delegation and the ex post involvement in the adoption of new legislation. In Germany, the *Bundestag* is allowed an ex post veto, but only on issues of particular political salience and only once executive instruments have been enacted. Also, the US Congress has found that extensive oversight of federal agencies ('police patrols') is extremely costly, and reliance on private interests to challenge decisions ('fire alarms') can be cheaper and in some cases more effective. Similarly, procedures such as 'ministerial responsibility' and budgetary controls can be less costly than on-going oversight and equally as effective in keeping the executive in check.

But the EP does not seem to be aware of this knowledge. The EP has developed a more sophisticated view of the Commission, in that the EP no longer sees the Commission as a permanent ally. Yet most of the EP's demands relating to the comitology system are less sophisticated. For example, key amongst the EP's demands are the abolition of the Council's executive powers, and the right to oversee all implementing measures well before they are enacted. The first of these demands is unrealistic considering the operation and legitimacy of the EU dual-executive, and the second would be a permanent and increasing drain on EP resources.

But there are alternatives for the EP. The EP could pass on much of the costs of scrutiny to private actors who are the subject of executive actions. And, through the right to censure individual Commissioners, the EP could give institutional bases to the principle of individual responsibility at the political level for administrative actions. Basically, in the BSE crisis, would the EP have preferred to threaten to sack Commissioner Fischler than review and approve every decision of the veterinary committee?

Executive power in the EU needs to be more accountable. In designing a system of parliamentary control of the EU executive, rather than 'make it up as we go a long', there is a depth of theoretical and empirical knowledge about parliamentary oversight and legislative–executive relations from which we can draw. Only by so doing will the EP be able to learn from the successes and failures of other parliaments' attempts to constrain run-away governments

Notes

1 *Immigration & Naturalization Service* v. *Chadha*, 462 U.S. 919 (1983).
2 *BverfGE* 8, 274, 319–22.
3 Council Decision, 87/373/EEC.
4 European Parliament document, A3-310/90.
5 European Parliament document, A3-417/93.
6 The Commission issued its initial opinion on the reform of the 1987 Council Decision on comitology in June 1998. Commission document, COM(98)380 final.
7 European Parliament document, PE 225.917.
8 European Parliament document, PE 226.626.

4

Postcards from the edge of integration?
The role of committees in EU environment
policy-making

Introduction: committee types and a 'committee method' in environmental policy

This chapter is concerned with the role of committees in EU environmental policy. This demands at least two main distinct tasks for study. First, it involves the analysis of a general committee method of bureaucratic politics for the policy sector. Second, this study examines the role of implementation committees as constituted under Article 145 of the TEU or what is more often referred to now as 'comitology'.

In regard to the first broad sense of a committee method of working, environmental policy has undoubtedly been influenced by a number of diverse committees. These in the main though can be divided into three types. First, there are those that are purely advisory committees which the Commission (sometimes in conjunction with the Council) sets up to help it determine policy. While these are often ad hoc, there exists examples which have been operative for quite a period, such as the environmental policy review groups where national environment ministry experts review policy in general with the Commission. All of these advisory committees share, however, the same essential feature that they relate to policy formation or design.

Second, there are various working groups and committees which one finds involved in the detail of the EU's arcane legislative process. For example within the opaque COREPER process there are working groups on environmental policy, although we do not know how many there are or how they are specifically constituted as no official list is available.[1] Indeed our information deficit is serious here, as to my knowledge there is no detailed account of COREPER's workings with regard to environmental policy. Yet we know they are in general vital in policy-making terms, as the COREPER processes routinely takes care of about 85 per cent of proposed directives or regulations before the environment ministers ever get to do a *tour de table* (Hayes-Renshaw and Wallace, 1996: 77).

Additionally, since 1995, the Council secretariat itself, as distinct from COREPER, has created its own specialised small committee of national experts, termed Directorate General I. Interestingly however, it has the lowest number of staff with just 15 persons (Hayes-Renshaw and Wallace, 1996: 102). It is simply too early to say what impact this special committee within the Council secretariat will have on COREPER and Council views on environmental policy. In the same way, the Parliament's Environment and Public Health Committee has come to be seen as a key player at the legislative stage of environmental policy. This is a role which it would look set to continue with, given the recent expansion of Co-decision in the Amsterdam treaty. However, while this committee has attracted the interest of environmental policy scholars, their accounts have tended perhaps to overstate key victories in the late 1980s such as on car emissions, at the expense of analysing the slow grind of more routine policy outputs where the power of the Member States has been more evident. In particular many have missed the fact that while the EP environment committee continues to chalk up impressive victories (EU Auto Oil Programme 1998, and the rejection of the Landfill Directive in 1996)[2], its views are not always endorsed by the Parliament as whole, as happened on the Packaging Waste Directive of 1994. In any event what is also forgotten by some commentators is the inability of the EP environment committee to achieve positive policy outcomes, beyond coaxing or threatening an occasionally bitterly divided Council to accept its amendments, with the power of a negative vote. Thus it can at best prevent bad or weak green laws being passed, but perhaps not fill the vacuum when such are dropped completely or when fewer environmental proposals ever reach table to begin with. Of all the committees studied here it is perhaps the one which is the greatest 'outsider' in terms of not having different institutional actors sitting within its structure or by being remote from decision-making power. Yet the Environment Committee is increasingly a manifestation of the growing maturity of the EP as an actor and it is clearly becoming adept at the opaque inter-institutional informal bargaining and 'corridor-politics' which dominates much of low level environment policy sector.

Finally, there are the comitology committees, or those governed by the Comitology Decision of 1987 and concerned with the production of secondary legislation through daughter directives, in EU speak, known as 'implementing measures'.

How important are these implementing committees for the environment sector? According to Demmke (1997: 28) DGXI itself relies formally on some 36 implementing committees, although the budget for 1996 confusingly lists 32 in the environment sector. The budget in this regard frequently underestimates the amount of committees operating, so there may be more de facto implementing committees operating in the environment sector than officially appears acknowledged.[3] Demmke suggests that just over half of the implementation committees in the environment sector were active for 1995, producing in the main positive approvals for the Commission's proposed secondary legislation.

It is significant that the majority of implementing committees in the environmental field appear to be Regulatory Committees of Type IIIa under the 1987 Comitology Decision terminology (Demmke, 1997: 29). In plain language this means that the Commission chairperson, who does not vote, must get express approval from the committee through QMV, before they can introduce any implementing directive or regulation. However, a crucially important caveat (see below) needs to be added. If the Commission loses the QMV vote, they can simply modify their proposal and then they must submit it to the Council who have to rule, again using QMV, within three months. If they do not do so and remain silent, approval is strangely assumed and the Commission can then go ahead and introduce its implementing law.

Demmke's assessments of a relative high reliance on implementing Committees by DGXI, some 36 out of 400 committees or about 7 per cent, needs however to be put in broader historical context (1997: 27–8). In 1989 for example, DGXI involved a total of some 3,157 experts (of which 1,397 were government experts and 1,760 were private experts) in their committee deliberations. This made them the fifth largest user of committees, measured in this way (Buitendijk and Van Schendelen, 1995: 41). We also know that measured in terms of total numbers of meetings for the same year, DG XI sponsored some 411 in total, which places them sixth in a table of DGs' committee use (p. 41). Of course these statistics are not only of limited use for being relatively out of date, but they also tell us little about their actual influence on proposals for Commission secondary regulation. In other words we need also to consider a qualitative assessment of their impact.

In that event, although legally and formally one ought to distinguish between committees and ad hoc working groups whose purpose is to inform and advise policy-making from those who are actually regulators in the sense of providing detailed harmonisation rules, in reality such distinctions may be academic. For if policy is 'evolution' as Majone would have it, then it is a little bit artificial to draw hard and fast boundaries between committees that set policy agendas and those that implement agreed policy: in reality all add to the making and breaking of policy outcomes. Indeed it is an important point to note that even implementation committees who meet after a Directive has been ostensibly agreed, nonetheless represent another chance where in the detail of secondary legislation Member States can influence the content of environmental policy. This is attempted, it is worth noting, largely free from formal parliamentary sanction which is not the case within the Co-decision process.

Undoubtedly therefore, the work of these various committees is in fact the nitty-gritty stuff upon which much of the low politics of environmental policy turns. Indeed in the case of implementing committees, technical rules are frequently the centre of conflict between contending interests of the Member

States, industry and environmentalists. That is to say, EU environmental policy is often contested and negotiated more in the opaque world of comitology and other ad hoc committees than it is at the higher level of policy debate between the Commission, Council and the Parliament. Obviously there are notable exceptions where the Council or some coalition of it together with factions of the Commission are clearly predominant in environmental policy, the carbon tax proposal being an obvious example. Yet frequently it will be a characteristic of the environment sector that Directives will leave complex and controversial points, often with cost implications, to be solved by implementation committees. This is not least because environmental policy is complex and relates to technically obscure and somewhat boring matters such as emission standards and BAT notices that could not possibly clog up the Council's brief. But also it is a product of the concurrent nature of EU environmental policy-making more generally. As it is more important for the Member States to get some agreement rather than no agreement, and because no one actor can be seen to systematically lose or win, it is then highly functional to have a realm where the technical issues can be dumped like 'hot potatoes' to be cooled down and sorted out later in the mundane world of comitology.

The case of the pesticide authorisation Directive of 1991 is a good example of this logic. Here the aim of the Directive was to create a streamlined and harmonised single point source for the authorisation of pesticides and related products. This basic Directive required a number of daughter directives be brought into force in order to give effect to the 'mother' directives provisions. Central in this was agreement on common scientific principles by which Member States should apply for end of line products which may contain approved pesticides or related ingredients. This was of course once again left in the lap of an expert regulatory committee to thrash out what these common principles might be. Not surprisingly the task took some time and indeed became quite politicised by 1994, with the European Parliament challenging the implications that this area had for the related question of pesticides in water. Indeed the Member States had done such a good job for themselves in bargaining a new regime on pesticides, that it provoked all out war from an enraged Parliament who saw this as lawmaking through the 'backdoor'. For what the expert committees had agreed in fact was de facto approval of levels of pesticides in groundwater which the original Directive had forbidden.

Not surprisingly the result of this was that the Parliament launched a successful legal challenge that struck down the putative Directive (ENDS 261, 1996: 45). Notwithstanding the brusque entry of the Parliament, showing in the process how much of an outsider it was, one is left nonetheless with an impression of the details of environmental policy being robustly horse-traded in the strange nether-world of comitology. Moreover this bears out the point that to implement environmental law, in this case through EC secondary legislation, is as important as to make it. The implementation phase allows the issue to be re-opened and re-bargained.

Another example of the type of detailed and sometimes contentious secondary legislation in the environmental field which comitology produces, is seen in two decisions taken by Committees of national experts formed under the 1994 Directive on packaging and packaging waste (ENDS 266, 1997: 45). These set out commonly agreed identifying details (such as numbers and acronyms) for certain types of packaging material and also what common format and approaches Member States' reports must take when giving annual packaging recovery statistics to the Commission. While it might be thought such decisions are relatively technical and innocuous matters, they can be important for firms' costs. Indeed European packaging industry sources seemed unhappy with the end result, feeling the new rules would add costs and complexity (ENDS 266, 1997: 45).

Harmonised measurement techniques are then a typical type of rule produced in a highly technical manner by comitology expert committees. Yet in this what is involved is not just policy complexity, but as argued above such rules are highly political in the sense of determining who will be the winners and losers under a given set of norms, an outcome de facto forbidden at Council level. One good example here was the decision to allow three distinct ways of measuring whether dioxin emissions were exceeding the strict emission limit set down by the 1994 Directive on hazardous waste incineration (ENDS 267, 1997: 37). In practice this allowed a German approach to be chosen or alternatively a US EPA method.[4] The UK however, exploited such technical disputes over measurement rules to argue that if harmonised procedures were not in place to give effect to strict common standards, then the entry into force of those standards should be delayed (*ibid.*). In other words we see here how Member States sometimes attempt to use the comitology process as a means of slowing down the extent of their legal commitments through technical details and adjustments.

Committees, 'ad hoc-ism' and flexibility in environmental policy-making

A generalised committee style of working is of course not neutral on the policy-making style which the environment sector displays. In this regard it is argued here that outside of the formalised standing implementation committees, or those permanent legislative environment committees of COREPER, the Council Secretariat and the Parliament, various ad hoc committees are evident in environmental policy. These spring up from time to time responding to agendas often set at quite a high level by the Member States. In other cases this ad hoc committee phenomenon appears responsive and reactive to developments and trends in environmental policy in ways which the small and overworked Commission cannot perhaps feasibly address, or perhaps be trusted by the Member States to empathetically examine.

The latter point is important as most academic commentators and even participants in the EU policy process have noted the tendency of DG XI in particular to be pro-environment and even of the Council of environmental ministers to be emboldened and assertive in their brief when they get together (Sbragia, 1996). The argument then is that these institutional insiders have a built in preference to talk up environmental standards. While this is certainly more than a little bit simplistic and inaccurate, it may be believed by certain Member States and industry lobbies. In such a context the reliance on expert committees which the Member States hand pick themselves effects a subtle permeation of the Commission. More importantly it steers early deliberations on policy direction, and is thus a useful way for Member States to redress the institutional balance in their favour and regain some control over policy agenda-setting.

A very good and recent example of such an ad hoc committee is the group of Member States' tax advisors on green taxes in the EU. This ad hoc group was set up by the Single Market Commissioner, Mario Monti, in April 1996 to examine the growing complexity of national carbon tax and other green tax regimes and what impact they were having on the single market. The group's wider remit was also to investigate the possibility that new green taxes could be introduced either at the Community or national level, or in some combined manner. In particular this 'group of wise men' was to examine whether green taxes could be used to reduce taxes on labour and thus create jobs, the so called 'double dividend' (ENDS 261, 1996: 41). This group of national experts, in most cases it seems designated personally by national finance and treasury ministers, but chaired and supported by the Commission, eventually produced a report in October of 1996 which was conservative. Nonetheless, they did steer policy substantively in the sense that they argued for further studies and affirmed that the EU level was the most appropriate level for energy taxes to be harmonised (*ibid.*). This reflects perhaps growing concern among some states at the proliferation of various national tax regimes on energy, notably in the Nordic states, all which could threaten to segment the single market and hinder the entry of domestic firms into neighbouring states' markets. Indeed the Commission and the Member States may have been encouraged to reclaim the initiative, after a series of bilateral and multilateral exchanges which culminated in a meeting, in January 1996, of the so called 'gang of six' green states[5] who wish to push ahead with the introduction of carbon taxes in the aftermath of the failed EU carbon tax proposal of 1991–92.

What is intriguing here is the confluence of a non-EU level of multilateral agenda-setting, together with a response by the EU institutions and some of the Member States to take up the issue of energy taxes again and re-examine it. It appears that other states, notably the UK and Ireland, are less enthusiastic about any re-examination of green taxes and want in particular to retain unanimity on environment related fiscal measures. Nonetheless there are still logical advantages on keeping an eye on and possibly restraining 'green' competitor states from producing results outside the EU realm which might be harmful to trade. In this vein it is noteworthy how what was originally a highly intergovernmental ad hoc temporary *'committee des sages'* has now become a more fixed permanent body of national experts which together with the Commission will continue to monitor national tax policies and the need for harmonisation and integration with other policy goals, such as the environment (ENDS 261, 1996: 41).

Perhaps the best known and most contentious example of ad hoc advisory committees in environmental policy was the Molitor Committee, set up in 1994 primarily at the instigation of Germany and the UK to examine the scope for de-regulation in EU policy spheres. Intriguingly one of their first ports of call on their quest to find suitable targets for de-regulation, was the environment sector. Their conclusions were a mixture of calling for novel and less invasive instruments, such as framework directives, but also stripping away old or irrelevant laws and generally avoiding environmental standards which placed European industry at a competitive disadvantage *vis-à-vis* North American and Japanese firms. By implication the future direction of EU environmental policy was to be a smaller corpus of simple framework laws, much greater national discretion, and a reliance on market based instruments generally. While the report attracted support from some quarters, it also contained its own dissenting contributors. Certainly, it attracted the ire of European environmentalists.

For example the European Environment Bureau (EEB), one of the main Environmental NGOs in Brussels, provided a trenchant criticism of the Molitor Group. As the EEB saw it, the group mainly focused its energies on a neo-liberal inspired critique of environmental policy and articulated a singularly pro-business view of environmental directives as making life hard for European business. Equally the European Parliament requested that the committee stop its deliberations, as they were worried about the legality of its basis.

The EEB concluded: 'Environment Ministers, the advisory Committee set up by DG XI (of environmental NGOs) were kept out of things. The whole system was bypassed so that the top of the hierarchy could impose a new environmental policy philosophy' (EEB, 1996: 36). Arguably, what the whole episode shows is that while expert advisory committees, may be relied upon by Member States to push new agendas in environmental policy, they are also doomed to attract the ire of established institutional actors precisely because such are jealous of being bypassed and sidelined. Moreover, the exercise may have been one of a more rhetorical rather than substantive nature, and one must be cautious about judging whether such ad hoc committees have the staying power to see their radical proposals through. Instead it is likely they serve more as venues for policy discussion and debate. Arguably, while there has been much talk of deregulation at the EU level, in practice the experience of these efforts remains quite mixed (Flynn, 1998). It is true there is less law being proposed, and a considerable degree of re-drafting and re-consolidation, but this arguably affords opportunities for re-regulation as much as de-regulation. None the less, while ad hoc committees of the Member States may be generating more heat than light in policy direction, they undoubtedly are an important feature by which Member States attempt to retain control of the established institutional framework for environmental policy.

Committees as expert scientific forums: less science, more negotiation?

Environmental policy inevitably involves questions of scientific expertise. While this is not much different from other policy sectors where there may be complex technical evidence to weigh (such as public infrastructure developments) what is distinctive about environmental issues is that they frequently centre on perceptions of risk and harm and especially the strange nexus between science and moral judgement. Thus some EC laws, such as those concerning sealskins and whaling are based more on moral sentiment backed by scientific evidence rather than a simple assessment of risk. Moreover, environmentalists will not just dispute scientific evidence within its own terms, they frequently also reject the legitimacy and basis of modern industrial society's scientific knowledge by arguing it is anthropocentric, state controlled or a slave to economic growth, etc.

All of this means that any environmental policy arena has to find a working institutional mechanism for the management of expertise. In this regard the various implementation committees are often staffed by national scientific experts on pesticides, chemicals, etc. Indeed it is striking the degree of dependence which the small Commission has on national scientific bodies for decision-making on scientific procedures, questions of measurement, and ultimately questions of risk. Significantly other institutions such as the Parliament have felt locked out of this process, and consequently somewhat ignorant. As a result the Parliament has set up its Science and Technology Office of Assessment (STOA) to provide it with expert evidence by which to confront the Council and Commission. While all of these observations are largely self-evident what has been missed by many commentators is the political implications of having so much of the EU's politics on environmental expertise handled within the opaque world of comitology and committees more generally. Arguably the political impact of such an institutional forum is that it has a strong tendency towards consensus and negotiation of expert evidence, rather than a more critical evaluation. More bluntly, committees provide an opaque venue where expert evidence can be slowly sifted by the Member States, until they reach a compromise.

A good example which illustrates the political opportunities and complexities of expert committees is the 'peer review groups' which are set up under the pesticide authorisation Directive of 1991 to examine the reports, called monographs, of each Member State's assessment of a given pesticide. In this case these 'peer review' working groups are quite obviously manifestations of national regimes and influence. The two main co-ordinating actors being the UK's Pesticides Safety Directorate (PSD) and the German Federal Biological Research Centre for Agriculture and Forestry (BBA), who both facilitate the organisation required for different Member States' experts to vet and 'peer review' each other. Once these have reached an opinion this is then submitted to yet another committee, a Commission working group and thence to a proper comitology regulatory committee, the standing Committee on Plant Health, which makes a final approval based on QMV (ENDS 261, 1996: 46). Yet note the sheer complexity and opacity of committee types involved here, blending various expert agents, mostly national, and providing multiple venues for the process to have sufficient flexibility. This has the advantage in that it provides more opportunities for negotiation, and compromise through the attritional forces of bureaucratic inertia and fits in very much with our conception of EU environmental policy-making as a concurrent venture where power, although co-ordinated by the nation states, is otherwise defused under their supervision and approval.

However, the way in which expert committees become focal points for negotiated scientific expertise is also politically significant because it surely affects individual policy outcomes. First and undoubtedly, the evaluation of scientific evidence is heavily politically controlled in the selection of national expert actors by domestic governments. Second this leads to a fairly small tight group, who see the scientific world in a pretty similar world-view, sharing epistemic backgrounds and each being sensitive to their political masters. There is no built-in channel for dissenting views and opinions, in the same way in which national evaluations of scientifically controversial proposals will frequently allow for, by selecting a balanced group of independent and government experts. Third and flowing from this, the character of such expert meetings is more akin to an academic seminar between national experts than a serious adversarial appraisal of risk. The opaque membership, the detailed agenda, the close informal and long standing contacts must all lean towards a distinctly 'clubable' atmosphere where there are many more incentives to reach agreement than not.

The primary idiom of such a forum is not scientific rationality but rather that of negotiation. This is borne out by Buitendijk and Van Schendelen, who through interview research found that the implementation committees they studied, (although not related to environment policy) had a strong emphasis towards reaching unanimity, and that this was regarded by participants as a reliable guide to the effectiveness of the committee (1995: 47). While there will be undoubted differences in working styles between individual committees it is suggested for the most part the institutional pressures are such that this consensual negotiation of risk is paramount.

The implications of this of course are that a committee methodology for questions of environmental scientific expertise, arguably loads the odds in favour of a deeply consensual style of working where controversy will be avoided. While this may be functional to integration it may mean hard decisions on risk are rejected in case they offend the lowest common denominator of national interest. Perversely then, rather than increase the flow of evidence and scientific argument, the expert committee system may actually reduce the level of genuine scientific debate and focus instead on reaching agreed outcomes around the practical questions of approving authorisation for products, practices, etc.

Perhaps the best example which illustrates these trends, are two distinct regulatory decisions where comitology came face to face with the problem of difficult scientific evidence in environmental policy. The first was the January 1997 decision to allow Monsanto to sell genetically modified soya inside the EU. The second was approval later in 1997 with regard to a Novartis[6] application to sell genetically modified maize. What is worth bearing in mind considering the politics of expertise here is that there were substantial grounds upon which any expert body might have delayed legalisation of sale or distribution of genetically modified foodstuffs pending further research.

For example, there was an important precedent from medical science for clinical trials evidence to be built up, which went unexplored. Equally the environment minister of Luxembourg argued more generally that the Commission's committees might have postponed considering any approval until further studies were carried out on the scientific risks involved (ENDS 266, 1997: 46). Indeed the UK's own Advisory Committee on Novel Foods and Process itself expressed fears that Novartis GM maize could involve transfer of genetic material to animals in feeds which would make them antibiotic resistant (ENDS 264, 1997: 41).

As a result, Austria, the UK, Sweden and Denmark out of an eventual total of 13 states all blocked the Novartis application in April 1996 when it first emerged. Yet this did not stop their application from progressing. What is interesting here is that the whole issue was transferred to the Commission for solving, as it remained deadlocked at Council level. Of course the Commission then sent the question to be examined by three regulatory committees under the comitology procedure: the Scientific Committee on Pesticides, the Scientific Committee on Animal Nutrition and the Scientific Committee on Foods. These three committees actually decided on 18 December 1996 to allow Novartis GM maize on the market, although the Foods Committee was a little more guarded[7] (ENDS 264, 1997: 41). The result of this decision was widespread controversy and several national 'bans' on Genetically Modified Organism (GMO) foods, seeds, or the marketing of such, by Austria, Luxembourg and Italy, as well as similar restrictive measures in other states.

Bizarrely, however, the role of a committee method did not end here, for the Austrian ban on GMOs was introduced under a special measure contained within the 1990 Directive that governs GMO releases. This provides that when such national bans are invoked under the Directive, a special ad hoc committee of national experts be set up to affirm or deny the continuation of the national ban. If they cannot reach agreement, then the issue will be returned back up to the Council of Environment Ministers. This procedure then kicked into gear by spring 1997.

Arguably this shows us a picture not so much of comitology in environmental policy as a realm of expertise, but rather committees seem to be trapdoors where policy problems can be pushed down from the Council to the Commission, or even upwards in a similar manner. In short, it is classic buck passing politics rather than genuine expertise. The problem becomes addressed in the creation of a more expert, but also more opaque and presumably less politically pressured group of negotiators who can attempt to find a solution to a thorny question which environment ministers cannot or simply do not want to solve.

Indeed one has to raise doubts about a true politics of expertise here more generally, insofar as in many cases the national participants of such committees are not just competent scientists or experts, but are usually national civil servants or otherwise open to political control and selection. Their desire to champion arguments which may be mediocre science but good national strategy must therefore remain a distinct possibility. More alarmingly one might cite some critics, who suggest that even where expertise is assumed it may not in fact be resident at all in the committee at hand. King and Lee (1997: 22) for instance have argued the expertise of the Scientific Committee on Pesticides was not that suitable scientifically as a background qualified to judge risks inherent with genetic material. There are also worries about regulatory capture regarding national pesticides and poisons experts vis-à-vis large chemical firms, or the lucrative practice of future employment contracts and consultancy payments.

In May 1997 the special committee of Member States' representatives formed under the 90/220/EEC Directive, approved the Commission's request to extend temporary labelling requirements to the Monsanto and Novartis products, as these were not covered by the Novel Foods Regulation which the Parliament had just rushed through around the same time in an attempt to force labelling of such products. This decision was despite notable opposition from the German delegation. On 9 April the Scientific Committees on Pesticides, Foods and Animal Nutrition also examined the Austrian and Luxembourg ban under Article 16 of the Directive (90/220/EEC) and concluded these were not justified. This implied action by the Council or legal proceedings, but the Council refused to act, pleading little internal agreement (ENDS 269, 1997: 29)

The Commission itself, left in such a leadership vacuum by the Council, finally came down off the fence in July 1997 when they published their draft labelling guidelines. These rejected any idea of the key demand by environmentalists, and the green Member States involved, notably Austria, for segregation of food stocks. This was because they allowed a category of label which had the words 'may contain GMO material'.[8] Finally the Commission in September 1997 reiterated its demand that the Austrian, Luxembourg and Italian measures hindering the free movement of GMO material should be dropped. This was despite the not unreasonable scientific arguments which the Austrian and their allies produced.[9]

Very swiftly then the policy descended into bitter controversy and quite a measure of uncertainty, as the demand to drop their national bans on GMOs provoked a stalwart response from both Austria and Luxembourg to the effect that they would rather see the Commission in court than given in. While Luxembourg appeared notably trenchant in its views promising to seek national higher standards under Article 100(a)4, in the event of losing a court battle, in practice some ground was conceded when the Austrians promised to remove the actual legal instruments which ban GMO imports in return for a voluntary agreement with industry not to import. Italy's position (they had banned the growth of GM Maize) then folded into relatively docile acceptance of the decision by the Commission that their approach was unwarranted.

This points to an important observation in the whole controversy, the ability of national governments to engage in what may be little more than shadow symbolic measures, which whilst appearing to make a tough stance, they know cannot prevail legally within the EU order. Thus the EU can become a functional scapegoat for getting through policies which at the national level would prove to be politically sensitive. To conclude the saga, even the Commission's demand that the national bans be rescinded was passed on to regulatory committees for legal confirmation, a decision which was to be reached under QMV. Thus we see at several stages in the controversy, the institutional focus through which the policy dispute was channelled was the Comitology system in particular and reliance on expert, advisory and regulatory committees in general. There is also a sense in which a 'committee method of working' is seen here as providing the right negotiating ground in which complicated legal and technical issues could be thrashed out and hopefully compromised on. One anomaly deserves mention however.

Committees and power in environmental decision-making: trapdoors for the Council?

This is the fact that the authorisation procedure as set up under Directive 90/220/EEC actually allowed the regulatory committee thus mandated to reach a decision apparently in the face of opposition by a hostile Council. From the point of view of those who endorse a state-centric view of the integration process this seems hard to accept, in so far as it suggests committees may be quite autonomous from the Council's power. Yet on the face of events this is precisely what happened in December 1996 and January 1997 when the original Monsanto and Ciba/ Novartis applications were cleared. According to some reports as many as 13 of the Member States were opposed to such authorisation (ENDS 272, 1997: 42). What then are we to make of power relations in such instances of environmental policy, that committees can become autonomous in their interests?

Certainly the Council has complained as much, and by September and October of 1997 it was promising that it would change the type of committee which would process such applications in future, so that no 'assumed approval' could be used by the Commission. This would be a type of regulatory committee which would allow the Member States in Council to reject an application from a given company if they could muster merely a simple majority, rather than a qualified majority as currently exists.

Yet more generally there is no loss of faith by the Council in committees attempting to solve problems about GMOs. Indeed apparently with Council approval, the Commission currently proposes an entirely new regulatory committee which would specifically be constituted to examine GMO effects on human health and the environment. Likewise this committee would be more controlled by the Member States in Council, for if it could not reach a majority opinion it would automatically have its opinions referred to the Council who could with a simple majority, rather than unanimity, reject any application.

Yet while the trapdoor effect may be about to be plugged, there is still arguably an over confidence in what tasks such committees are fit to do. For example the Commission proposed under its review of Directive 90/220, that the committee mentioned before would also evaluate ethical concerns. This is a strange move in many ways, as expert national scientists of biotechnology may not be, on their own, the most well equipped body to consider complicated ethical issues as distinct from technical ones.

To recapitulate the morale of the story told here, it is important to remember first that controversy with GMOs was caused as much by the way in which the comitology procedure dealt with the issue as in the fact that the subject matter is contentious in its own right. Second, a policy 'trapdoor' effect is evident: the original meeting in April of the regulatory committee failed to get a qualified majority for approval of the Ciba/Novartis product. They therefore referred the matter upwards to the Council of Ministers. However, rather than take a decision, a formal vote was avoided. This strange situation of course all resulted from the arcane decision rules adopted for the regulatory committee under Directive 90/220/EEC. Either the Council has a choice of adopting the authorisation with a qualified majority, which was impossible in this case as about 13 states rejected the committee's view that approval should be granted, or they amend it acting unanimously. But this will nearly always be impossible to reach and in any event France, who had sponsored the Ciba/Novartis application, would have probably rejected an amendment of the proposed approval notice.

The best interpretation to put on this is that the Member States were clearly unhappy being boxed in by perverse comitology rules which they had originally designed. To be more probing one might also note though, that they were also conveniently relieved of taking a contentious decision themselves. This view is borne out by at least some anecdotal evidence in the form of the Belgian newspaper *Le Soir*, which managed to leak the discussion of the GMOs issue by the collegiate commission, in a story which suggested that Commissioners seemed predominantly concerned with the commercial pressures associated with the policy rather than environmental or health concerns (ENDS 267, 1997: 38–9). Indeed, Greenpeace were less circumspect, calling the entire comitology procedure inherently undemocratic as a means by which the Council could absolve itself of responsibility for approving GMO food (ENDS 257, 1996: 41). Therefore it is argued here the 'trapdoor' effect sustains rather than challenges an account of environmental policy-making which is state centric. The Member States find in it a convenient method of buck passing for a policy which would inevitably attract criticism whatever the decision, either from industry or environmentalists.

In case one thinks that the GMOs example is a special case where such a 'trapdoor' tactic was evident by the Council and the Commission, broadly the same problem-solving approach has been used even for fairly routine policy disputes. For example this was evident in the details of the EU's Eco-management and Audit Scheme (EMAS). This provides companies with a voluntary programme to prove their own green credentials either through the unified Commission designed scheme as set down in the Directive, or else through an approved national scheme which is deemed of similar quality as the EMAS approach. Such national schemes are then examined for compatibility by a 'committee of national experts'.

Yet here again we see the bizarre decision rules of the comitology process at work. In early 1996 both the Irish and Spanish national eco-audit schemes attracted the displeasure of this committee of national experts, chiefly led by the German delegation. This was despite a Commission suggestion that the Irish and Spanish schemes were compatible with EMAS. The result was that the committee of experts referred the issue to the Council of Ministers, who deftly and perhaps cynically refused to vote on the issue at all. Of course, once the Council failed to agree, then the Commission could legally act in the absence of disapproval and assume that they actually had approval. Consequently they approved the Irish and Spanish national schemes notwithstanding the opposition of the German delegation and other experts in the field (ENDS 253, 1996: 43; and OJ L34, 13 February 1996).

Committees and the democratic legitimacy of environmental policy

Environmental policy is popular with most Europeans. Indeed Eurobarometer surveys continually produce evidence to suggest that the EU is viewed as a key arena where many would like to see environmental policy decisions taken. Moreover, in countries such as Austria and Denmark, the EU's comparatively good record for environmental action has been offered to otherwise sceptical segments of their electorates as an important positive aspect of integration. Therefore while this is not the place to rehash arguments about the EU's democratic deficit, it is clear that a lot of what legitimacy the EU does have rests on competent performance in popular policy sectors such as the environment: the legitimacy of technocratic policy competence as it were.

Yet it goes without saying that the opaque and complex committee and comitology structure described above is not readily comprehensible, never mind accountable to even well informed citizens. Indeed in some cases all we really know about certain committees is that they exist, but we cannot always be sure at times who actually sits on them. Sometimes indeed private actors can end up discussing complex issues of European law inside implementation committees. For example under the EMAS Directive several Member States appear to send commercial representatives to thrash out the details of the scheme with the Commission. This is all very well, but we may have worries about whether these representatives can distinguish between a commercial private interest and a broader national or European one.

Even more bizarrely, there is the phenomenon of the so called 'sleeping committee', whereby the Commission keeps a particular committee alive merely on paper labelled under one heading as a cost centre for budgetary allocation, but in practice this committee in fact may be working on something other than its official title suggests (Buitendijk and Van Schendelen, 1995: 42). More especially the sheer scale of the enterprise suggests it may be practically impossible to supervise the estimated 1,000 various implementation committees alone. In this regard Buitendijk and Van Schendelen's estimate, that comitology involves an incredible 50,000 representatives of the Member States and private bodies annually, must represent a serious challenge to making the EU process more transparent and democratic (1995: 40). In fact the Comitology procedure has been for many years now an acknowledged democratic black hole which successive attempts, such as the Comitology decision of 1987 and the inter-institutional agreement of 1994 have tried to solve (see the chapter by Simon Hix in this volume for a more comprehensive analysis of accountability issues).

The fact that even the recent IGC largely failed to produce any substantial reform or simplification of the 'comitology procedure' is also a cause for concern. Indeed recent reports confirm that although some pressure continues to grow for change, the likely direction this will take is conservative and focused on just giving more rights of participation to the European Parliament rather than addressing wider questions (Turner, 1998: 2). Yet such a move will merely make the Parliament at best but another insider within comitology and not render, the interests of surely legitimate national parliaments a chance to supervise these committees. Arguably this continues then with the classic manifestation of the democratic deficit.

In this regard it is useful to recount the observations of one senior Dutch civil servant on comitology in particular. He noted simply how he knew little of who, from the Dutch government, actually attended comitology meetings in the environment sector. He could get no lists of participants, or minutes of their meetings, but he might meet them or hear about their work incidently. Overall though, he seldom felt he knew what they discussed and in his own words, 'had to beg them for little bits of information'. If this is the situation with regard to the relatively efficient Dutch civil administration one wonders about how other countries keep tabs on what their delegates get up to in Comitology or committee workings.[10] More especially this clearly has the makings of a democratic nightmare, if not at the very least a severe policy co-ordination challenge for national administrations.

Of course on the flip side it is important to point out that in some cases the use of committees has been benign and actually furthered democratic legitimacy, accountability and transparency, a fact which most commentators miss. One example of this was the regulatory committee which oversaw the application of the Directive on Eco-Labels, which was balanced with an associated Consultative Forum. The latter brought together environment, consumer and business interests and from a democratic view point has to be seen as quite a progressive development.

Indeed it is important to note here that the Regulatory Committee set up under the eco label Directive of 1991 did make some very tough decisions which European textile manufacturers in particular were unhappy about. In this case they prohibited the use of some 25 pesticides in any cotton which would claim the label, and placed other technical demands such as which bleaching agents could be used by those firms seeking the label (ENDS 254, 1996: 27–8). The fact that these decisions were greeted it appears by a large measure of hostility on the part of textile manufacturers does show us clearly that regulatory committees in the environment sector are not inevitably pro-business in their orientation, and that they can obviously decide rules which have important environmental implications.

Yet in this light it is alarming perhaps that the Commission by late 1996 felt that this much troubled eco label scheme was faltering with only a small number of companies participating due to an alleged overly rigid and non-business friendly institutional structure. As a result they proposed abolishing this relatively balanced institutional structure with a consultative forum, and it is now to be replaced by a private corporate agent, the European Eco-Label Organisation (ENDS 263, 1996: 19). This development must surely raise questions about the assured quality of any future eco labels awarded, once non-commercial interests are left less involved in the institutional set up.

Conclusion

Arguably, this chapter has reached perhaps some surprising conclusions in the overall context of this book. For one thing, while it seems ad hoc committees can spring up with aplomb and map out radical changes in environmental policy, it is not clear they have the institutional staying power to effect changes. Moreover, the reliance on advisory committees and even implementation committees by the Member States, suggests a picture of these actors attempting to control a formal Commission and Parliament which they regard as rather too environmentally friendly. It is not that the Member States are simply hostile to more green laws, but, rather, that they want to be in relative control of the process by which environmental policy is agreed.

Therefore it is a somewhat paradoxical finding of this chapter that the opaque reliance on actor based networks of committees is itself largely a product of Member States' desires to retain flexible control and influence over a policy which otherwise could easily dissolve into a low hierarchical jungle of various networks with diffuse power. While this does not simply sustain a more state-centric view of the integration process, it does arguably demand that we accept a greater sophistication in such theoretical accounts. Networks may at first look diffuse and autonomous but in fact turn out to be widely permeated with Member State actors sitting inside the various advisory, expert or implementation committees described here. More especially one can argue that environmental policy specialists ought to be more attentive to such committees, revealing as they are of the political dynamics at the heart of policy. For too long perhaps, we have settled for relatively simplistic accounts of institutions in environmental policy-making: a green Parliament battling against a reactionary Council, while a divided Commission stands by. In practice, the political alliances are complex and may differ from issue to issue in environmental policy, a frequently overlooked phenomenon by researchers. What is certain though, is that somewhere at the heart of an environmental policy dispute a committee will be playing a central part.

In that regard one other strong finding of this chapter is that the role of committees is unquestionably becoming more controversial in environmental policy. The Molitor group for example provoked bitter hostility. Equally, the Parliament with regard to the pesticide Directive of 1991, has shown a willingness and ability to fight the use of such committees as a means by which the Member States subtly re-negotiate details away from their prying eyes. Moreover, the continuing GMO dispute and even the Bovine Spongiform Eucephalopathy (BSE) crisis throws up important questions about the role of implementing committees in general. Are they really expert enough to make good scientific judgements free from the urge to please national interests and negotiate consensually? Are they being used by Council to take hard and unpopular decisions in environmental policy that it would rather not be seen taking? Conclusive evidence cannot perhaps be offered here, but this chapter has been unambiguous in suggesting that such questions are genuine and give cause for concern. In any event for the democratic legitimacy of environmental policy it was argued these issues need to be addressed. However, what was also acknowledged was that implementation and advisory committees can have a part to play in making policy more rational and even democratic, if they are properly constituted.

This chapter ends by noting then, that the various types of advisory, expert and implementation committees will probably continue to play an important part in policy. Beyond what they are formally meant to do, such as approve secondary legislation, it is evident they offer a flexible means of policy debate and agenda setting of particular attraction to the Member States. They also offer forums where questions of scientific risk can perhaps be evaluated, or potentially negotiated if not horse-traded, again suiting Member States. Finally, implementation committees provide venues where the details of environmental policy compromises that have been agreed beforehand as directives, can later be thrashed out in the comfort of a pragmatic and opaque committee. In other cases, implementing committees can be used as 'trapdoors' through which unpopular or difficult legislation can be passed. Unquestionably, these features are becoming more evident to the actors within the environment policy process, as was clear in the EEB criticism of the Molitor group. To conclude then, it is perhaps as likely that a reformist agenda will emerge from such actors, keen to curtail the abuses (as they see it) of a committee method of working which now lies at the heart of environment policy.

Notes

1   Indeed there can be little certainty if the picture Hayes-Renshaw and Wallace paint is true: some 3,000–4,000 officials meeting everyday from Member State governments in about 50 committees and about another 150 on-off groups. Or that some working groups just form and meet but once (1996: 70, 97).
2   The European Parliament's environment committee led the way with respect to their rejection by a huge majority in May 1996 of the Landfill Directive proposed by the Commission in mid summer 1994. In this case while familiar 'ego' disputes over legal basis and slowness on the part of the Council in responding to the Parliament were present, there were also substantive environmental concerns evident. The proposed common position would have allowed Member States a large discretion in exempting landfills in rural and dispersed areas (ENDS 256, 1996: 39).
3   The reason why the budget underestimates the number of implementation committees existing is because Commission only publishes a financial review of the costs of committees for which consultation is mandatory (those who come strictly under the 1987 comitology decision, so called A2510 committees). Other, ad hoc 'sounding out' committees are given no financial reports (Buitendijk and Van Schendelen, 1995: 40) As this is the surest way of knowing the existence of committees we cannot even know just how many exist at one time.
4   (See OJ L113 Vol. 40, 30 April 1997).
5   Usually thought of as Denmark, Austria, Sweden, and with less certainty, Finland, Netherlands and Germany. The latter particularly is regarded by some as not qualified to claim a green status, given the pressure which re-unification have put on German willingness for tough green laws. However, together these states form a blocking minority under QMV in the Council, so they can at least in theory prevent green laws being undermined by the other states. In terms of a formal sense of alliance, while it does appear there are substantial bilateral civil service and political links, there is little formal coherence. Norway additionally seems to be involved in such ad hoc bilateral and multilateral exchanges.
6   In fact at the time, the company in question was the Swiss chemical and pharmaceutical firm Ciba, which later merged with another firm to form Novartis.
7   They suggested for example that it was merely 'on the balance of evidence' that risks were low and promised that they would review the issue again at a later date.
8   This was suggested to be in line with best international practice but they did concede that the 'may contain GMOs' label should be limited in use through tough rules which specified that whenever testing can confirm the presence of GMO material then it should be done.
9   These were: (1) that the Novartis GM maize in particular included a modified genetic marker which could, if found in animal feeds, pass on resistance to the antibiotic

ampicllin among animals and even possibly humans; (2) a second gene in such maize was based on a bacterium, Bacillus thuringiensis (Bt), which could help spread resistance among insects to its current use in organic pest control (ENDS 272, 1997: 41).

10 It is important to be cautious here, as it may be hard to generalise from the Dutch case. In fact while the Dutch civil service is regarded as highly competent and displays often high technical expertise as opposed to 'generalist' staff, it is very fragmented. No genuine unified national civil service exists and each ministry is quite distinct in its approach to administration (Andewig and Irwin, 1993: 176–80). Yet such sectoral fragmentation, does not explain why two policy actors in the environment sector are so poorly co-ordinated. It would appear the comitology process has a distancing effect of its own.

$\mathcal{A}$NNA $\mathcal{M}$URPHY

5

In the maelstrom of change
The Article 113 Committee in the governance of external economic policy

Introduction

The 113 Committee originates in the Rome Treaty as a 'special committee, appointed by the Council to assist the Commission' and consult it in international trade negotiations. It was established as part of the decision-making apparatus for the common commercial policy, itself a central element of the Rome Treaty. Since 1958, the completion of the customs union, successive rounds of General Agreement on Tariffs and Trade (GATT) negotiations on trade, key rulings of the European Court of Justice, four enlargements of the EC, and the completion of the internal market have had considerable effects on this policy. The 113 Committee has been under constant pressure to adapt to these changes in its policy-making environment and to the increased complexity of issues to be addressed. It has been implicated in general debates on efficiency and democratic accountability in the IGCs leading to the Maastricht and Amsterdam Treaties. In addition, the committee itself as an institutional actor faces competition for influence in the Commission and Council, in the shape of COREPER and Council working groups.

A perennial issue affecting the work of the 113 Committee relates to ambivalence concerning the scope of the common commercial policy and disagreements between the Commission, on the one hand, and the Member States, on the other, on the competence of the EC/EU to enter into trade negotiations on specific issues. Internal divisions over the competence to act raise questions regarding the division of responsibilities between the EC/EU and Member States both in internal decision-making and in external representation in multilateral trade negotiations. This affects the capacity of the EC/EU to negotiate effectively with other trading partners (the unwieldy nature of the EU in successive GATT rounds has been much criticised [Patterson, 1983]. In addition, the existence of three separate domains or pillars of action in EC/EU external relations – the

European Political Co-operation (EPC)/CFSP, Justice and Home Affairs (JHA) and EC – raised questions of policy coherence and the hierarchy of decision-making instances. Decisions taken in pursuit of objectives under the CFSP, for example, have implications for trade (indeed the principal policy instruments are trade-related) but may not involve close liaison with the 113 Committee.

This chapter reviews the role of the 113 Committee in EU decision-making and its evolution since 1958. In many ways this mirrored developments in EU governance. There has been a continuous struggle between the Member States and the Commission over competence to act, punctuated by landmark interventions by the European Court of Justice. Developments in international trade and in multilateral trade negotiations created pressure for an expanded interpretation of the common commercial policy and for the EC to act in unison. The pace of internal integration also altered policy parameters. Nonetheless, the 113 Committee remained at the centre of policy-making and developed new levels of operation in order to manage its business. Member States resisted calls to involve the European Parliament in decision-making and, likewise, Commission proposals to limit the role of the committee to that of consultation only on international negotiations. By the 1990s, however, the committee was stretched in terms of maintaining oversight of trade policy, managing its own agenda and operating effectively with an expanded membership. This raises broader questions for EU governance as the Union faces into a new round of World Trade Organisation (WTO) negotiations and enlargement to the east.

The working procedures of the 113 Committee

The role of the 113 Committee in policy-making is two-fold: it consults with the Commission on trade matters and assists it in the conduct of negotiations on the Common Commercial Policy (CCP) with external partners. The fact that the committee does not formally vote can be seen as a source of weakness or at least ambiguity in its relationship with other parts of the EU machinery. It acts as an important clearing house for the Commission, but should the Commission wish to ignore the wishes of the Committee or some of its members, it can place its proposals directly on the Council's agenda through COREPER (in practice, this rarely happens). The committee's work is facilitated by much informal contact between Member State representatives and various parts of the Commission. Individual Commissioners or representatives may also float ideas to the full committee or individuals before they are agreed by the Commission. In this way, individual Commissioners may use the committee to strengthen the case for adoption of his/her initiatives.

COREPER, in contrast to the committee, has a stronger influence in decision-taking and is the channel through which 113 Committee items are filtered to the Council (see Figure 9). As a result, the 113 Committee's formal role remains advisory. On the other hand, as policy has been channelled through

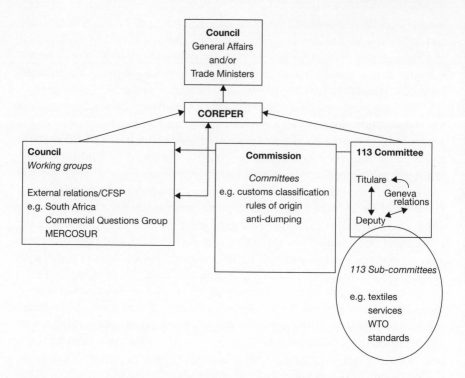

Figure 9 The 113 Committee in EU policy-making

representatives of the Member States in the committee, opinions of the 113 Committee are rarely overturned by the Council and are sometimes treated as if they were official decisions of the Council. Although it does not formally vote and Council decisions are taken on the basis of qualified majority, the committee seeks consensus amongst the members. At a minimum, it tries to ensure that there is no blocking minority before passing matters upwards to the next level of decision-making. Conscious efforts are made not to ignore or isolate individual Member States.

The 113 Committee lacks openness[1] and transparency concerning its work. The EP has no formal input into policy-making under Article 113, despite efforts to acquire a right of co-decision in negotiations leading to the Amsterdam Treaty. This was rejected by the Member States who saw this as complicating decision-making. Some did favour greater involvement of the EP in order to enhance democratic accountability. In practice, the European Parliament is kept informed of the conduct of external trade negotiations, maintains informal contacts with the Commission and Member States and in the case of the Uruguay Round agreements was formally submitted the final package for approval. Such measures fall short of giving the Parliament an effective voice in decision-making. Industry and lobbying groups too lack formal relations with the Committee. Formal consultative processes may obtain at national level or with the Commission.

The 113 Committee has traditionally been divided between a liberal north (centred around Germany, the Netherlands, Denmark, Luxembourg and, on non-agricultural issues, Ireland) and a protectionist south (centred around France, Italy, Greece, Spain and Portugal) in its deliberations (Hayes, 1993: 146–60; Murphy, 1996a). There is some evidence that enlargement to Austria, Finland and Sweden has strengthened the liberal bloc. Each Member State however, even the most liberal, has adopted protectionist positions on certain issues (e.g. textiles, steel). The fragmented nature of decision-making, coupled with the search for consensus means that narrow sectoral interests can prevail over collective interests, as in the case of the final stages of the Uruguay Round negotiations and in negotiations on association agreements with the Central and Eastern European states (Pelkmans and Murphy, 1992; Smith and Rollo, 1996; Murphy, 1996a). Nonetheless, most critiques of EC policy-making on trade accept that while it is not liberal in all cases, such as bananas, the general trend has been liberal, in line with the philosophy of the internal market and in view of the constraints of the multilateral trading system, reinforced by a strengthened dispute settlement mechanism in the WTO (Woolcock and Hodges, 1996). The question of whether the balance of views in the committee has tipped in favour of a more liberal approach to trade will be tested in the preparation of the EU's negotiating mandate for the forthcoming round of WTO negotiations.

The working philosophy of the committee is best expressed by its concentration on collective problem-solving. It is a rather pragmatic committee and has demonstrated flexibility in its working procedures and in its relations with the Commission so as to negotiate effectively with the outside. Debates over issues of competence can be linked to overall trends in decision-making, as was the case in debates on Article 113 in successive IGCs on Treaty reform. Member State objections that the EC/EU lacks the competence to act often conceal opposition to policy initiatives, although others reflect a more principled approach to Member State involvement in the EC/EU.

The committee also experiences some difficulties in the organisation of its workload as a result of an expanded agenda, an expanded membership and the usually short notice given to the Member States of the agenda. While some items for the agenda are known in advance, the detailed agenda of the Deputies meeting may only be circulated a few days ahead of the weekly meeting, leaving little time for preparation and consultation. A review of the functioning and organisation of the committee, undertaken by the Dutch Presidency in 1997 (Johnson, 1998: 63 and author's interviews) pointed to the tendency of the Commission to rely on oral communications to the Committee and to table written proposals late in the day. While this technique may reflect a desire to impose its views on the Member States, this trend is also related to the sheer pressure of scheduled meetings with external partners and the need to act quickly. This can lead to superficial consultation and increase pressure on the committee to accept the

Commission's proposals in order to meet external deadlines. This practice also reflects the fragmented nature of policy-making in the Commission, where internal rivalry (within and between directorates and Commissioners) and difficulty in reaching agreed positions can cause delay in the submission of positions to the committee.

The expanded membership of the committee following successive enlargements, while not adding greatly to the diversity of views on any given issue, does complicate discussions in the 113 Committee. Usually, some fifteen items are tabled on the agenda of the Committee and even the presentation of initial national responses to an item can take one to two hours. It is the norm for each state to seek to express a view on each issue in order to have this written into the official record (with a view to its domestic audience and/or the media).

Since 1997, some organisational steps have been taken to overcome these weaknesses – for meetings at Deputy level (see below), there is more regular use of e-mail in advance of meetings, attempts to obtain relevant Commission documents before meetings and the submission of written documents by Member State representatives to the Presidency. Other moves have been made to shorten the agenda of meetings and limit Member State interventions but few substantive changes have been introduced. The initiative to alter working procedures lies largely with the Presidency which due to lack of interest or resources has not pursued the Dutch Presidency review (1997).[2]

The Common Commercial Policy: Member States in defence of their powers

The Common Commercial Policy was one of the first areas in which the EC acquired exclusive competence (under Articles 110-15). Article 113 states that:

> the common commercial policy shall be based upon uniform principles, particularly in regard to changes in tariff rates, the conclusion of tariff and other trade agreements, the achievement of uniformity in measures of liberalisation, export policy and measures to protect trade such as those to be taken in the event of dumping or subsidies.
>
> The Commission shall submit proposals to the Council for implementing the common commercial policy.
>
> Where agreements with third countries need to be negotiated, the Commission shall make recommendations to the Council, which shall authorise the Commission to open negotiations.
>
> The Commission shall conduct these negotiations in consultation with a special committee appointed by the Council to assist the Commission in this task and within the framework of such directives as the Council may issue to it.

One of the most significant features of Article 113 is that, since the end of the transition period (1968), decisions on the CCP are taken by qualified majority. This means that the Member States are quite sensitive to the issue of policy scope as this affects their influence to shape policy and negotiate with non-EC partners. First, consensus remains the basis for decision-making in areas in which competences are shared between the EC/EU and Member States or remain at the national level; and, second, where competences are not exclusive to the EC/EU, the question of who represents the EC/EU in external negotiations remains open. It was also noteworthy that the European Parliament was not given any voice in decision-making under Article 113.

The competence issue remained contentious throughout the development of the CCP given that the Treaty failed to provide an exhaustive list of policy instruments or prescribe its scope. The question of policy scope was also critical to the EC's participation in GATT negotiations whose agenda moved initially beyond tariffs to encompass non-tariff barriers to trade and, in the Uruguay Round (1986–94), to new areas of trade in services, intellectual property and investments which did not fall within the scope of the CCP. The Commission did not have an automatic right to represent the EC and the Member States in these new areas. As the section below on external representation demonstrates, a pragmatic solution was found in which Article 113 procedures were followed without prejudice to the issue of competence which was to be resolved at the conclusion of negotiations. This suggests that where there is a common will to act, disputes over competence can be resolved.

The European Court of Justice, in its rulings and opinions, played a key role on determining the EC's competences under the common commercial policy. First, in the AETR case, 22/70, it determined that where the EC has adopted internal rules in a given policy area, it automatically acquired exclusive competence to enter into international agreements in those areas.[3] It further extended the EC's area of competence when, in 1977,[4] it ruled that the EC had the power to enter into international agreements where this was necessary to attain Treaty objectives even in cases where internal powers had not been exercised (Johnson, 1998: 9). This appeared to give considerable powers to the EC and led the Commission to argue that external competence flowed automatically from internal Treaty provisions where EC participation in international agreements was necessary to attain a Treaty objective. The Court rejected this far-reaching argument (Opinion 1/94, Bourgeois, 1995: 780–2) and, later,[5] stated that such power relates only to cases where international agreements are necessary to achieve objectives which cannot be obtained by the adoption of autonomous rules.

Further pressure to expand the CCP arose from the dual structure of EC external relations. This surfaced in Commission proposals to radically overhaul the CCP and the 113 Committee in negotiations leading to the Maastricht Treaty. In order to achieve coherence in external relations (as between foreign and security policy and commercial policy), the Commission argued for a transformation of the common commercial policy into a common policy on external relations. This would comprise of *inter alia* economic and trade measures in respect of services, capital, intellectual property, investment, establishment and competition, export credit and credit insurance schemes (Article Y17) [Bulletin

2–1991: 108]. New decision-making procedures would be introduced. The Commission wanted to establish the principle that, for every power conferred on the union for internal matters, a corollary power to act in the external domain would exist.[6] Once those powers had been exercised internally, Union competence to act in the external domain would become exclusive (p. 97). The Member States opposed these proposals although, in view of ongoing Uruguay Round negotiations, the Luxembourg Presidency did support the inclusion of trade in services in the CCP. Thus, the issue of the precise scope of the CCP remained unresolved.

Also rejected were Commission proposals to reduce the role of the 113 Committee in decision-making. It proposed that its role change from one of assistance in external negotiations to mere consultation (Article Y26) [Bulletin 2–1991: 95]. This would effectively end the practice where representatives of the Member States are directly involved in negotiations or accompany the Commission in such. Not surprisingly, this proposed erosion of Member State influence was opposed.

The Commission also failed in its attempt to increase democratic accountability and transparency of decision-making by giving a voice to the European Parliament in the common commercial policy. It suggested that the Parliament be consulted on policy and, in certain cases, give its formal assent to trade agreements. The Member States opposed any formalisation of consultation with the Parliament under 113 while accepting that its assent should be given for certain kinds of international agreements.[7] Their general view was that this would introduce greater complexity and delay in decision-making and impinge on the confidentiality of negotiations with the outside. Instead, the practice whereby the Parliament is kept informed of progress in negotiations through its committees and in Commission statements to the Assembly continues.[8]

The resultant Maastricht Treaty failed to make any significant changes to the CCP (Maresceau, 1994: 18–19). A new provision, Article 228a, clarified the legal basis and decision-making procedures to be followed when introducing trade sanctions. Until then, such decisions were taken in the context of EPC and the 113 Committee's role was minimal even though it was clear that such decisions affected the common commercial policy. The choice of legal base determined decision-making procedures and whether the European Parliament would be consulted (cf. Nuttall, 1992: 264–5). The sanctions question raised the broader political issue of complementarity between the CCP and EPC/CFSP as clearly actions taken in each domain could have implications for the other. Article 228a made it clear that decisions would be taken in the context of the CFSP and on the basis of qualified majority (some Member States had argued in favour of unanimity).[9]

The European Court of Justice next entered the fray when, in 1994, it gave its Opinion on the competence of the Community to conclude the Uruguay Round.[10]

The Court established new parameters for Article 113 but, in contrast to earlier judgements which interpreted EC competences widely, its interpretation of the CCP was quite restrictive. It determined that:[11]

- the EC has exclusive competence to conclude multilateral agreements in the area of trade in goods (including goods covered by the ECSC and EURATOM, the European Atomic Energy Community)
- with respect to trade in services, cross-border services which are electronically transmitted are analogous trade in goods (and fall within the exclusive competence of the EC)
- responsibility for other cross-border trade in services which require the movement of providers or establishment within the EC is shared between the Community and the Member States
- trade in intellectual property, with the exception of trade in counterfeit goods, is a competence of the Member States

In their submissions to the Court, the Commission's arguments in favour of incorporating services into Article 113 had been resolutely opposed both by the European Parliament (for reasons linked to its lack of power under Article 113) and the Member States (which wanted to maintain maximum leverage in decision-making). The Council had argued that the Commission was attempting to extend competence through the judicial door when this had been rejected by the Member States in the IGC leading to the Maastricht Treaty (above). The Court agreed that a narrow range of services fell within the ambit of the CCP.[12]

This opinion would have implications for decision-making in the EC/EU and the representation of the EC/EU in multilateral fora such as the World Trade Organisation. The existence of shared competences between the EC and the Member States in services and intellectual property could also frustrate the implementation of new dispute settlement procedures in the WTO. These, for the first time in the history of the GATT, permitted cross-retaliation between the sectors of goods, services and intellectual property whereby violations in one sector could henceforth be addressed by taking corrective action in another sector. If the Community was given the right to retaliate in the areas of services or intellectual property it might not be able to exercise it because the Member States retained competence to act in those areas. The Court, echoing the views of the Council an European Parliament, advocated a political solution to the matter: it declared that there was a 'duty of co-operation between the Member States and the Commission' with respect to their participation in the WTO.

The issues of both policy scope and competence resurfaced in the IGC leading to the Treaty of Amsterdam. The Commission (1996) argued that the Court had not resolved the key issues and that changes were necessary to adapt to new developments in international trade and enable the EU to negotiate effectively in the World Trade Organisation. It also bemoaned the inadequate co-ordination between the Member States and the Commission in sectors in which competences were shared and the negative impact that this had on the Union's unity of action in non-GATT fora such as the International Labour Organisation. It argued that the Union's competences should be expanded and that the Commission should be the sole external representative of the EU. Member State opposition meant that changes agreed in the Amsterdam Treaty were less ambitious. A new paragraph was inserted into Article 113:

> The Council, acting unanimously on a proposal from the Commission and after consulting the European Parliament, may extend the application of paragraphs 1 to 4 to international negotiations and agreements on services and intellectual property insofar as they are not covered by these paragraphs

This amendment reflected both a reluctance on the part of some Member States to extend the competence of the Community to new areas and a distrust of the Commission which, some Member States argued, did not consult adequately with the Member States in the final stages of the Uruguay Round negotiations (*Agence Europe*, 1997a, 1997b; Woolcock and Hodges, 1996). The Treaty amendment is restrictive in that (1) Article 113 can now be applied on a case-by-case basis only to international negotiations or agreements in the areas of services and intellectual property (i.e. there was no open-ended transfer of competence); (2) Article 113 can be extended to these named areas only (for example, it did not cover direct investments even though negotiations on such were on-going in the OECD and were expected to feature on the WTO's agenda in the future). In effect, the status quo was retained insofar as unanimity would be required to authorise the EC to act on behalf of the Member States in these cases (Blin, 1998: 451, 453). On the other hand, the new provision does allow decisions to extend the application of Article 113, which would imply a change of decision-making procedure from unanimity to qualified majority, to be taken without amending the Treaty itself. Finally, the European Parliament was given an explicit right of consultation in decisions to extend competence, but none with respect to the operation of Article 113 itself. Despite vociferous attempts, the European Parliament failed to obtain significant powers in this area.

The 113 Committee and interaction with EC/EU institutions

The 113 Committee is part of the machinery of the Council, having established at the outset, in 1958, that the Presidency rather than the Commission should chair it. The Presidency can exert an important influence on the agenda and work of the committee through strong chairmanship and discipline of committee members. In practice, the 113 Committee is consulted by the Commission on all key aspects of trade policy. The Commission however has the sole right of initiative in decision-making and is the external representative of the EC in multilateral trade negotiations (this does not preclude efforts by individual members to exercise influence in each of those domains). The relationship between the Commission and the 113 Committee is marked by both tension and co-operation. In addition to attempts to carve out a greater role for itself in external representation, the Commission may also attempt to strengthen its own institutional profile in trade policy through tactical moves (e.g. delayed tabling of proposals to the committee which leave little time for discussion and by direct recourse, over the heads of the committee, to the Council). Commission representatives may also float proposals and ideas to the committee before formally tabling them to the full Commission e.g. in late 1998, Sir Leon Brittan tabled ideas for a transatlantic partnership to the 113 Committee before they were approved by the Commission.

From the 1970s onwards, the expanding agenda of GATT negotiations demanded the establishment of a second level of policy-making in the committee. The so-called full committee (titulaires) continued to meet once monthly supplemented by weekly meetings at deputy level (also considered to be the 113 Committee). Committee membership is determined by the Member States and the constitution of national delegations can vary according to topics or level of the meeting (experts from national capitals and officials based in Brussels may accompany the members of the committee). Procedures for policy co-ordination at the national level vary from strict central control in France to looser co-ordination in Ireland by the Department of Industry and Trade (Johnson, 1998: 45–6). The titulaires are based in national capitals (generally at the level of Assistant Secretary) and are usually drawn from Trade and Industry Ministries in accordance with the division of responsibilities in the Member States. Many of these are long-standing members[13] and their meetings tend to be less formal (and involve fewer officials) than those of the deputies. The deputies are usually drawn from the Member States' permanent representatives based in Brussels, with the exception of the larger Member States and those in closer proximity to Brussels. They focus on more technical issues while political ones and issues on which there is no prior agreement amongst Deputies are handled by the titulaires. Both titulaires and deputies direct the work of the 113 Committee which also meets at a subordinate level in Geneva (where representatives of the Member States meet to prepare and consult on GATT/WTO issues). The latter's brief is to liaise with the Commission in detailed preparations for and negotiations in the GATT/WTO. Occasionally its members also attend the higher-level 113 Committee meetings in Brussels where key negotiating positions are agreed. The deputies may also meet in Geneva or elsewhere on the occasion of Ministerial meetings of the GATT/WTO.

In addition to establishing a second level of work, the 113 Committee also set up a number of specialised sub-committees to deal with issues such as textiles, steel, trade in services, the mutual recognition of standards and the WTO, each of which works closely with the Commission. Co-ordination between the 113 Committee and the sub-committees is generally good, assisted by the fact that there is some overlap of membership with that of the deputies committee. Johnson's argument (1998: 55) that the 113 Committee does not have sufficient oversight of their work is contested by current members of the committee.[14] This alleged lack of oversight is also linked to the quality of policy co-ordination in

Member State capitals. In contrast, the committee however has little formal oversight of the work of specialist committees in trade-related areas, chaired by the Commission, including those dealing with rules of origin, customs duties and anti-dumping. These committees report directly to the Commercial Questions Group in the Council.[15] Failure to take adequate account of the political implications of seemingly technical issues handled by these committees, such as customs classification, can however implicate the 113 Committee by triggering trade disputes with external partners or violation of WTO rules.

The negotiations in which the 113 Committee assists the Commission can be bilateral, multilateral, sectoral or global. It also sees itself as having an important role in ensuring the coherence of the EC/EU's external relations and the unity of its action but has considerable difficulty in managing this (see above). Inter-bureaucratic rivalry amongst different levels of policy-making involving the Member States has emerged in the late 1980s and 1990s. The expansion of EU activities in the CFSP, extension of preferential trade agreements, bilateral relations, electronic commerce and specific trade strategies such as the Transatlantic Agenda[16] and the expanding agenda of the WTO place considerable demands on the capacity of the 113 Committee to maintain oversight of EU action which impinges on the common commercial policy. In the 1990s, its main focus is on GATT/WTO business. Initiatives formulated in Council working groups, especially those handling bilateral/ regional relations, increasingly include measures affecting trade, e.g. concerning South Africa and MERCOSUR, the free trade area in Latin America. The 113 Committee is concerned that they may not accord sufficient attention to trade issues given that policies are driven by other concerns. Similar 'spillover' effects appear with respect to policy-making on internal EC/EU matters where, for example, a decision taken by Environmental Ministers to ban the use of leg-hold traps can trigger accusations of a breach by the EU of WTO rules. In similar vein, decisions taken by Agriculture Ministers could have unforeseen consequences for the EC's obligations under the GATT/WTO, e.g. with respect to animal welfare and veterinary standards. The principal challenge facing the 113 Committee is to acquire full oversight and direction of trade policy – it only discusses the main elements rather than the detail of trade matters taken up by Council working groups. It's ability to lead policy is further hampered by the absence of formal ties to the working groups and the fact that they report directly to COREPER which prepares decisions for the Council.

This tricky relationship with Council working groups is exacerbated by the fact that membership of the 113 Committee and the working groups does not overlap and that policy co-ordination within national capitals may be weak or fraught. The expanding agenda of multilateral trade negotiations, on the one hand, and the increased complexity of EU business on the other, blur the boundaries of EC/EU and international policy. Much of the 'internal' business of the EU has trade policy effects while much of the business of the WTO concerns market regulation (and therefore has significant 'internal' effects). The expansion of the multilateral trade agenda into areas such as environment and labour standards also raises issues of democratic accountability and involvement of non-governmental organisations in the policy process. They also place strain on policy-making procedures which were not designed to cope with such issues or objectives which may not, in substance, be about trade (e.g. part of the motivation to extend WTO rules to cover labour standards and environmental protection is driven by efforts to strengthen international rules in these areas rather than to promote trade liberalisation).

The Dutch Presidency review of 1997, above, reflected these strains and indicated concerns that the committee lacked visibility and presence both with respect to internal policy-making instances and to external representation. The first related to its relationship with COREPER and the General Affairs Council. There is some competition with COREPER – which has a direct line of communication to the Council and a formal voice in decision-taking. COREPER also meets directly before Council meetings, unlike the titulaires who no longer assemble at the margins of Council meetings,[17] and therefore has the last word in devising solutions before Ministers become involved (Johnson, 1998: 53). In addition, the General Affairs Council does not devote sufficient time to trade issues. Although Trade Councils have been convened, usually on an informal basis, opinion is divided as to whether Trade Ministers should convene regularly or whether the General Affairs Council, which has broad oversight and is driven by more powerful Foreign Ministers, should remain the primary ministerial-level forum for policy-making.[18]

These concerns reflect a sense in which the committee sees itself as an institutional actor, anxious to retain its place as the primary forum for discussions on trade policy. This identity has been shaped by socialisation and its long history and strong continuities in committee membership. Johnson (1998: 46) points to the frequency of informal contacts which facilitates policy-making. He, echoing those who lament the passing of the small community of officials dealing with EPC, argues that an expanded membership has seen a reduction in this 'community feeling'. In any case, this community feeling does not deter individual members from their primary objective of promoting and defending national interests.

External representation and negotiations with the outside

The Commission negotiates on behalf of the EC in international fora on Article 113 issues. It has established itself as the sole EC representative and, in successive GATT rounds, won increased independence to negotiate even though the Member States remained contracting parties to the GATT. The practice has been that the Commission represented the views of the Member States but that they retained the right to speak and represent themselves in areas in which they had competences. Nonetheless, disputes arise as to whether it exceeds the mandates given it by the Council and whether it keeps the Member States, through the 113 Committee, fully informed about the conduct of multilateral negotiations. Some disputes are bound to arise as any negotiating mandate has to leave some room for manoeuvre and hence scope for differing interpretations. In general, working relations with the Commission are good. On increasingly rare occasions, individual Member States intervene in their own right as in the latter stages of the Uruguay Round, when France argued that the Commission had exceeded its mandate. There is a strong institutional constraint against such individual action as it weakens the collective power of the EC and may allow negotiating partners to exploit differences. Such action and the questioning of the EC's competence to act in specific cases may also be a cover for Member State opposition to particular EC/EU positions or reflect failure to reach joint agreement (Hayes-Renshaw and Wallace, 1996: 141).

While the Commission negotiates on behalf of the Member States in the GATT/WTO, the Member States are consulted before and after each significant round of negotiations. In addition, the Member States may accompany the Commission in formal meetings of the WTO Council and in formal negotiations but generally do not speak. The 113 Committee is responsible for on-site co-ordination and representation but the sheer number of negotiating sessions and simultaneous meetings may mean that Member States cannot always be represented. In addition, all Member States are entitled to attend informal negotiations which are critical to the finalisation of GATT/WTO deals although this may not be practicable. Non-participation can generate tension and accusations of lack of adequate consultation or respect for negotiating mandates by some Member States. The Commission's negotiating mandates – which are confidential – can be amended by official decisions of the Council although this can be difficult and time-consuming (Pelkmans and Murphy, 1992).

In the latter stages of the Uruguay Round the Council agreed a 'Code of Conduct' for the EC's approach to negotiations on services[19] as a mechanism to facilitate and formalise negotiations on issues falling outside the scope of Article 113 or where the EC's competence to act was disputed. The Commission would continue to negotiate on behalf of the Member States and inform the Member States as far in advance as possible of all discussions and negotiations to be held with other parties (formal and informal). It would ensure that representatives of all the Member States were in a position to attend all relevant meetings and negotiations with third parties (they could also request the Presidency to attend on their behalf). Finally, the Commission would circulate any notes produced by the GATT Secretariat and other participants, including the Commission itself, which had not been sent to the Member States directly. The Council could itself review progress in negotiations and consider re-formulating negotiating objectives or issue new mandates to the Commission as appropriate (Opinion 1/94: 81–2). The provisions of the proposed Code revealed certain tensions between the Member States and the Commission concerning adequate information and consultation about negotiations it engaged in – for example, the French government argued for the possibility of suspending negotiations where necessary and that all positions taken by the Commission should be based on agreements reached in the Council according to the relevant Treaty provisions. Where no consensus obtained, the Member States should be free to express their views in the WTO (Opinion 1/94: 100).

Discussions on a general Code of Conduct took place in 1994/95 but were abandoned in early 1996 in view of the then ongoing IGC. The Member States were reluctant to restrict their possibilities for action given the criticism of some of the Commission's conduct in the latter stages of negotiations in the Uruguay Round on agriculture when it was accused of exceeding its negotiating mandate from the Council. Such accusations and fears surfaced again in the Commission's negotiations with the United States on the suspension of the Helms–Burton Act (April 1997) and led some Member States to demand a protocol in the Amsterdam Treaty which would detail the obligations of the Commission in international negotiations (this was subsequently dropped but nonetheless reflected continued Member State suspicions). In practice, the Member States proved capable of acting in unison and exercising leadership in the Uruguay Round negotiations on services and in responding to new challenges such as the Helms–Burton and d'Amato Kennedy laws which claimed extra-territorial effects.[20]

No code of conduct has since been agreed with respect to EU participation in the WTO or in its dispute settlement proceedings. In view of disagreements over the Commission's role in the latter (particularly in cases which do not clearly fall within the scope of Article 113 or where individual states rather than the EC are accused of breaching WTO rules), a so-called 'non-decision' was taken by the Member States which established the principle that the Commission should co-ordinate response(s) with the Member State(s) in question. The alternative approach of codifying Member State and Commission roles would, according to committee members, require a formal decision of the EU in each case – both a time-consuming and cumbersome approach. The informal approach retains flexibility and leaves open the question of whether individual Member States can take an action in the WTO. Although few cases have tested this approach, the Commission, up to late 1998, co-ordinated responses with the Member States e.g. with Ireland in its defence against charges of infringement of GATT rules on intellectual property rights. It remains to be seen whether all states will work with the Commission should proceedings be initiated against them or should they wish to take a case in the absence of agreement in the 113 Committee.[21] The committee's institutional bias in favour of collective action can, however, be expected to continue.

Conclusion: EU governance and the 113 Committee

The evolution of the 113 Committee in many ways mirrors that of the governance of the EC/EU. The committee has developed new working mechanisms in response to an increased workload and membership and is itself an example of multi-level governance. In essence, its working habits and relations between the players remain unaltered – no fundamental overhaul of either its legal base or working methods has occurred since it was established. The Dutch Presidency review (1997) of the functioning of the committee revealed significant shortcomings in the organisation of its work, its capacity to exercise effective oversight of trade policy and maintain a strong internal and external presence. While some argue for a clarification of its procedures and working methods, others argue that codification might in fact reduce flexibility and efficacy e.g. with respect to a Code of Conduct in the GATT/WTO. Yet, it remains the central mechanism through which the Member States exercise control over trade policy (Johnson, 1998: 62). For most, its primary purpose is to serve as a means to facilitate decision-making.

Disputes over the competence to the EC to act reflect a tussle for control of policy between the Commission and Member States. Successive interventions by the European Court of Justice testify to the powerful integrating force of EC law, on the one hand, and inter-linkage between internal integration and external action, on the other. While the committee had a certain 'community-feeling' in the past, the complexity of decision-making and expanded membership have reduced this. The sheer number of delegates attending meetings is now a hindrance to the committee's work – some insiders would go so far as to say that this increases the relative influence of the Commission. Moreover, it is present in all key policy-making instances in the EU and may have a better overview of all issues relating to commercial policy.

The committee still retains a sense of institutional identity in the EU system, particularly at titulaire level, in its concerns to remain the primary trade policy forum for the EU. This is expressed in competition not just with the Commission but with working groups in the Council. There are also elements of tension between the national and EU level (e.g. disputes of over the Commission's interpretation of negotiating mandates and division of competences); inter-bureaucratic rivalry between the 113 Committees, COREPER and Council working groups; and the blurring of policy boundaries as a result of Europeanisation of domestic policies and increased multilateralisation of trade policy. A powerful dynamic in policy-formulation is the collective desire to solve problems – this leads to co-operative behaviour including with the Commission – and to maintain a collective identity in international negotiations. The awareness that failure to reach agreement will give other decision-making instances greater leverage over trade policy may act as an incentive to representatives to resolve issues within the committee. Exceptions do occur and reflect the sensitivity of an issue for a particular Member State which, regardless of community-feeling, will not be persuaded to alter its position. In conclusion, the 113 Committee is generally treated by the Member States as a framework for collective action but can be said to have a certain institutional status in its own right. Some like the French, tend to take the high ground on issues of competence but pragmatic solutions are generally found which, although they may not satisfy the purists, facilitate progress in decision-making.

Notes

1   A Committee representative suggested that the Commission is an important source of information for the media and that contentious issues will be made public (author's interview, October 1998).

2   For example, the decision to convene a standing chair's working group on the functioning of the committee was not put into effect by successive Presidencies (cf. note 19).

3   Case 22/70 [1970] European Community Reports (European Community Reports) 263.

4   Opinion 1/76 [1977] European Community Report 741 (Rhine navigation case).

5   Opinion 2/92, 24 March 1995 (The Organisation for Economic Co-operation and Development (OECD) National Treatment Instrument).

6   It argued that this would codify principles laid down by the Court of Justice (Bulletin 2–1991: 108).

7   Its assent must be given in the case of association agreements (Article 228a), agreements which establish a specific institutional framework by organising co-operation procedures and agreements which have budgetary implications or which involve changes to acts adopted under the co-decision procedure.

8   The practice is not entirely satisfactory as, in 1995/96, the Council failed to consult the Parliament on an interim trade agreement with Russia (*Agence Europe*, Europe Daily Bulletins No. 6658, 2 February 1996).

9   Moreover, the scope of such sanctions could exceed that of the common commercial policy in that the amendment refers to the interruption of economic relations (MacLeod *et al.*, 1996).

10   With respect to establishing the WTO, the General Agreement on Trade in Services and the Agreement on the trade-related aspects of intellectual property rights, including trade in counterfeit goods.

11   Opinion 1/94, 15 November 1990 [1994] European Community Report 2871.

12   The supply of cross-border services which do not involve the movement of persons was deemed to be within its ambit whereas the supply of services which required the movement of the supplier, consumer or a commercial presence in the territory in which the service is supplied were deemed to be outside Article 113. Transport services too fell outside the scope of Article 113. The Court also decided that intellectual property rights did not fall within the domain of Article 113 although trade in counterfeit goods did. In these cases, competences were shared between the EC and the Member States.

13   Johnson (1998) notes that Titulaires representing Italy, Germany, the Netherlands and the UK did so continuously for at least ten years while one senior official of the Council Secretariat attended meetings from 1958 to 1996. The regular titulaires lunch also provided an important informal forum for discussions and, according to Johnson , was critical to problem-solving up to the 1970s.

14   Authors interviews with two committee representatives (at deputy and titulaire level). They also note that some sub-committees meet infrequently while others are due to be phased out e.g that on textiles.

15   In the early years of the EC, the 113 Committee vied for influence with the Commercial
       Questions Group (a Council working group). The latter was set up to report on the prin-
       ciples of trade policy and operational issues to COREPER and was the preferred inter-
       locutor of both the Commission and certain foreign ministries (Johnson, 1998: 18–19).
       In the 1960s, for example, it co-ordinated EC policy on multilateral trade liberalisation
       and bilateral relations with Japan. The 113 Committee was relegated to handling tech-
       nical issues but, over time, its expertise and proximity to national ministers made it the
       principal channel for trade policy. From the 1970s onwards, the role of the Commercial
       Questions Group dwindled to that of managing administrative issues.

16   In this case, COREPER created a special working party to examine the agenda. France
       issued a statement indicating the need for the 113 Committee to be involved in perma-
       nent consultations on issues in which the EC is competent to act (*Agence Europe*, Europe
       Daily Bulletins No. 6643, 12 January 1996).

17   Some Member States argued that the practice of convening on the margins of Council
       meetings should be reinstated so that they could assist in the final stages of decision-
       making. Others argued that the Committee should be prepared to submit final propos-
       als to the Council and, where serious difficulties existed, elaborate clear options for the
       Council (based on authors interviews with Committee members, October–November
       1998, and Johnson 1998).

18   This review was discussed at an informal meeting of the 113 Committee (Deputies),
       Noordwijk, 6 May 1997 and circulated to the Titulaires meeting in May 1997. It was
       agreed that a permanent Chairman's working group would be set up to prepare recom-
       mendations for improvement of the functioning of the committee (under the responsi-
       bility of the Presidency). This did not become operational.

19   Council decision 11 October 1994.

20   Blin (1998) notes that the Union responded by basing its decisions on the CSFP and arti-
       cles 113 and 235 of the EC.

21   In 1998, the Netherlands, for example, did consider taking individual action in the
       Phonogram case (against Canada) in the absence of agreement in the 113 Committee,
       but the issue never came to a head.

Andreas Faludi, Wil Zonneveld
& Bas Waterhout

6

The Committee on Spatial Development
Formulating a spatial perspective in an
institutional vacuum[1]

Introduction: an exceptional committee

In early 1992 the Committee on Spatial Development (CSD) held its first Brussels meeting. Since then it meets on average four times a year. So what? On any average working day, Brussels may play host to a dozen such committees. (Nugent 1999: 52) The CSD, however, fits into none of the known categories. It does not come under the comitology system as described elsewhere in this volume, nor is it a Council working party. Nonetheless, the CSD obtains the facilities, like interpreters and so forth extended to more run-of-the-mill committees (Faludi and Zonneveld 1997).

A much-heralded opinion is that, in the absence of a Commission *compétence* for spatial planning, formalisation of the CSD is a non-starter. This has not deterred some Member States from arguing for the CSD being given formal status. Our sources (in the main the archives of the Dutch Spatial Planning Agency and interviews with some of the actors concerned) show Germany having done so at the ninth EU Informal Meeting of Ministers responsible for spatial development policy at Madrid in 1995. (More about these meetings is to be found below.) So far, this has been to no avail. The result of the informal status is that, contrary to standard practice, a Member State rather than the Commission holds the chair. In fact, it has always been the Member State holding the Presidency that did so, a situation that, as will become evident below, has been formalised under the Dutch Presidency. So the closest analogy seems with Council working parties. Made up of officials from Member States and the European Commission and chaired by the Presidency, such parties deal with the final drafting of nearly all legislative and policy proposals coming before the Council of Ministers (Schäfer 1996; Van der Knaap 1996).

As it is, the CSD rests on a delicate deal struck between Member States and the Commission. Naturally, there have been ups and downs, but the CSD is a going concern. It has produced a unique planning document, the 'first official draft' of the 'European Spatial Development Perspective' (ESDP) that EU spatial planning ministers could take cognisance of at their June 1997 meeting at Noordwijk in the Netherlands (European Commission 1997a). This was followed by the unpublished 'first complete draft' presented to the ministers at Glasgow in 1998. At their next meeting in May 1999 in Potsdam ministers have given the nod to a definite ESDP. Although not a formal document but rather of the nature of an informal agreement, the signs are that the ESDP will result in a twelve-point Action Programme involving Member States and the European Commission. This is to be adopted at yet another ministerial meeting at Tampere under the current Finnish Presidency in 1999.

So what is the CSD? How did it come into being? How does it work? Which were the main issues? Does the CSD signify a move towards 'joint governance' in the area of spatial development between the European Union and the Member States?

Whatever the answers, clearly the CSD engendered a new discourse on the spatial development of the Community. Setting up the CSD in fact signified the intent, even in the absence of a formal *compétence*, of Member States to co-operate with each other and with the European Commission. However, a number of issues remain unresolved. Where spatial development policy is concerned, the traditions of Member States are vastly different. As Williams (1996) shows, it is difficult, if not impossible to transpose terms that are central to these traditions into other languages. So the reader will not be surprised to learn about much initial confusion. Clarifying issues requires re-inventing notions that countries with well-established spatial planning traditions take for granted. The focus here is on planning principles and spatial planning concepts.

Planning principles are about the form, preparation and application of plans, including not only statutory plans, but also other forms of policy statements. In the case of the CSD, why are planning principles important? The reason is that in the absence of a European Union *compétence* there is much uncertainty as regards them. Thus there is uncertainty concerning the application of any CSD planning document, once it is produced, as well as about the way such a document should come about in the first instance. These are difficult issues because the European Union is not an ordinary planning subject, like local, regional and, in some countries anyway, national authorities acting in this capacity. So what will Member States do with whatever planning document emerges? Will they adapt their policies? Likewise, what is the European Commission going to do? In other words, will those to whom the document is addressed apply it more or less as intended? Answers to these questions are as yet elusive. However, they surely were in the participants' minds when considering how, in the absence of a formal planning subject, European planning could and should proceed. In such situations, planning principles in fact relate to institutional design. Creating committees of whichever kind and devising their operating procedures are the stuff of such design, the end being that of improving co-operation and common understanding.

The other notion that we focus on, that of spatial planning concepts, relates to perceptions of spatial development and how to handle it, now and in the future (Zonneveld 1989). Spatial planners need to interpret the spatial make-up of the territory that they are concerned with and to convey their ideas to others. This involves symbolic representation of the territory, or of parts thereof, in the form of icons, diagrams and/or maps. In short, spatial planning involves creating images (Faludi 1996). Indeed, as Kunzmann (1996: 144) points out: 'In the end visualised concepts can contribute more to achieving certain political goals than legal and financial instruments. Visualised spatial symbols, for all their vagueness, can reduce complexity enormously.' As we shall see though, on a transnational level conceptualisation and visualisation are difficult.

Reaching consensus within the CSD on planning principles and spatial planning concepts is a forbidding task. Within Member States, so-called planning communities have been of crucial importance, with the Netherlands a prime example. (For an account of research on the Dutch planning community see Faludi 1998.) Such communities unite heterogeneous groups that, through a process of social learning, have nevertheless succeeded in formulating joint planning principles and spatial planning concepts that they constantly apply and modify in their day-to-day practice. In so doing they have developed certain fundamental values, so it is possible to describe them as 'epistemic communities'.

An obvious question for us to pursue is therefore whether the CSD, composed of representatives of countries with sharply divergent planning traditions, forms the nucleus of an epistemic community. If so, then the institutional design of the CSD has had a measure of success.

In what follows we first give an account of the establishment and the working of the CSD. Then we discuss the issues outlined in this introduction. Against the backdrop of the introductory chapter of this book, we seek to provide answers to the question as to the type of governance the CSD represents. In the last section we explore the outlook for the CSD.

Filling an institutional vacuum

It is not surprising that the European Community (EC) should have formed a platform for co-operation regarding spatial development. Many of its policies have a spatial impact, so much so that European integration may be seen amongst others as a spatial project (Swyngedouw 1994; Kuklinski 1997; Zonneveld and Faludi 1998). What is perhaps surprising is the time that it has taken for the EC to enter this field. The European Parliament adopted a resolution calling for a European spatial planning policy and a planning scheme as early as 1983.

For another five years, this initiative met with no response from the European Commission. However, the Commission had reasons to be reticent. As indicated, the EC Treaty gives the Commission no spatial planning *compétence*, so there was an institutional vacuum. An additional complication was the question as to who within the Commission should take the lead. After all, 'whether spatial planning should link up to regional policy, environmental policy or transport policy; policy areas for which Brussels has separate Directorate-Generals' (Fit and Kragt 1994: 463) was of much consequence for the future shape of spatial planning.

The situation changed profoundly in 1988. There was the prospect of vast increases to the Structural Funds, mainly due to the accession of Spain and Portugal and the ensuing high priority for overall cohesion in Europe. The budget was set to rise from 6300 MECU (million ECUs) in 1987 to no less than 9100 MECU in 1989. The same year the regulations regarding the Structural Funds for the next programming period – 1989–93 – underwent a thorough overhaul. A new Article 10 was included in Council Regulation 2083/93 for the largest fund, the European Regional Development Fund, or ERDF (Martin and Ten Velden 1997; Bastrup-Birk and Doucet 1997). This article empowered the Commission to finance pilot projects on spatial development and also 'studies aiming to identify the elements necessary to establish a prospective outline of the utilisation of Community territory'.

The idea behind Article 10 had come from the French planning agency DATAR (Délégation à l'Aménagement du Territoire et à l'Action Régionale) and had reached the Commission via the consultative Committee for Regional Policy. According to DATAR, a thorough appreciation of the spatial position of European regions was a prerequisite for a more effective use of the Structural Funds. As a result of this French initiative, and even though at that stage that term was not in fact invoked, spatial planning became part of the European Community's regional policy.

Although at the time an advocate of a European Community spatial planning *compétence*, the Netherlands knows no such coalition between spatial and regional policy as proposed by France. The so-called Compendium of planning law compiled by an international team of experts for the Commission describes this as the regional-economic approach. Under it 'spatial planning has a very broad meaning, relating to the pursuit of wide social and economic objectives, especially in relation to disparities in wealth, employment and social conditions between different regions of the country's territory' (European Commission 1997b: 36). In contrast, the Dutch pursue what the Compendium describes as a 'comprehensive integrated approach' focusing on land use with special emphasis on balancing major housing development and open space. Similar approaches prevail in other northwest European countries. After 1988 there have been many efforts to marry these divergent approaches. Inevitably, this resulted in conceptual confusion, even as regards the very notion of planning as such. One of the outcomes is that both spatial planning as well as spatial development policy have become terms of good currency.

In 1989 the French, with the Dutch and the Portuguese operating discretely behind the scenes, organised the first meeting of ministers of the Member States of the European Community responsible for spatial planning. This meeting would become the first of an unbroken succession of so far more than a dozen meetings. It bears emphasis once again that the status of these meetings was, and still is, informal. So the meetings can take no formal decisions. Instead, it is the privilege of the Presidency summing up the proceedings to put the consent of the meeting on record. When the first meeting was held, the EC Treaty even failed to mention planning altogether. It is useful to remind ourselves though that, initially, other policy areas now firmly rooted in the *acquis communautaire* – such as environmental policy – likewise had to make do without a firm Commission *compétence*.

The second meeting took place at Turin. The third one held in 1991 at The Hague was important for the institution building that it triggered. One of the aims was to come to an agreement about establishing what was beginning to be described as a Committee on Spatial Development. A term invoked before in this chapter, 'spatial development' represents the outcome of social learning and mutual adjustment. According to Williams (1996, p. 48) the Dutch had wanted this committee to be named the Committee on Spatial Planning, but other Member States found this unacceptable. The search was on for a term with fewer connotations of state-activism and top–down intervention. Indeed, spatial development is as neutral as the weather: you can be neither for nor against it.

The need for a Committee on Spatial Development was clearly felt. Until then, it was up to the Member State holding the chair to prepare the meetings. (Note that this was before the chair went to the Member State holding the Presidency of the EU as a matter of course.) The first idea had been to hold meetings of senior planning officials under the umbrella of the comitology system. Indeed, in the margins of the Committee for Regional Development some meetings had already taken place involving directors and directors-general, with the Commission in the chair. However, this practice was regarded as unhelpful.

The Dutch proposal at The Hague to establish a CSD was accepted by other Member States and the Commission alike. Within a matter of a few months, the Dutch National Spatial Planning Agency produced draft terms of reference. It is standard procedure for a committee operating under the comitology system to have such terms of reference. However, the terms of reference have never been approved. The reason is that Member States adhere to an important principle that stands in the way of formalisation. It is that, other than with comitology committees, the Commission is *not* to be in the chair. Rather, one of the Member States has the chair, with the final Dutch proposal formalising the link with the rotating Presidency of the European Community, later the European Union. According to the Dutch proposal, however, the European Commission was to be given the secretariat.

It is worth noting that a similarly constituted Committee for Regional Policy had existed during 1975–88. The new regulations for the ERDF had spelled the end of that committee.

As indicated, this unresolved issue notwithstanding, the CSD held its first meeting in 1992, to be followed over the years by many more meetings, mostly at Brussels. Under Article 10 of the new regulation for the European Regional Development Fund (ERDF) the European Commission pays for the expenses of two committee members per delegation and, even though not falling into this category, the CSD can make use of the services of interpreters extended to ordinary 'comitology' committees. In fact, the Commission considers the CSD as presently constituted as an anomaly and would prefer it to be reconstituted as a consultative comitology committee. So far, however, the Commission has tolerated the present situation.

Leadership conflicts within the CSD

In June 1992, at their fourth meeting the European spatial planning ministers expressed satisfaction with the start a few weeks earlier of the CSD's operations, and this put a temporary end to discussions within the CSD regarding its position. What was important was that the Dutch minister, supported by his Danish, French and German counterparts, argued for a vision on European spatial development, this vision to include policy proposals. The German minister emphasised that this was a task for the CSD. It would take another year before the final decision to prepare such a vision was taken. Prior to the fifth ministerial meeting at Liège in November 1993, the Belgian CSD delegation (in fact the Walloons, who under internal arrangements allowing one of the regions to represent the country, something that had been made possible by the Treaty of Maastricht) announced that their minister would make proposals as to the formulation of a European spatial 'plan', described by them in French as *Schéma de développement de l'espace communautaire*.

Styling themselves an informal ministerial council rather than a meeting, the EU ministers gave a sympathetic reception to the proposal to prepare what since then is being described in English as a European Spatial Development Perspective (ESDP). Since then, preparing this document is the chief rationale for the CSD's existence, and working on it has without doubt proved crucial to its development.

The ministers operated on the basis of the subsidiarity principle. This became a kind of meta-planning principle. Thus, the ESDP was to be the product of Member States because it was, after all, the Member States who were responsible for spatial planning. However, Member States were not the exclusive owners of the ESDP. On the contrary, there was every reason to involve also the European Commission and more especially the Directorate General XVI, Regional Policy and Cohesion. It became standard practice at CSD meetings to discuss DG XVI's work. The idea was that a future ESDP would provide the spatial framework for policies of the European Community. The spatial interrelations between various policy areas are (or should be) the rock-bottom concern of the ESDP. The European Commission and in particular DG XVI need to be well informed about the ESDP so as to be able to apply it properly.

The idea was to engage in experimental learning, but during the Greek Presidency following the Liège informal council there was a leadership conflict between the German delegation and DG XVI. The latter administered a questionnaire to the Member States and on that basis submitted a document. This is a procedure often used by the European Commission, but the impression was that DG XVI thereby wanted to gain a central position. The Germans, being next in line for the Presidency and strictly opposed to any substantive Commission influence as they were, had prepared a document of their own hoping that this would form the basis of further work. The CSD sent both contestants back to their respective corners. Thus Member States felt that DG XVI had taken insufficient account of their replies, whereas the Germans had created the impression of wanting to impose their ideas (otherwise complementary to those of other delegations) on the CSD. This leadership conflict notwithstanding, the Greek Presidency achieved a great leap forward in the development of the CSD. (The Greek delegation had been reconstituted, representing the Ministry of the Environment.) Based on the preparatory work of both DG XVI and the Germans, a joint document was prepared. This included a rough outline of the future ESDP, traces of which are still recognisably present in the existing document. It also included eight contributions written by two or more Member States each. This was the first time that the CSD as such had produced a document. This so-called 'Corfu paper' (after the location where the informal ministerial council met under the Greek Presidency) was subsequently presented to the ministers. The planning principle that the CSD, and not the Presidency, prepare ministerial meetings came to be known as the 'Corfu method'.

After Corfu the CSD approach, however, was for the Presidency, sometimes after consultation with the Commission and other delegations, to propose the work programme. Finding it difficult to adapt to its less-than-central role, once more DG XVI could not desist from taking the initiative. However, in principle it was up to the CSD to take decisions, and it was their opinion that counted. Still, up to and including the Italian Presidency in the spring of 1996, the CSD did not speak with one voice, and so its influence was small.

The domination by politics

Successive Presidencies had much scope to influence things. Some brought this discretion to bear more deliberately than others. In 1994 at Corfu and at Leipzig the agenda was more or less fixed. The aim was to lay the foundations for the ESDP. This is precisely what between them the 'Corfu paper' and the 'Leipzig principles', both of them produced following the 'Corfu method', did.

In the absence of clear CSD guidance, the French Presidency went more or less off on a tangent. Involving all delegations in a scenario exercise, the French introduced an innovative method of work. Under their energetic leadership, every Member State had to submit a trend scenario for its own territory, from which the strong-headed French intended to derive a European scenario. However, national elections interfered, and so there was not enough time to fulfil the ambitions of the French. What resulted was a puzzle of fifteen pieces, each consisting of several puzzles in turn. The joint formulation of spatial planning concepts for the European Union turned out to be difficult. The various maps produced by the Member States each reflected a home-grown planning tradition. However, the beneficial consequence of the scenario exercise was that Member States became more familiar with spatial planning and that their delegations got much more actively involved in the ESDP process.

Following the French example, the Spanish and Italian Presidencies, too, set other Member States to work. No commonly accepted spatial planning concepts emerged. The Spanish were not even capable of producing a document that could gain the approval of the CSD, and at Madrid the ministers had to make do with a lower-status document presented only by the Presidency. This posed a threat to the whole ESDP process. The subsequent Italian Presidency introduced a new theme into the discussions, that of the cultural heritage (Rusca 1998).

An important reason for internal divisions holding up progress was uncertainty about the impact of a future ESDP on European funding. This was a politically very sensitive issue. Neither the Spaniards nor the Italians due to assume the Presidency in early 1996 had any desire to get entangled in discussions, the long-term consequences of which were unclear. They had a point, the firm assurance, on Spanish instigation, by Commissioner Wulf-Mathies at Noordwijk in June 1997 that the ESDP would have no short-term implications for the allocation of the Structural Funds notwithstanding. After all, the Commissioner herself added that the ESDP might influence, if not the allocation of funds, then at least the implementation of policies. Also, the ESDP process paid more attention than hitherto to economic opportunities, defined mostly qualitatively, occurring in strong regions. As a consequence, deficiencies of weak regions as measured by quantitative indicators, playing such a major role in the allocation of funds, were no longer the exclusive area of concern.

Turning the CSD into a work force

Already during the run-up to Corfu the practical problem became apparent of how the CSD, diverse as it was, was to produce concrete texts. There were various initiatives to set up working parties. On the instigation of the Commission, an 'ESDP-troika working group' was established under the Greek Presidency to deal purely with the 'technical' side of the ESDP process. They were to produce drafts on the basis of which the CSD could formulate a political platform. As a planning principle, the strict distinction between technical reports and political decision-making was doomed to fail. Delegations were suspicious of the intentions of DG XVI, and so, even though not members of the troika, many of them participated in the working group simply to monitor developments. In this way the working party became a clone of the CSD, thus rendering the distinction between 'political' and 'technical' aspects of the work irrelevant. Not surprisingly, before the Leipzig meeting, the working group was put to rest.

Under the French Presidency of the first half of 1995 another working group called Task Force was instituted. Once again this was intended to answer to the need for a flexible and efficient arrangement under the umbrella of the CSD. As before, the Task Force was to limit itself to drafting documents on behalf of and according to briefs by the CSD. Delegations were allowed one representative each for whom the Commission footed the bill for expenses. However, the terms of reference were never approved, nor was the CSD capable of formulating a 'technical' brief for the group. After a couple of meetings, the last one in June 1995, the Task Force faded out of existence.

The status of the whole exercise gave cause for concern. During the Spanish and Italian Presidencies there were repeated calls therefore for formalisation. At the Madrid informal ministerial council in late 1995, both the Commission as well as the Germans presented such proposals. The underlying motives were very different though. Commissioner Wulf-Mathies who, unlike her predecessor, Millan, saw advantages to spatial development policy on a European level, proposed to incorporate spatial planning in the EC Treaty by amending article 130b. Thus spatial planning would come under the umbrella of economic and social cohesion, an unambiguous *compétence* of the Commission. As against this, the central German concern had always been that of restricting, rather than expanding the influence of the Commission (Faludi 1997). Contrary to what many may think formalisation implies, the Germans saw formalisation as a way of checking the Commission by defining spatial development policy as an intergovernmental power. So in Madrid the Germans submitted a position paper proposing to remodel the CSD into a 'standing committee' under the umbrella of the Council of Ministers. A Council Committee would entail that the secretariat would go from the Commission to the Secretariat-General of the Council of Ministers, with the Commission being restricted to observer status (Nugent 1999: 121–2). However, neither the German nor the Commissioner's proposal got much of a hearing. There had been no prior consultation by either proponent of formalisation, nor had they lobbied delegations for their support.

At a CSD meeting in April 1996, the Germans once again proposed to reconstitute the CSD as a committee under the Council of Ministers. However, according to the Legal Service of the European Commission such a committee in an area of policy where the Council lacked a *compétence* was unprecedented. Thus the Commission advised caution, a position supported by France. At subsequent CSD meetings, attention for this issue faded. Obviously, most delegations still lacked any clear idea as regards formalisation. In fact, the institutional void in which the CSD operated was not much of problem. Anyway, it was 'all hands on deck' for the CSD engaged in writing the ESDP, and there was no time to consider thorny, long-term issues.

A breakthrough

Work on the actual ESDP started under the Irish and the Dutch Presidencies. Prior to that, during the Italian Presidency the troika had begun to come into its own as an effective platform of co-operation. To organise work as efficiently as possible, the troika proposed a new form of organisation that the CSD duly accepted. The three fundamental principles were that ultimate responsibility was to rest with the CSD; that the troika was to receive a mandate to produce the texts and to set up a writing group; and that the troika was to co-ordinate the work. The writing group was duly formed, bringing together one representative each from the four troika members. The troika screened their work prior to submission to the full CSD. Drafts went back and forth until the texts were acceptable. In the meantime, the troika kept the CSD up to date. In addition, a cartographic group was formed to work under the writing group.

The mandate for the troika changed the mood. Scepticism gave way to a sense of purpose. However, and although the work was now in the hands of no more than four people, problems persisted. Formal CSD discussions had never been able to generate a common appreciation of key concepts and this now formed the stumbling block. The previous Presidencies had produced a profusion of amorphous survey material. To arrive at a common terminology required extensive discussions, and it was only after much effort that the first draft could be submitted to the CSD in December 1996. Subsequent so-called multilateral discussions with three Member States at a time generated sufficient consensus, and in June 1997 the ministers received the 'First official draft' of the ESDP with approval.

So far we have discussed planning principles. As regards spatial planning concepts, progress has been slow. Discussions evolved around the production of maps. Maps are an important element in spatial development policy. In fact though, the ESDP includes few maps and even fewer that relate to policy.

As indicated, in setting up a cartographic working group to produce the maps, the troika followed the same approach as with the texts. However, political sensibilities meant that any maps produced should leave no room for ambiguity during interpretation. Thus, agreeing on the maps required even more social learning than agreeing on the texts. The upshot was that the troika was unable to present the CSD with draft maps until one month before the decisive Noordwijk meeting. At this late stage, a number of delegations who had not been involved swept most of the maps from the table. As far as social learning was concerned, these delegations lagged enormously behind the writing and the cartographic group. What became painfully evident was how long the way was to the formulation of European spatial planning concepts.

In the end four rather non-committal maps were put in the appendix of the Noordwijk document. They carry the ominous proviso: 'This representation is only an illustration of certain spatial elements referred to in the text of the First Official Draft of the ESDP ... They in no way reflect actual policy proposals and there is no guarantee that the elements displayed are exhaustive or entirely accurate.' This reminds the reader of the disclaimer going with films that any resemblance to reality is purely the result of coincidence!

Having discussed it the previous day, on 10 June 1997 the ministers gave the go-ahead to the 'First official draft' of the ESDP. The Dutch Presidency duly noted this in its conclusions. Even this weak form of agreement was not as uncontroversial as one might have hoped. Up until the very last moment, Spain was trying to demote the ESDP to a Presidential document rather than to a document that represented the sense of the whole meeting.

What followed were consultations on the ESDP in the Member States and within the Commission. These were designed to bring the ESDP to the attention of the spending departments at a European, national, regional and local level. By thus generating consensus, the hope was that, though informal, the ESDP would nevertheless have an impact. The attention of non-governmental interest groups and of the academic community was also sought. The goal was to increase awareness of the need for and the issues in European planning. Last but not least, the ESP, COR and the European Parliament gave their opinions. Such consultations seem unusual in an area of policy outside the EC Treaty. This may be seen as yet another way of filling the institutional void in European spatial development.

Altogether the twelve months prior to the Noordwijk meeting represent something of a breakthrough. Working arrangements within the CSD and in particular the writing group proved to be effective. After all, in contrast to previous futile attempts, within a relatively short period of time, the draft ESDP came into being. However, looking at the content of the document, there are casualties to account for. Achieving consensus proved only possible by avoiding politically delicate issues. Giving expression to spatial planning concepts in map form proved to be near impossible. This is a serious problem. Like nothing else, cartographic representation seems of the essence of spatial planning.

Making up the balance sheet

This chapter began by positing that the CSD was difficult to categorise. In a way, Article 130s of the EC Treaty gives the Council powers to take measures in the field that the English version describes as 'town and country planning'. However, this is nothing like the *compétences* for the seventeen policy areas defined in titles I to XVII of the EC Treaty. There was never even the slightest chance of Article 235 (Article 308 under the new Treaty) being invoked for the purpose of giving the European Commission a *compétence* for spatial planning either. Nevertheless, the Commission of the European Communities, as it was then called, together with the Member States (to be more precise the ministers responsible for spatial planning) proceeded to set up a committee to consider the spatial development of the European Community. So on one important count the CSD is, after all, comparable with committees operating within the European Union: it forms an expression of joint governance.

What this might imply has been the object of continuous debates ever since the CSD came into existence. At the beginning the role of the CSD seemed merely that of a discussion platform comparable to committees existing within other forms of multilateral co-operation, such as the Benelux and the Council of Europe. However, the reader should take note of two very obvious differences between the European Community and the latter two organisations. First, within the European Community it is possible to pool sovereign powers. Second, the European Community pursues policies that in many cases are highly relevant to spatial development, for instance the agricultural policy (title II), the trans-European networks (title IV) and economic and social cohesion (title XIV).

Potentially, the work of the CSD could have a twofold impact. First, existing spatial planning powers of Member States could be eroded by shifting powers little by little to the Community, such as has been the case in the area of environmental policy. Second, Member States could insist that the European Commission takes account of the spatial effects of ongoing European policy. Both options have been discussed in the CSD, in particular since the end of 1993, when the decision to formulate a spatial perspective document had been taken. In the end, it was decided that the ESDP was not to infringe upon the powers and responsibilities of the Member States. In particular Germany has tried to go one step further. In the run-up to the Treaty of Amsterdam, it attempted to put a permanent check on the expansion of spatial planning powers of the European Community by defining spatial planning as an area of intergovernmental policy (Faludi 1997). Nothing has come from this, and so the 'first official draft' of the ESDP says that: 'the existing competences of the responsible institutions for Community policies have to remain unchanged' (European Commission 1997a: 6). Clearly, European spatial development policy operates within small margins. In fact, throughout its existence the CSD has performed a constant balancing act involving sixteen artists on the high wire simultaneously: fifteen Member States, each having their own interests in mind, alongside the Commission, the latter obviously also pursuing policies of its own. As far as balancing acts are concerned, this feat seems unparalleled.

The introduction to this chapter indicates the tools for analysing the CSD and its operations, i.e. the two notions of planning principles and spatial planning concepts. Generally, both are considered as more or less of equal importance. This is based on the normal situation in countries or regions with established planning traditions. However, our analysis shows the situation of the CSD to be anything but normal. In fact, as we know, the Commission considers the CSD an anomaly. Be that as it may, the CSD had to create itself and its planning tradition from scratch, so to speak. This put issues of institutional design at centre stage, and so discussions of planning principles got priority over those concerning spatial planning concepts. Anyhow, their potential impact on the allocation of European funds has meant that European spatial planning concepts were a bridge too far. A number of Member States found the form of expression that such concepts almost naturally take, i.e. maps, unacceptable. At first glance, this seems to suggest insufficient social learning and that the CSD is still far from being an epistemic community proper.

Be that as it may, the gradual emergence of planning principles in itself also represents social learning. Albeit slowly, Member States and DG XVI have been able to agree on a document identifying policy issues, whilst at the same time steering clear of the danger of infringing upon existing, or imposing any new *compétences.*

What is plausible also is that DG XVI and the Member State representatives have mutually influenced each other's perceptions, not only as regards planning principles but also as regards spatial planning concepts. One indication is the emergence of a common vocabulary, partly in Euro-English. A term like spatial planning, which simply did not exist when the CSD started its operations, illustrates this. An example drawn from the category of spatial planning concepts is that of urban networks (Minister of Housing, Physical Planning and the Environment 1991). Although not entirely unprecedented, the network concept has entered into common parlance mainly as a result of the work of the CSD. There has been recognition also of spatial differentiation in Europe, and this in itself represents progress.

As far as the concrete work of the CSD is concerned, a number of conclusions suggest themselves. A first one is that the attempt to break problems down into political and technical issues has been a dead end. This sheds light on persistent, but so far unsuccessful efforts to form a network of research institutes, the European Spatial Planning Observatory Network (ESPON). (But note the so-called Study Programme designed to pave the way for ESPON.) As the name suggests, this network, too, would be based on the assumption that researchers can discharge technical duties based on a brief by the CSD. To repeat, so far to identify issues or themes that are neutral or 'technical' in character has proved illusory.

Another conclusion is that the CSD was more adept at dealing with spatial analysis than with policy. Reading through the draft ESDP, this becomes only too evident. Also, it is certainly no accident that the ESDP eschews any attempt to render policy more concrete in the form of projects. After all, such a step would require political commitment, clearly a commodity in short supply at the CSD. (But note, once again, that the agenda for the near future includes an action programme.)

What is also striking is the absence of a permanent chair, as found in comitology committees. As a consequence, the agenda of the CSD fluctuated in line, as the reader will remember, with the preferences of the rotating Presidency flanked by other troika members. It was only during the latter stages when the mood was one of now or never that the CSD showed itself capable of breaking with this pattern. As will be remembered, the trick was to form a small drafting group drawn from the members of the troika and leaving this group to get on with the production of the first draft of the ESDP.

Undeniably, according to our sources, DG XVI, too, has fulfilled an important role in ensuring continuity. DG XVI found it difficult though to adjust to a situation in which it had no exclusive right of initiative. It is for this reason that we have highlighted the leadership conflict under the Greek Presidency during the first half of 1994. Even after finding a solution ('the Corfu method') DG XVI had difficulties abstaining from taking the initiative. An example, not mentioned in our analysis above, was the presentation of so-called 'terms of reference' for the preparation of the ESDP under the Italian Presidency during the first half of 1996. DG XVI even wanted to have bilateral meetings with Member States without the Presidency present. This is only one example of a *faux pas* made by DG XVI during the first years of the work of the CSD, but we have no indication of similar irritants occurring after 1996.

It is important to briefly address another dimension of the problem of spatial development policy. It is the relation between DG XVI representing the European Commission on the CSD on the one hand and other Directorates General on the other. In the past this relation has not appeared to be close. Those in the know characterise DG XVI as operating fairly independently from other Directorates General. This is problematic because in principle at least the ESDP should have a bearing on spatially relevant policies of those other Directorates General. Indeed, not to mince words, according to at least some Member States, the very rationale of the ESDP is to get a grip on these policies as they affect the development of their territories. At the same time, as we have seen, potential implications of the ESDP have been neutralised by the insistence, repeated at Potsdam, that it will not affect the existing *compétences* of the European Community. It is relevant to note, however, that the positions may be shifting. DG XVI is involved in the set-up of an interdepartmental working group with a brief to streamline discussion with the other Directorates General. So attention to what these other players are doing is bound to increase.

Something that this analysis has been unable to demonstrate but which can be deduced from the positions of those concerned is the wide divergence between the mandates of the various delegations and how this affects the way they operate. For instance, there is a gap between the representatives of federal states such as the Federal Republic of Germany and Austria and those of countries like the Netherlands and Denmark. In the Federal Republic, responsibility for spatial planning rests largely, and in the case of Austria even wholly, with the states, or *Länder*. This implies that national representatives must constantly look over their shoulders. As far as this is concerned, these two federal states are eclipsed by the third, Belgium. In Belgium all planning powers have been devolved to the three regions: Flanders, Wallonia and that of the Brussels

Capital. The federal government has no planning role. This required some kind of special arrangement. Accordingly, each of the Belgian regions is represented on the CSD, but during meetings they must speak with one voice. Coordination between the three regions alternates between them (Houvenaghel 1998). The consequence was that in fact the Belgian Presidency of the second half of 1993 fell to Wallonia. In the run-up to Noordwijk it was the turn of Flanders to represent Belgium. In fact, both Flanders and Wallonia are in the midst of a fundamental reform of their respective planning systems (including the drafting of strategic planning documents) and so pressure of work prevented both to pay much attention to the ESDP process. More than once, their representatives failed to show up, even when they were members of the troika during the Greek Presidency, following immediately upon the Belgian Presidency. It should be noted though that there is every sign of the situation improving and that the representation is being streamlined.

By way of contrast, Dutch representatives for instance, endowed as Dutch national planners with some real powers, feel less constrained. Besides, Dutch political culture gives a fair amount of discretion to civil servants. So the representatives of the Netherlands are reasonably free from any direct political interference. This has certainly not been the case with for instance the Spanish representatives. The reason is extreme political sensitivity about even the slightest potential implication of the ESDP for the distribution of the Structural Funds and the Cohesion Fund. (Interestingly though, with Agenda 2000 out of the way, for the time being such misgivings seem to have dissipated.)

In short, on the CSD, each delegation is under an obligation to take into account a specific set of circumstances and/or stakeholders. So it seems reasonable for the procedure to have included manifold consultations on the 'first official draft' of the ESDP. One beneficial consequence of consultations might have been that the ESDP process has become somewhat more transparent to outsiders. So far the work of the CSD has taken place in the proverbial back rooms. Only a handful of cognoscenti has been able to follow it, making use of such personal contacts with members of the CSD as they might have. This is perhaps the greatest challenge for the CSD: how to generate support outside the inner circle of civil servants and their fellow travellers.

Outlook

The CSD have availed themselves of the results of the various consultations. Also, on the insistence of Austria and Germany, concern for the expected accession of new Member States is being added. As indicated, the ESDP process came to a conclusion in May 1999. The Finnish Presidency is focusing on the so-called Action Programme.

Meanwhile, the Austrian Presidency organised a 'CSD seminar' in Vienna on 'The Future of European Spatial Development Policy – CSD and ESDP after

1999' (Austrian Presidency 1999). Having been a seminar rather than an official meeting, participants were free to air their views. It was not the intention to draw conclusions either, but rather to open up avenues leading past Potsdam. Invited to consider the future of the CSD, the current Finnish Presidency is indeed following up these discussions.

Suffice it to say that the meeting perceived a danger of the ESDP process fading out of existence. One of the reasons was felt to be the informality of the whole exercise, and so formalisation of the CSD one way or the other was considered overdue. This is remarkable since the unpublished 'First complete draft' of the Glasgow ministerial meeting of only a few months earlier had referred to some Member States having persistent doubts about formalisation. Be that as it may, the Germans continue to pin their colours to the option of a Council working party, but beyond that there are still no firm ideas as to how to proceed. There are, of course, the Interreg IIC programmes, Interreg IIC being a so-called Community Initiative, in this case to promote transnational co-operation in the field of spatial planning. Interreg IIC programmes (soon to be replaced by Interreg IIIB programmes for the period until 2006) arise out of the ESDP. However, they absorb much energy, and it may just be that the resolution of organisational and procedural issues will have to wait until these programmes, alongside the accession of new members, generate enough of a momentum for considering a new version of the ESDP. At the same time, it is precisely these programmes that may generate the momentum for a new round in the ESDP process.

In the interim, much work needs to be done. For technical work in depth, it has long been considered essential to set up the observatory network ESPON. However, according to 'The Task Force on the Definition of the Institutional, Legal and Financial Frame of the European Spatial Planning Observatory Network (ESPON)' reporting to the CSD in October 1998, this is a complicated issue. What transpires is that, under a recent ruling of the European Court of Justice, to obtain European funding for such a network it is insufficient to get a 'budget line' approved (difficult though this may be in itself). No, the European Court insists on an article of the EC Treaty being invoked. The only article that presents itself is Article 308 (ex-Article 235). Under it, the Commission can propose to the Council of Ministers to view the establishment of ESPON as necessary for achieving the aims of the common market. Such a proposal would have to obtain unanimous approval. The only other option is that of ESPON being set up under an international treaty. That of course requires unanimity, too. So far, unanimity as regards ESPON has been out of reach, but maybe now the thorny issue of Agenda 2000 and the reform of the Structural Funds is out of the way unanimity will become a possibility.

The explorations of how to set up ESPON highlight a feature of European policy-making, which is the centrality of the EC Treaty when it comes to doing real business. The importance of formalisation of the CSD and the ESDP has not escaped the European Parliament. In April and May, the Commission for Regional Policy discussed the ESDP. As indicated, it concluded that the intergovernmental process had reached the end of the line and that it was time for a communautarian policy, with a formal ministerial council and the CSD as a permanent feature. As we know, the European Parliament has argued for a communautarian policy in this area before, without the European Commission and the Council of Ministers acceding to its demand, so this call for action still far from settles the future of the Committee on Spatial Development. The wait is on for what proposals the CSD will produce and for what ministers will decide at Tampere in Finland in October 1999. (They decided to postpone resolution of this issue until the next French Presidency, in the second half of 2000!)

Note

1 As far as the operations of the Committee on Spatial Development are concerned, this chapter is based largely on a Masters thesis, 'Europees ruimtelijk ontwikkelingsbeleid op zoek naar evenwicht', written in 1998 under the supervision of Wil Zonneveld by Bas Waterhout at the University of Amsterdam.

AMY VERDUN

7

Governing by committee
The case of monetary policy[1]

Introduction

Monetary policy-making in the European Union (EU) has a relatively successful record of integration. It also happens to have had at least two very strong
committees – the Monetary Committee (MC) and the Committee of Governors
of Central Banks (CGCB) – to help co-ordinate Member States' policies. However, both were eventually superseded. The CGCB was first incorporated in the
European Monetary Institute (EMI) which was subsequently incorporated into
the European Central Bank (ECB). The MC was dissolved on 1 January 1999
and replaced by an Economic and Financial Committee that has much of the
same tasks and duties as the MC has had.

The MC and the CGCB were very influential, though little was actually
known about them. They operated in an ambience of secrecy. No minutes were
taken of their monthly meetings. The reason they were influential is that their
proposals usually became the basis of European monetary policy-making (Kees
1987; Italianer 1993: 54). Much of what went on in these committees fed its way
into the final decision-making process. This chapter examines how influential
the MC was in the policy-making process, and how this came about. It also looks
at the interactions within the committee, the relationship of the MC with the
European Commission, the ECOFIN Council and the Member States. In particular it analyses the role of knowledge, socialisation and policy learning. The
chapter discusses to what extent the case of monetary policy can shed light on
the more general process of policy-making in the EU, and what can be learnt
from the case of monetary policy about 'governing by committee'. The implications of this mode of governance on transparency and democratic legitimacy is
also briefly touched upon.

The structure of the chapter is as follows. The first section discusses the historical and institutional framework and reviews the previous literature. The

second section provides an analytical framework for understanding how the MC influence occurred. The third section discusses the role of knowledge, learning and socialisation, and uses the 'old boys club' metaphor to clarify the nature of the MC. The section also compares the monetary case to other cases and evaluates this mode of governance. The final section draws some conclusions.

Historical and institutional framework of the MC

Even though the introduction of the single currency from 1999 is one of the most novel developments in the European integration process, the co-ordination of European monetary policy has been around since the late 1950s. To assist Member States in co-ordinating their monetary policies, an advisory committee was called for in Article 105 of the Treaty of Rome. The MC was in operation for close to four decades. In that period it was influential in streamlining monetary policies. The Maastricht Treaty changed its mandate and listed a set of areas where the MC contributed to the preparation of the work of the Council (Treaty on European Union, Art. 109c). It also stipulated that at the start of stage three of Economic and Monetary Union, which took place on 1 January 1999, the MC was transformed into an Economic and Financial Committee (EFC). The main difference between the MC and the EFC is that the latter will have more than an advisory status and play a stronger role in the preparing of Council meetings (Treaty on European Union, Art. 109c, see Treaty of Rome, Art. 105; see also Italianer 1993: 67–9).

Another influential advisory committee was set up in 1964, the Committee of Governors of Central Banks (CGCB). Its formal creation was a result of a request by the ECOFIN Council (the Council of Ministers of Economic and Financial affairs) to have a committee similar to the MC which would help co-ordinate central bank policies. The CGCB was taken up in the European Monetary Institute (EMI) when it was created on 1 January 1994, as part of the second stage of Economic and Monetary Union (EMU). The CGCB consisted of central bank governors from the Member State central banks. Like the MC, it was influential and helped shape the policies of the European Community (EC) and contributed to the harmonisation of Member State policies.

As is the case with other advisory committees in the EU, the MC consisted of representatives of the Member States. Each Member State had two representatives on the MC. One representative came from the Treasury/Ministry of Finance or Economics, the other came from the national central bank. They usually were the head of the Treasury or his deputy, and the '*sous-gouverneur*', i.e. the 'number two' of the central bank[2] (Kees 1987: 258). In total the MC consisted of a chairperson, two top officials from each of the Member States and two European Commission officials. In addition, two 'observers' from the European Central Bank (ECB), formerly the EMI, and the secretary of the MC were invited to take part in the meetings (Westlake 1995).

Committee members viewed each other as technical experts who were exceptionally well placed to know what was politically feasible. This technical expertise was in fact envisaged in the constitutional set up of the Committee. The statutes of the MC, in fact, stipulated that they be independent experts, not representatives of Member States as is the case with the Committee of Permanent Representatives (COREPER) (see Italianer 1993: 81). The MC Statutes article 5 stated: 'Members of the Committee and alternates shall be appointed in their personal capacity and shall, in the general interests of the Community, be completely independent in the performance of their duties' (Monetary Committee 1994: 118). However, the MC 'national' members had very good contacts with their national Finance Minister and often also with their Prime Minister. Continuity of membership was also a strong feature of the MC. The committee members typically served on the committee for many years, five to eight years, and some as long as seventeen. They were drawn from a larger community of monetary experts. Membership by personal capacity, the frequent meetings and the consensus decision-making culture of the MC implied that committee members got to know and trust each other which created an atmosphere of confidence in the committee.

The MC had as one of its main tasks to prepare the ECOFIN Council Meeting. Even though COREPER also helped to prepare the ECOFIN Council, the MC was the more important preparatory body (see also Bakker 1995; Hanny and Wessels 1999). The MC usually met once a month (except in August), during one day, or if need be half a day before. If the agenda was long, the 'alternates' were asked to have a separate meeting to discuss the more technical matters. The alternates were top officials who could replace MC members: one was a senior official from the national central bank and the other came from the Ministry of Finance. The alternates could also attend the MC meetings unless the MC decided otherwise. However, according to the MC's statutes (article 8) alternates could not take part in the discussion nor vote (Monetary Committee 1994: 118). After an ECOFIN Council meeting the MC received a 'mandate' on which ECOFIN wished to seek the MC's advice.

With the mandate provided, members began to discuss the issues on which the ECOFIN Council wanted an 'opinion'. By these discussions they established which issues could be settled, and which issues remained unresolved. The MC almost always came to consensus decisions. Anything that got into an *impasse* was fed back into the ECOFIN Council and the MC asked the ECOFIN Council for 'guidance', i.e. the MC informed the ECOFIN Council on the prevailing political divisions and asked how the MC should proceed from there. Often the ECOFIN Council would make it clear that there were also still political divisions within the ECOFIN Council in those particular areas where the MC could not come to a consensus. The MC *could* vote if it wanted to, but it preferred consensus decision-making (Westlake 1995; interviews with DG II and MC officials 1996, 1998).

The MC had an interesting mix of politics, expertise, and technical knowledge combined in one committee. Because the members know each other, as well as the national politicians, so very well, there was quite some leeway for discussion. One European Commission official stated in an interview that 'the monetary committee was probably the most influential committee that there was'. The reason mentioned was that the members relied on their own expertise, that of others, and the fact that they knew that the committee members had a good sense of the political support that they could expect from both the Finance Minister and the Prime Minister. At the same time they had quite some room for manoeuvre especially because the Finance Minister and the PM both placed a lot of confidence in the committee members of the MC. Also, according to the Treaty their status in the committee was that of independent experts. So they had a special mix of being 'above politics' and 'embedded in politics'.

In official terms, the MC was an advisory committee to the European Council and the ECOFIN Council. It did not officially take decisions or draft formal proposals. MC members were very keen to point that out. According to its statutes, its formal role was to promote co-ordination of policies of the Member States in the monetary field, and review the monetary and financial situation of Member States. Its main activities were focused on the working of the European Monetary System (EMS) which included decisions surrounding the entry and exit of currencies in the ERM and re- and devaluations, preparing of EMU, drafting economic reports on Member States, formulating of the EU's broad economic guidelines, the co-ordinating of international monetary policy, e.g. International Monetary Fund (IMF), World Bank and international currency concerns. The MC reported regularly to the Council and the Commission. In several cases the Council or Commission had actually to obtain the MC's opinion. In addition, the MC had the power and obligation to draw up opinions on its own initiative in order to fulfil its tasks (MC Statutes, Monetary Committee 1994: 117–18).

Although the MC generally did not propose formal decisions, the ECOFIN Council could ask it to formulate an 'opinion' on a certain subject. Yet, when the final outcome of ECOFIN was examined, it was clear that many of the ideas originated in the MC, and/or were expanded and elaborated there. Formally this committee did not have a very influential or powerful position, but in practice it was a very important committee. Andreas Kees, a former member of the MC, observes: 'Seldom does a meeting of economic and finance ministers pass without a request for preparatory work and a statement from the Monetary Committee. No important monetary decision in Community history has been taken without preparatory work by the Committee' (Kees 1987: 260). Formal proposals were put forward either by the Commission or COREPER (Westlake 1995). However, in practice the MC was quite influential because in the last instance the proposals the Commission drafted reflected very clearly the outcome of the consensus reached in the MC. The MC was usually careful not to go too far towards creating a possible proposals, because it needed to be clear that it is the Commission, not the MC, that drafts the proposal. Thus a delicate balance was maintained. Formerly, when the Commission initiated proposals it could ask the MC for advice. But key informants are clear to point out that the actual consensus behind proposals, and often even the wording of the proposals originated in the MC.

There were two special features of this committee. First, the MC chose its Chairperson for a period of two years from amongst its midst. The Chairperson attended and joined in the ECOFIN Council meetings, and could speak on behalf of the MC, which was unique compared to other advisory committees (Westlake 1995). The Chair usually went to a member from a larger Member State. Second, the European Commission Directorate General Two (DG II) hosted the secretariat of the MC, which was different from most committees which were usually hosted by the Council secretariat.

As for the issue of hierarchy in the MC there appears to be a complex set of influences at stake. Martin Westlake (1995: 261) stresses that 'the larger Member States and those with stronger currencies in general [tend] to pull more weight'. Interviewees have stressed the importance of personality, relationship and long standing building of confidence. A representative from a smaller Member State with a good reputation and a strong argument was also able to steer the consensus in favour of his/her direction. There seemed to be very little partisan politics. Expertise and reputation seemed to have been more important.

Yet the famous powerful potential of the Franco-German axis was also omnipresent in the MC. That is, if the Germans and the French agreed on a proposal, or if they had the same ideas on a certain question, it was likely to pass the committee. An example was the Euro-X Council. It was basically a watereddown version of the original French proposal to have an economic government (*gouvernement économique*) flanking the ECB. The Germans opposed this suggestion, as they believed it would cripple the independence of the ECB. Yet, once the French proposal was rephrased and a clear indication was given that it would *not* obstruct central bank independence, the Germans were in favour. According to one DG II official, it is certain that the Germans and French would have already had an agreement on the French proposal prior to coming to the meetings. MC members have frequent contacts before the actual meetings take place. Many politically sensitive issues would have been discussed in the corridors and by telephone prior to the official MC meeting. Another split in the MC is emerging with the introduction of the euro in only 11 of the 15 Member States (see Hanny and Wessels 1999).

In the actual meeting an issue is addressed (or a proposal is made by one of its members). Then there followed a *tour-de-table*, in which everyone made comments. When everybody had spoken, and the chairperson felt that there was consensus on the topic, he – only men have held the Chair – would formulate a consensus opinion. He would not do that if he felt there was disagreement, as the MC aimed at reaching consensus opinions. The Chairperson had a leading role in this process. He determined the course of the deliberations and decided whether or not to have the MC take a position. These positions usually took the form of the Chairperson's reports or statements to the Council. This procedure allowed the Chairperson to draw up a report that did not have to be approved word for word by the members of the MC. It thus enabled the quick delivery of policy statements and permitted the statements to be above the lowest common denominator (Kees 1987: 259).

If there was clear disagreement the formulation of an opinion on that item would be postponed and the MC would inform the ECOFIN Council that there was no consensus on that issue and asked for more clear 'guidance'. Officially the MC could vote, but the Chairperson avoided that situation occurring. According to article 6 of its statutes each of the MC members has one vote. Article 10 of the MC statutes states that an 'opinion' of the MC can be adopted by 17 votes. The statutes are based on the 12 Member States, thus with the expansion of the EU to 15 the majority threshold was expanded accordingly to 20.[3] In the MC a minority could set out its views in a document attached to the opinion of the MC (Monetary Committee 1994: 118–19). Though this situation is avoided, sometimes recommendations were indeed put forward that have been only accepted by a majority. This was the case, for example, when the Monetary Committee gave its advice on requirements of EMU for budgetary discipline (Italianer 1993: 62).

Though the institutional setting of the MC is understood, not a lot is actually known about the influence of the MC or how it operated. In addition to the accounts provided by a former member of the MC (Kees 1987, 1994), several scholars have provided a clear general overview of the working of the MC. Martin Westlake (1995) draws the picture that the MC was a different type of committee that had achieved much by keeping the monetary issues labelled as 'technical' and had kept them out of the political domain. Glenda Rosenthal (1975) has focused on the socialisation and learning aspect, as well as on the elitist, exclusive nature of the committee, and how that influences the decision-making process. John Woolley (1992), drawing on Kees (1987) had depicted an influential body in which the process of idea formation and knowledge was the product of frequent exchanges and long standing membership in a committee in which like-minded souls were present. Kees (1987) provided a very interesting insiders' account of how the MC affected policy-making, how important the interaction between the various MC members were, as well as the political weight the MC had because of its particular role in the consultation process. Hanny and Wessels (1999) point to a mixture of elements that made the MC so influential. They refer to its particular institutional position, that of a two-level network, inspired by the two-level game analogy (Putnam 1988). In their view the outcome was more than the sum of the parts. Applying Wessels' fusion thesis (Wessels 1997, 1998) they find that the MC was able to move from being a purely advisory committee to a decision-making body, i.e. it helped shape the EU (Hanny and Wessels 1999).

Yet, these limited number of accounts about the MC only draw part of the picture of the workings of the MC and its influence on the policy-making process. In interviews with this author, Commission officials and members of the MC stated that they were not at all surprised that there was so little known about the MC. It operated in total secrecy. In part this was done because the MC discussions and decisions may have had significant effects on the financial markets, especially as regards the Exchange Rate Mechanism (ERM) of the EMS. A second reason was of course that the negotiations between the various delegations are easier if there are no leakages to the press.

Knowledge, learning and socialisation: epistemic communities and policy learning

Let us now turn to the process within the MC. Various authors have stressed the importance that the MC members operated in their own personal capacity. Their selection depended on their high reputation on monetary issues and their capacity to maintain close contacts with national politicians in order to be well informed about what they could agree on and discuss. Let us examine the socialisation process and the knowledge sharing process that went on within this committee.

What did it mean to have these committee members share knowledge, experience and policy learning, and socialise? These concepts are notoriously slippery and difficult to define, and therefore to research. For the purpose of this chapter let *knowledge* be defined as: *the objectives of policy-making, and the policies that are considered desirable to achieve this objectives, as well as the acceptance of a specific set of causal relationships that underlie the way policies affect policy objectives. Learning* is then defined as: *the process whereby an individual changes his 'knowledge' based on experience and evaluation of past policies and ideas. Socialisation* is defined as: *the phenomenon of exposing individuals to one another whereby they start to 'learn' from one another.* What is important here is not whether these definitions apply to all possible situations in contemporary political analysis. On the contrary, they serve only to clarify what is meant in this chapter by these terms.

Knowledge on what monetary policy should aim at, and which policy would serve to obtain that aim, has gone through considerable change since the late 1960s. Kathleen R. McNamara (1998) has set out how this process took place with regard to the ERM in the 1970s and 1980s. The total package of knowledge changed from being more Keynesian and interventionist to being more anti-inflationary, monetarist and inspired by neoliberalism (see also Hall 1989). Marcussen finds a very similar result in his study of changes in ideas over economic policy-making in Denmark, Sweden and The Netherlands. Learning took place at different times in different places, and occurred with different central actors at a time. But in most countries it was the monetary experts in Ministries of Finance and central banks that were the forces behind this learning.

The monthly meetings of these experts since the inception of the Monetary Committee and other similar committees has facilitated this process.

What is seen here in the case of the MC is similar to what other authors have found in the case of foreign economic policy in the US. Authors who examined the role of ideas in foreign and trade policy (Goldstein 1993; Goldstein and Keohane 1993), and in macro-economic policy-making (Gourevitch 1986, 1989a, 1989b; Hall 1986; 1989; Jacobsen 1995), and foreign economic policy by using an institutional approach (Ikenberry 1988), also found that ideas of experts were crucial for understanding the outcome of the policy-making process (see also Yee 1996). Another body of literature examining the impact of communities of experts or 'epistemic communities' (Haas 1992), comes to the conclusion that not only the ideas are powerful, but also the common acceptance of certain causal links and the importance of the existence of a common policy aim (see also Verdun 1998a). Elsewhere I have argued that the monetary experts that drafted the Delors Committee were part of a larger epistemic community. Their participation in the Delors Committee, however, enabled them to come up with a consensus result. To draft an acceptable EMU blueprint it was important that they belonged to a wider epistemic community, and thus shared notions of causal relationships about monetary policy, policy tools and outcome. On the other hand, the exposure to each other in meetings enabled them to focus their attention to obtaining a common goal: EMU (Verdun 1999).

Getting a hold on the socialisation process which goes on in these committees of monetary experts is a difficult endeavour. What stands out is that part of the socialisation has occurred prior to these members obtaining the position they hold. They all tend to have gone to similar schools and universities, have learnt similar doctrines of economic philosophy and have updated their information so as to fully accept the neoliberal anti-inflationary philosophy of the 1980s and 1990s. Here is where policy learning comes in. The experiences of the 1970s and 1980s have made many monetary experts convinced that expansionary monetary policy does not work, and that anti-inflationary monetary policies needs to be pursued.

Thus, before even arriving into the position of office, the monetary expert has shown his/her capacity to conduct policies in a certain way, to have learnt certain 'rules' and has accepted certain causal relationships. Upon obtaining membership in these committees, be it the MC, the CGCB, or the above-mentioned Delors Committee, these members start to learn from each others' perspectives. Because they operated in these committees as experts rather than political representatives, they were more willing to be convinced of the position held by other experts on the committee. Thus, the socialisation process and learning continues in these committees; it was an ongoing process.

The cognitive approaches serve to explain why the policies could converge towards common policy objectives and similar approaches to monetary policy in Europe. Yet, more research is needed to understand exactly how this knowledge is obtained and how socialisation and learning happens. It is also important to discover why monetary experts in some countries conformed faster to these new sets of ideas than those in other countries. It also begs the question whether there are preconditions within the Member States that made the monetary experts in a given country more keen than those in other countries on adopting these new 'monetarist' 'neoliberal' ideas about policy-making.

The debate in Europe on the role of committees (comitology) has often focused on the agenda setting and the process of policy formation in these bodies. The literature focusing on the cognitive dimension and that on comitology together help us understand that the process occurring in these committees does not nicely fit into a box of either 're-nationalisation' nor 'supranational policy-making'. Clearly if any label would need to be put on these committees it would be that of 'trans-nationalism'.

An old boys' club

As mentioned above the mode of operation in these committees was purposefully 'secretive'. No minutes of the meetings were taken, and the officials were very careful in speaking to the press. The Commission officials were not at all allowed to discuss MC issues with the press. This rule was put in place because far too often information would be leaked and the media would state the source as 'Brussels'. There was also a clear division of what is 'in the public domain' and what remained secret. And secrecy was the dominant attitude. It was even difficult to ask for a list of the members and alternates of the MC, even though one could easily calculate it by identifying the persons in the top ranks of the national Member State central banks and Ministries of Finance. In earlier years the MC published names of the members in an annex to its annual report. In later years the names of the members were no longer included, and more recently no annual report had been published at all. By contrast, the Committee of Governors of Central Banks started to publish annual reports in 1992 (CGBC 1992, 1993).

Once a member of the MC, that member usually stayed in for many years. The culture within the committee was one in which people got to know each other, learn about each others' sensitivities and those of the respective national political situation. All in all the development of trust, confidence and a sense of 'belonging' created an atmosphere of an old boys' club. A MC member, interviewed in October 1996, himself used this term to illustrate the atmosphere of the committee. Hanny and Wessels (1999) use exactly the same metaphor to describe the atmosphere they find, on the basis of interviews. Glenda Rosenthal (1975) studying the Monetary Committee in the 1960s and early 1970s, came to a similar conclusion.

This secretive nature, as well as the individual committee member's attitude of being 'above' national governmental politics can lead to concerns over democratic accountability, responsive and responsible modes of governance. It is clear that there are instances where democratic control did not occur in the process, but that the politicians were held accountable at the end of the process. But, if it is significantly clear that an advisory committee prepares decisions so that the final outcome of the ECOFIN Council often resembled the consensus coming out of the MC, one can wonder if democratic accountability is served by this overly secretive ambience. The main problem in the EU more generally is that there is no European public debate, only the various national debates. This implies that national representatives can open up the debate about the 'national' side of the discussion. Yet, the 'European' side of the discussion is in any case a problem. With this strong secrecy an added feature, European citizens may easily feel excluded from the general debate about policy-making. Elsewhere I have discussed in more detail the problems related to the institutional design of EMU and in particular the lack of a political, and/or economic counterpart: see Verdun (1996, 1998b, 2000).

What the experience with these committees however *does* show is that the committee members could be socialised, and obtained significant credibility, to influence the Member State governments' policies and attitudes. The interaction between the individual MC member, its national government, and the other committee members was a very delicate one. Many a compromise proposal was made possible by this 'two-level game'/'trans-national' natured position of the MC member (on the role of trans-national actors see Cameron (1995); on two-level games, see Putnam (1988)). As mentioned above, Hanny and Wessels also identify this two-level characteristic to be the reason for there being more than a lowest-common-denominator outcome, a finding shared by Kees (1987, 1994).

A positive side effect of this mode of operation is that it becomes easier to create a policy that everyone can accept. Consensual decision-making has the advantage that everybody needs to be willing to water down their position if required. This can occur without a loss of face to the outside world. In other words, though weak on democratic accountability and transparency, it is strong on creating a common sense of policy direction, and strong commitment to a common goal, which they can collectively defend. Its legitimacy thus was based on this policy effectiveness (for a further discussion see Verdun and Christiansen 2000).

Nevertheless, there was an element of both re-nationalisation and supranationalisation in the working of the monetary committee. Supranationalisation occurred only in so far as one considers the committee members having a common policy objective in mind which they wanted to achieve – in the case when the common policy objective had an element of supranationalism, such as the setting up of the European Central Bank. The element of 're-nationalisation' is present in that the MC in fact accounted for a degree of 'intergovernmental' bargaining in so far as that occurred in the days and weeks prior to the MC meetings. Still, one should not underestimate the degree of common focus that the members of the committee had *a priori*, and the degree of learning that went on during the years that the MC members were participating in MC meetings. The problem with the 're' in the word *re*-nationalisation is that it refers to a novel trend in which Member States try to 'win back' power from European institutions. However, the workings of the MC had not changed since its inception. If anything the MC had been given more power. In fact, there were no indications that the Member States had tried to win back power by operating through their MC members.

At the core of the above discussion lies the question of whether the MC was involved in technical matters or political ones. The MC itself, as well as the Member States had worked hard at giving the signal that monetary policy was a matter for technicians and that thus it was a-political. It had subsequently on various occasions asked the MC to deal with issues of co-ordination of monetary and exchange rate policies. It was however very doubtful whether monetary policy can be considered purely 'technical'. Claudio Radaelli (1999) in this regard makes the argument that in fact the crucial political negotiations as well as discussions at the European Council at Maastricht in 1991 make clear that intergovernmental bargaining still plays an important role. However, a number of important decisions had been taken in the MC prior to that the December 1991 European Summit, such as the criteria for entry to the EMU, i.e. the convergence criteria (Italianer 1993). The exact figures of the convergence criteria were determined by MC, that is the level of the budgetary deficits (3 per cent of GDP), height of the public debt (60 per cent of GDP), inflation rates and exchange rate measures. Thus, it is clear that monetary matters were dealt with as both political and technical.

Summarising, the monetary case differs in comparison to others in a number of ways related to the way the committee is composed, where its secretariat is based, and the role of the Chairperson of the MC. It also appears to be a committee that was more influential than most ('It was the most influential committee' according to some observers). Its powerful position came from a variety of sources: the fact that monetary policy had been considered 'technical', the fact that the MC members had complete confidence of the respective Finance Ministers, that the MC members stayed in the committee for many years – thereby increasing the chances of policy learning while at the same time an ambience of confidence was created. Also important is the fact that the Chairperson drew up reports when he felt there was consensus on the issue, whereby it was not even necessary that all members agreed to all of its details.

Of course, the monetary case is special for another reason. As has been the case with the other important committee – the CGCB – the MC was fully institutionalised within the EMU/EU framework. Interestingly, these committees also were strong advocates of EMU, including the particular *kind* of EMU, that has now been established in the EU. Perhaps lessons can be drawn about the usefulness and desirability of having the committees institutionalised as has happened to the MC and the CGCB.

Finally, the mode of operation of these committees poses questions of democracy, legitimacy and accountability – in particular the lack of public and general political debate over what the aim should be of monetary policy-making (and monetary integration) in the EU. The effectiveness and efficiency is high, but the feeling of alienation is high among the general public and significant parts of the national political scene in the Member States.

Conclusions

This chapter has shown that the Monetary Committee (MC) was influential in creating European monetary policy. The MC was a forum for policy learning and policy co-ordination. An exchange of knowledge occurred between the members. The fact that they were often members for many years led to socialisation and learning. Yet, the members were already part of a closely knit community of monetary experts prior to becoming part of the MC. The dynamics of this committee still needs to be further researched in order to clarify exactly how this dialectic of the individual (the member) and the collective (the MC) occurred, both internally (towards each other) and externally (towards national governments, the Commission, and the Council). The ideas and suggestions coming out of the MC were frequently the basis of decisions adopted at the ECOFIN Council. The reason why this committee was so influential is because its members enjoyed a high degree of trust by their respective Finance Ministers and Prime Ministers, and that the committee operated on a basis of finding consensus. With the start of stage three of EMU, the MC was transformed to become the Economic and Financial Committee. It will play a stronger role in advising the Council on monetary matters. It is interesting that this committee has evolved and become further embedded into the decision-making process of the EU.

The cost of its success, however, will be found in the process not being very transparent, accountable, responsive, legitimate, and thus not very democratic. The newly established European Central Bank should take notice of these concerns and aim at being as open and transparent as possible. As for the comparison with other committees it should be noted that this route from committee to institution is uncommon, save for some exceptions (see Ben Tonra's chapter (8) on the CFSP in this volume). Yet, it is a possible logical next step. Other committees can learn from the democratic concerns over the mode of operation of the monetary policy committees, and make sure their record is better.

Notes

1   This chapter is partly based on material acquired through interviews with members of the Monetary Committee and DG II officials which were conducted in October 1996 and September 1998. The author wishes to thank these interviewees for their frankness

and openness. An earlier version of this chapter was presented at the Third Pan Euro-pean Conference on International Relations, organised by the European Consortium for Political Research (ECPR) Standing Group on International Relations (IR) and the International Studies Association (ISA), Vienna 16–19 September 1998. The author wishes to thank participants and the editors of this volume for useful comments on an earlier draft. The usual disclaimer applies.

2   The terms used by the various countries for this rank differed throughout the Member States, i.e. vice-governor, director, director-general, etc. (see for example, Annex 1 in Monetary Committee 1959, 1960).

3   The new Economic and Financial Committee (EFC) that replaces the MC at the start of EMU is able to adopt opinions that are supported by a qualified majority (*Treaty on European Union*, Art. 109(3)).

Ben Tonra

8

Committees in common
Committee governance and CFSP

Introduction

The issues surrounding the committee structure of the Common Foreign and Security Policy (CFSP) often appear to be the mirror image of those traditionally associated with comitology. In the first instance, the development of committees within CFSP should not be confused with the 're-nationalisation' occasioned by the development of committee structures in other policy sectors. The decision-making dynamics between the first and second 'pillars' of the Union (the European Community pillar and the CFSP pillar) are strikingly different. Policy control within the second, CFSP pillar of the Union, is predicated upon national control and this has traditionally been the *sine qua non* of foreign and security policy co-operation within the Union. As a result, the committee structures established within CFSP have been devised as a means of ameliorating the perceived defects of strictly intergovernmental decision-making rather than seeking any 'return' to national control or an augmentation of national inputs to collective policy-making

At the same time, it would also be incorrect to see the development of committee structures within CFSP as being the means through which this area of policy is becoming 'communitarised'. The association of the Commission with CFSP policy-making is precisely that – 'association'. Commission ambitions in the early 1990s to constitute itself as the core of a new foreign policy system for the Member States of the Union came to nought (Allen, 1998). The committee structure as currently constituted provides for a Commission input to policy-making but the locus of control is situated firmly and unambiguously with the Member States through the Council and the Council Secretariat. This has recently been evidenced in the Amsterdam Treaty by the decision to situate the CFSP Planning Cell within the Council Secretariat and the decision to appoint the Secretary General of the Council Secretariat as the new High Representative of CFSP.

Finally, the purpose of the committee structure established within CFSP is not that of technocratic issue-management but one of substantive political debate and decision-making. To that extent, again, CFSP committees differ from many of their counterparts within the main EU policy portfolios. The core function of the CFSP committee structure is to share information, to exchange analyses, to agree upon collective policy positions, to establish collective policy actions and then to pursue the implementation of these actions. Thus, while CFSP committees certainly include a managerial function their primary aim is core policy formulation.

Models of governance in CFSP

Despite the foregoing differences, the analytical question pertaining to the CFSP committee structure remains the same as for other committees within the European Union, 'What is the nature of European governance at the coal-face of CFSP policy-making and implementation?' As has been suggested above, the answer to that question is not to be found in simple dyadic terms. CFSP is neither a framework of classic intergovernmental co-operation nor a nascent supranational foreign and security policy. While public arguments about the trajectory of policy-making may continue to be framed in these terms they are singularly unhelpful to the analyst who is seeking to make sense of contemporary decision-making and policy-making. At least three models of governance might be considered when looking at CFSP structures.

The first model is based upon the socialisation of national foreign policy actors and the creation of something like an epistemic community within CFSP structures. Several early writers on CFSP (Nuttal, 1991; De Schoutheete, 1986) noted the formation of a certain *esprit de corps* among early participants in the Political Committee (PoCo) of European Political Co-operation (EPC being the 1970–93 precursor of CFSP). The Political Committee was established by the 1970 Luxembourg/Davignon Report to bring together the senior foreign policy officials of the Member States responsible for political affairs – who often carry the title of Political Director within their foreign ministry. A sense of fellow feeling and of community among these senior officials had, it was claimed, led to a 'consultation reflex' in which these national policy-makers sought to accommodate the concerns of their PoCo colleagues in policy formation. This did not take the form of any 'loyalty transfer' which had been foreseen by early neo-functionalist theorists of European integration, but it was nonetheless significant in creating a common set of norms and expectations by which a collective 'European' foreign policy identity was being created.

More recently, some analysts have drawn attention to the increasing institutionalisation of CFSP caused by an enlarging Union and the need to accommodate the participation of a greater number of policy actors – from both the national and the European level. This has had the effect, they argue, of reducing the sense of community shared by key national foreign policy actors. In effect, the 'family atmosphere' within PoCo has been lost (Tonra, 1997). Crucially, the attempt to compensate for this reduced sense of fellow-feeling by deepening bureaucratic structures (through increasing the frequency of meetings, by broadening the committee structure and by merging Council and CFSP working groups etc.) has not been wholly successful. As a result, rather than seeing any true 'Europeanisation' of national foreign policy-making, what is being witnessed is a 'Brusselisation' of foreign policy structures – a shift in the physical and psychological locus of national decision-making to Brussels-based intergovernmental institutions (Allen, 1998).

A contrasting analysis of CFSP committee structures posits them as a particularly sophisticated means of bureaucratising national interests. Collectively, the fora established for information sharing, policy analysis and the pursuit of agreed joint actions has created a complex system in which national interests are bargained and bought-off in long-term trading. Such trading is not limited to the single commodity of foreign policy – trade-offs may also be made between other EU 'markets'. Thus, the lesser foreign policy interests of Member States may be exchanged for Community-based socio-economic interests located closer to the top of their hierarchy of national interests. Such an analysis sees governance in this context as characterising neither Europeanisation nor Brusselisation but simply a bureaucratisation of foreign policy-making.

Expectations and distinctive features of CFSP committee structure

As we review the committee structures within the Common Foreign and Security Policy and seek to assess what model of governance exists therein, it is perhaps useful to remind ourselves of Member State expectations in pursuing co-operation in this field. The explicit ambition of the Member States, as expressed in the agreements establishing EPC and later CFSP, was to create a 'European voice' in world affairs. This voice was initially to be established by sharing information on and analyses of world events and, where possible, to then act in concert in support of agreed policy positions. This was to be achieved by the construction of a committee structure through which Member State foreign ministers and senior foreign policy officials would meet regularly, discuss selected world events and come to an agreed position. This structure was later to be supported by a systematic sharing of information through a telex system (COREU) managed by a distinct echelon of officials – European correspondents.

The structure thus established did not, however, deliver upon the explicit expectations made of it. The 'European voice' created was sporadic, often vague, usually rather ponderous and always limited in its expression. As a result, the Member States, pursued a course of ad hoc reforms and adjustments to these structures. Such changes were then validated *post hoc* by formal intergovernmental agreements and later, with the 1987 Single European Act, by way of treaty change.

There are some unique features in the committee structure supporting CFSP that should be noted. The first of these is that the Commission has been a long-standing observer of and only more recently an active participant in CFSP. Originally excluded from the operation of EPC – except in so far as it might be invited to offer its views – the Commission was gradually brought within the ambit of regular EPC policy discussions. This process began quite early in an ad hoc fashion but was only slowly formalised until the 1981 London Report codified the Commission's working association with EPC at all committee levels (ministers, political directors and working groups). This was not given legal force, however, until the Single European Act allowed that 'The Commission shall be fully associated with the proceedings of Political Co-operation' (SEA, Article 30.3[b]). However, so long as the material discussed within EPC was limited to issues strictly defined in terms of 'traditional foreign and security policy' the Commission's role in such deliberations remained limited (Cameron, 1998: 99).

With the end of the Cold War the Commission's policy horizons broadened. The foreign policy implements available through Community structures (where the Commission had a central role) such as trade, aid, economic assistance and political dialogue took on a much higher profile and a more central place in the 'tool box' of Member States' foreign policy. As a result, the Commission assumed a more central role in policy deliberations and through both the Maastricht and Amsterdam treaties was integrated more fully into CFSP structures and given a joint right of initiative alongside the Member States.

While the Commission has ultimately become a central actor in the CFSP drama, the European Parliament remains firmly in the wings – and at best wrestles with the job of off-stage prompter. Parliament has, unsurprisingly, been highly critical of the way in which foreign policy co-operation has developed, demanding (to little obvious effect) the institutional changes and dedication of political will necessary to create a truly collective foreign and security policy (European Parliament, 1994). Parliament, however, has no access to the committee structures of CFSP except in so far as the Parliament must be consulted and informed by the Presidency, may question the Presidency on its conduct of CFSP and, in theory, its opinions must be taken into account by ministers.

The limited roles accorded to both Parliament and Commission might suggest that CFSP committee structures are simply a subset of intergovernmental co-operation within the Council. However, the situation is rather more complex than this. In fact, EPC/CFSP committee structures have been traditionally shielded even from the intergovernmental realm of the EC/EU, i.e. from both the Council Secretariat and COREPER (the Committee of Permanent Representatives – Member State Ambassadors to the EC/EU institutions).

The determination of Member States to ring-fence foreign and security policy co-operation from the EC/EU arena led them to create, in effect, a parallel track of intergovernmental committees (see Figure 11). Thus, the EPC Secretariat was kept physically and politically distinct from that of the Council, the COREU telex system shared information exclusively through European Correspondents in the foreign ministries,[1] the foreign ministry-based expert working groups fed their analyses into the Political Committee and the Political Committee set the agenda for Foreign Ministers meeting in the exclusive context of EPC. Only with considerable (and ongoing) difficulty has this system been fused onto that of the Council. Under the Treaty on European Union (TEU) signed at Maastricht, EPC/CFSP expert working groups were merged with those that traditionally handled external relations issues in the Community pillar. A new (and still problematic) working relationship has been established between the Political Committee and COREPER so that foreign ministers meeting in the General Affairs Council now deal with CFSP and Community issues from a single agenda submitted by COREPER and into which PoCo has fed its contribution (see Figure 10).

In sum therefore, the institutional dynamics behind the CFSP committee structure are quite distinct from those operating within other EU committees. One further point must be made in this context. The committee structure sustaining CFSP is arguably the furthest removed from democratic control and national parliamentary scrutiny. With the European Parliament denied access to a substantive policy role, national parliaments might be expected to fill the resulting vacuum. This, of course, is not the case, due to the absence of any norms for parliamentary accountability in the Member States and the traditional distance between parliaments and foreign policy (Caporaso, 1996) more generally. Similarly, interest groups and other foreign policy lobbyists are given no formal access to CFSP committee structures. Their expertise and specialist knowledge etc. is not called upon – except in so far as they may be utilised by national foreign ministry officials participating in various working groups. The only formal access of NGOs etc., to the policy-making sphere is through the direct lobbying of national governments (using traditional instruments) and through the European Parliament – which, as has been noted above – has itself no direct input to policy-making.

The failed divorce of foreign and security policy co-operation from European integration

While Member States were agreed in 1970 that a European voice in world affairs was a necessary corollary of European integration – and indeed a necessary step towards political union – they were very sensitive as to how it might be developed. The 1970 Luxembourg Report established a minimalist, intergovernmental and informal machinery designed to facilitate co-operation in the field of foreign policy. At its heart it comprised twice-annual meetings of foreign

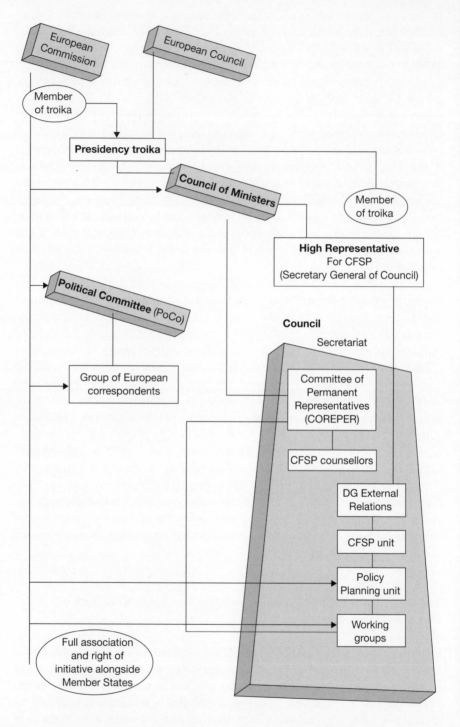

Figure 10 CFSP institutional structure, post-Maastricht and Amsterdam

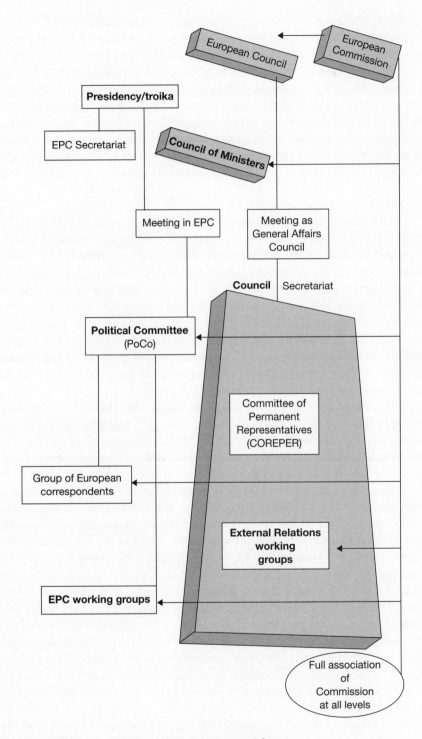

Figure 11 EPC institutional structure, pre-Maastricht

ministers and quarterly meetings of the national foreign ministries' Political Directors. This system of committees was explicitly divorced from the institutions of the then European Community – including the Council of Ministers – with separate meetings of the same Foreign Ministers being conducted for EC business and for EPC matters. It soon became clear, however, that there were practical deficiencies in this division of labour. First, the boundaries between political co-operation and economic integration were unclear and, second, it soon emerged that many of the tools necessary to pursue foreign policy objectives (sanctions, trade agreements etc.) were within Community purview. Moreover, the European Commission was anxious to ensure that agreements in the framework of EPC did not cut across its own responsibilities (EC Bulletin, no. 6, 1971).

The Paris summit of October 1972 sought to address this issue of EC/EPC co-ordination. In the first instance, the summit communiqué accepted that the Foreign Ministers should consider the potential political impact of EC policy. Then, where foreign policy discussions had a 'direct bearing' on EC activity, 'close contact' was to be kept with Community institutions (EC Bulletin, no. 10, 1972).

A report presented to the 1973 Copenhagen EC summit reviewing the operation of EPC, re-stated its original aims and catalogued several by now well-established features of the process. This Copenhagen Report also defined a more specific role for working groups to study particular issues and formalised the establishment of the COREU multilateral telex system.

The Copenhagen Report also sought to address the relationship of political co-operation with EC institutions and a joint Dutch–Belgian proposal was agreed which doubled the annual number of meetings (or 'colloques') between the European Parliament's Political Committee and EPC Ministers from two to four. The Dutch also won agreement for their proposal that PoCo would be directed to 'draw to the attention of Ministers proposals adopted by the European Parliament on foreign policy questions.' It was also agreed that Ministers could 'instruct the political co-operation machinery to prepare studies on certain political aspects of problems under examination in the framework of the Community' (EC Bulletin, no. 12, 1973). Despite these linkages between the Community and EPC, the summit participants felt the need to underscore again the separate nature of each process. They stated that: 'The political co-operation machinery, which deals on the intergovernmental level with problems of international politics, is distinct from and additional to the activities and institutions of the Community which are based on the juridical commitments undertaken by the Members States in the Treaty of Rome.' This division was not legal pettifoggery. It reflected a political distinction between perceived 'high politics' (issues of peace and war) and 'low politics' (issues of socio-economic welfare).

In response to the strains imposed on EPC by events in 1979 and 1980, the Foreign Ministers agreed to incorporate a number of revisions to EPC commit-

tee structures at the October 1981 London summit. First, the workload of ministerial meetings was streamlined, by keeping on the agenda 'only those items of
major importance ... [which] should contain either precise recommendations
or clearly defined options'. Second, they agreed to strengthen the Commission's
level of participation in EPC. Third, they agreed the formal establishment of the
'troika' system.

The Troika had been an organic development within EPC in which the Foreign Ministers and officials holding the present, previous and subsequent Presidency-in-office of EPC co-operated to ensure substantive and procedural
consistency. The London Report institutionalised this process. It also provided
a limited administrative support structure with one (usually junior) official
from the preceding and succeeding presidency being seconded to the foreign
ministry of the state holding the current Presidency-in-office. These officials
remained in the employment of their national foreign ministries, but were at the
disposition of the Presidency, 'work[ing] under its direction' (EC Bulletin, no.
3, 1981). This ultimately became the model for, and precursor of, the EPC Secretariat set up in 1987.

The establishment of a Secretariat had been controversial almost since the
beginning of EPC. While there was broad agreement that the Presidency needed
some administrative support and logistical coherence, several Member States
were anxious to forestall the development of any permanent secretariat that
might be seen as the beginnings of a large-state *directoire*. Moreover, the physical base of such a secretariat was also a major issue. To have its seat in Brussels
implied proximity (spatial and psychological) with Community institutions
and thus raised the fear of an unacceptable *communitarisation*. Similarly, a
headquarters in Paris (as the French Government had long suggested) would be
the final seal to a model of strict intergovernmentalism and thus unacceptable
to those Member States who saw EPC as temporary aberration from a Community 'norm' in policy-making. These divisions meant that EPC worked without
a formal secretariat for 17 years. Every six months the limited support staff
underpinning EPC moved house and changed in composition – with the entire
archive of EPC being physically moved every six months to the next Presidency
capital.

Following the settlement of a series of contentious budgetary issues at the
June 1984 Fontainebleau summit, and the subsequent report of the Ad Hoc
Committee on Institutional Affairs (also known as the Dooge Committee), the
Council of Ministers called an intergovernmental conference of two working
groups to consider proposed treaty revisions. The first comprised the Member
States' Permanent Representatives to the EC, the Commission and the governments of applicant states (Spain and Portugal) to consider revisions to the existing Community treaties. The second group, made up of the political directors of
the 12 foreign ministries concerned itself with EPC. Title III of the resulting
Single European Act (SEA) codified European Political Co-operation in an
international treaty for the very first time. Although there were few innovations

from existing practice, the treaty did provide the erstwhile roving 'secretariat' with a permanent base in Brussels and a formal structure. This new Brussels base also served to draw in the working groups. The practice developed from 1987 for more and more working groups to meet in Brussels rather than in the Presidency capital as had previously been the rule.

Despite some objections, the EPC Secretariat was housed in the same building as the Council Secretariat. However, it was located on a separate floor of that building (at a nominal 1 ECU rent payable annually by the Presidency) and could only be accessed by its own staff. As part of its formal agreement with the Council (facilitated through an exchange of letters), a limited infrastructural support was also supplied by the Council Secretariat's services to the EPC Secretariat. There was, however, no formal policy interaction between the two. The EPC Secretariat's structure was based upon 'an expanded troika'. The 17 members of staff comprised officials from the current, two preceding and two subsequent Presidencies (a total of five diplomats) plus an archivist, small administrative and communications staff (again, seconded from preceding and subsequent presidencies) and a Head of Secretariat appointed by the Foreign Ministers of the Member States.

While the SEA had, in effect, put down on paper that which was already in operation, the negotiations which led to the November 1993 Maastricht Treaty initially promised much more. The European Council summit meeting of 28 April 1990 instructed the Foreign Ministers to undertake: 'A detailed examination [of] the need for possible Treaty changes.' As a result, two intergovernmental conferences (IGCs) were set up. The first drew up treaty-based proposals on EMU and the second studied options for European Political Union (EPU). The second of these IGCs was designed to look at four aspects of political union, including a reassessment of the Community's international personality and the prospect for a common security and foreign policy. A focus of study here was the prospect of integrating EPC and security policy co-operation into the decision-making structures of the Community, thus eliminating the remaining distinctions between EPC and Community structures.

In the event, however, and despite the efforts of an ambitious Dutch presidency, Member States were determined to maintain a formal distinction between the decision-making processes of CFSP and 'Community' business. At the same time, however, they were willing to accept the principle of a single institutional framework. In effect, this meant eliminating the parallel track of intergovernmental structures that had grown up alongside those in the Community sphere. In practical terms this meant integrating the Ministerial agenda of CFSP with that of the General Affairs Council (GAC), merging the working groups of CFSP with their analogues in external relations and integrating the new CFSP secretariat with that of the Council as a whole.

This wholesale merger was not unproblematic. As might be imagined, there were substantial battles for administrative supremacy. COREPER for example, which set the agenda for the GAC, could not allow itself to be 'instructed' by colleagues in the Political Committee in drawing up that agenda for the GAC. Similarly, the Political Committee (whose members in several Member States were senior to their colleagues in COREPER) was sensitive to any suggestion that 'their' issues on the ministerial agenda might be second-guessed by their COREPER colleagues. In the merger of substantive working groups too there were difficulties.

In most Member States the policy distinctions between COREPER and PoCo reflected the internal structural organisation of Member State foreign ministries. In most of these, there existed a traditional division between economic and political sections that was reflected in the Community/EPC division of labour. In working groups for example, the foreign ministry officials who worked within the EPC Asia Group would have been those from their ministry's political division while it would often have been colleagues from the economic section that would have sat in on the Community's Working Group on Asia. Where two groups existed, merger – which on the face of it was wholly logical – required decisions as to who, in future, would participate, who would speak for the national delegation and which established working methods would predominate. In several instances, however, EPC/CFSP working groups – having no Community counterparts in areas such as human rights, non-proliferation and consular affairs – continued (initially) to operate as heretofore.

Surprisingly – in view of the long and sensitive history of its establishment – the merger of the EPC/CFSP Secretariat with its Council analogue was less problematic. While the physical and metaphorical 'doors' of the new CFSP unit (situated within the Council's own External Relations DG) were thrown open to their Council colleagues, established working procedures and structures remained largely untroubled. There was certainly the potential for greater substantive co-ordination within the 'foreign policy' portfolio but the essential features (and/or weaknesses) of CFSP remained the same. This was particularly the case in the context of the six-monthly rotating Council Presidency and the implications that this had for the composition and working methods of the CFSP unit.

By the time the 1996 IGC on further treaty revision was underway, many of the changes wrought by the Maastricht Treaty were still taking root. COREPER and PoCo had come to a *modus vivendi* in which the former set the overall agenda for ministerial discussions in a Union context and integrated the more specialised contribution of their PoCo colleagues. Increasingly, as the two agendas merged, COREPER was drawn further into CFSP waters since its own remit was to ensure consistency and coherence in the work of ministers. COREPER was now at the core of the foreign policy system and developed its own structures accordingly. A new echelon of CFSP Counsellors was established within COREPER to discuss issues such as the financing of CFSP which was now 'Community' business (Allen, 1998: 53).

In the merged working groups, the 'Community style' ultimately predominated. The acculturation of participating officials (whether they originated from the Community or EPC/CFSP side of the house) to 'Brussels' proceeded apace. This was also the case even where no 'merger' of working groups had occurred (e.g. in the area of human rights) but where working practices and meeting venues were gradually harmonised and groups increasingly focused upon the 'Brussels machine'. One result of this was the 'withering away of the old "club" atmosphere' (Regelsberger, 1997: 79) and a consequent integration of personnel, styles and agendas.

In many ways the changes ultimately proposed by the Amsterdam Treaty continued the trajectory towards greater Council control over the 'foreign policy' portfolio. The design of the Policy Planning and Early Warning unit gathers together officials from the Council Secretariat, seconded personnel from the Member States and officials from both the Commission, and the WEU. Crucially, this new unit will report within the Council Secretariat to the new High Representative for CFSP (the Council's Secretary General) who will, in turn, be responsible to the Presidency and Ministers of the Council. The appointment of the High Representative is designed to provide a more coherent personal and political focus for CFSP. This also feeds into a revised troika arrangement that is to be comprised of the High Representative, the Presidency and the Commission. Previous and/or succeeding Presidencies may also be called upon in particular circumstances.

In sum, the development of support structures and the committee framework sustaining CFSP represents at least three moves. First, it has eliminated the structural differential between EPC/CFSP and Community business. The implications of this move are, however, contested. While it would not be possible to argue that there has been any substantial 'communitarisation' of policy and/or decision-making (as feared in the early days of EPC) there has undeniably been a shift towards standard Community norms in terms of participation and working method. This has been achieved at the expense of the old informal 'club' network. The impact of the acculturation effects of collective policy-making upon national foreign ministries and foreign policies has yet to be fully assessed.

The second move has focused command and control over what might be dubbed the 'foreign policy' portfolio of the Union within the Council. This is an intriguing development. On the one hand a classic federalist conclusion would have been to envisage the Commission (as arguably the central 'Executive' institution of the Union) as the core player in the foreign policy drama. Instead, the Council is being adapted – with a higher political profile and greater substantive policy-making capacity – to take on this classic executive function. The question which then arises is the nature of policy-making within this evolving institution – classic intergovernmentalism (zero-sum, traded interests and lowest common denominator policy-making) or something more and/or different?

The third move – and a consequence of the preceding two– is the contribution being made to the development of a Union-centred foreign policy personality. Two key objectives in the historic development of a collective foreign policy voice (alongside effectiveness) have been consistency and coherence.

What appears to have emerged is a compromise between a truly collective (and hence quasi-federal) foreign policy structure that would have been centred in the Commission and the preservation of independent-but-co-operative national foreign policy systems. This, however, must give rise to future challenges. While consistency is the *leitmotif* of these changes – it must still be acknowledged that the differing decision-making structures between CFSP and External Relations is likely to give rise to contradictions. If EU 'foreign policy' is properly to be seen as having integrated the political and the economic then surely the nature of decision-making must ultimately reflect the logic upon which such an integrated structure is based?

Structure and nature of CFSP committees

The structure of committees within CFSP reflect the move from a strict intergovernmentalism (explicitly divorced from the institutions of European integration) towards a Brussels-based working method. The Member States remain at the heart of the system. At all levels within the committee structures – from meetings of ambassadors in third countries and international organisations, through the European Correspondents, the working groups and the Political Committee – Member State diplomats comprise the core of the policy process. However, in the search for added value (and so as to overcome the intergovernmental dynamic of lowest-common-denominator politics) the Member States have sought to develop a new institutional logic for CFSP. This logic is both bureaucratic and epistemic.

In terms of a bureaucratic logic the struggle has been between the Commission as the locus of institutional interest and the Council. For its part, the Commission has vigorously courted the CFSP. Its logic is clear – consistency and coherence in foreign policy cannot be achieved in a bicephalus institutional structure. To this end the Commission has sought to position itself at the centre of a unified foreign policy structure. Moreover, its dedication to this end has even moved it to replicate perceived weaknesses in the structures of national foreign ministries. The 1993 establishment of DG IA to handle CFSP, for example, mirrored the division in many national foreign ministries between political and economic affairs – a division which the Commission had long insisted (in its criticism of the EPC/Community divide) was illogical. The 1995 move under Commission President Santer to sub-divide 'foreign policy' among four Commissioners on the basis of four regional portfolios went some way towards re-integrating political and economic issues but at the potential expense of co-ordination. To compensate for this the President created the *Relex Group*. This brought together the six Commissioners and supporting senior officials whose policy responsibilities dealt with some aspect of foreign policy (Cameron, 1998: 62–3)

The Commission's efforts have not paid off. In the Amsterdam Treaty, the

Commission's attempt to extend its own external trade competence to include trade in services and intellectual property was rebuffed in favour of a mechanism whereby the Council might extend such competence on a case-by-case basis. More broadly – and despite its best efforts – the Commission is in effect a sixteenth non-voting member of CFSP with acknowledged special competences and a unique ability to present an integrated policy perspective to the Member States.

It is the Council, however, which has thus far won the battle of bureaucratic logic. The Council Secretariat – too often overlooked in the Union's institutional pantheon – has emerged as the central bureaucratic actor in CFSP. As noted above, it has been re-structured and significantly politicised as a means of giving CFSP both a planning capacity and a political profile. In some ways this development is experimental. For many years, the Council Secretariat has been a crucially important behind-the-scenes actor. During their presidencies, for example, smaller Member States have successfully relied upon it for administrative support and in the skilled drafting of presidency texts – even in the sometimes charged atmosphere of IGC negotiations. What is now proposed however – a task thrust upon it rather than one actively sought – is that the Secretariat should engage in a political high-wire act. In this new, and often cruel spotlight, the role of the Secretary General (wearing the hat of CFSP High Representative) will be crucial. So too will be the success of the Policy Planning and Early Warning Unit. The question is whether the Council Secretariat has the capacity to fulfil the responsibilities being placed upon it. Its successes and/or failures will be keenly studied.

Because the Member States are uncomfortable in seeing such a sensitive area as foreign and security policy drawn within the 'Community machine' they have chosen to follow a bureaucratic logic which has turned toward an adapted intergovernmentalism

The set of committee structures established through CFSP have as their aim the construction of an effective, coherent and consistent European foreign policy. It is difficult, if not impossible to see the creation of same being achieved on the back of a strict intergovernmentalism. Accepting this, the Member States have therefore sought to adapt intergovernmental structures towards a model of collective policy-making that is premised upon intense, highly structured, regular, permanent and ever closer policy consultations. Crucially – and distinguishing this level of policy consultation from any other form of diplomatic activity – this framework is situated within the institutional structures of an integrative political project. It is this that establishes something other than an intergovernmental bureaucratisation of foreign policy and something more than a Brusselisation of national foreign policy systems.

According to long-standing participants in this policy structure the added-value provided by EPC in its earlier days was an informal sense of shared community and fellow-feeling. In its fusion with Community structures that has been allegedly lost. However, what appears to be nonetheless constant is the development of a sense of common identity and sense of collective purpose. The informal 'consultation reflex' in which Political Directors sought to accommodate the views of their fellows in an almost personalistic fashion has given way to what might be described as a formal internalisation of shared norms and precedents. This internalisation is in turn being strengthened and developed through its institutionalisation in committee structures.

One crucial point to bear in mind here is the fact that the participants in this process of internalisation are not national civil servants but national diplomats. As a result, the culture of national diplomatic corps may be significant. In all Member States, recruitment to the diplomatic corps is distinct from that to the general civil service. While the openness of the diplomatic corps varies from state to state, it is nonetheless an institution of some distinction and set apart from the national civil service. In order to be effective diplomats must also have the capacity to understand and thus to empathise (at least to some degree) with their host government or diplomatic colleagues. It is for this reason that most national diplomatic corps insist that their officials rotate between national and overseas postings. Moreover, in some Member States the very idea of area or subject specialisation by diplomats is shunned in favour of a culture of 'generalists'. In sum, diplomats – as a category of national officials – share a culture and mode of thought which is at least distinct from that of national civil servants and is perhaps more open to the possibilities of shared and mutually beneficial interests.

Thus, between the evolving institutional and committee structures of CFSP – which have the effect of fostering the internalisation of norms and values – and the temperament of the national diplomatic corps, an epistemic community may be seen to be created. At this point, however, it is crucial to distinguish between this epistemic community – this sharing and internalisation of norms – from the transfer of loyalty expected under traditional neofunctionalist analyses. It would be more correct to say that national interests are being transformed within a European context and that national foreign policies are being Europeanised. In other words, the identity of national foreign policies is changing. This process is certainly most evident among smaller Member States (Tonra, 1996) but some studies suggest that it is also appreciable in the foreign policies of larger Member States. In any event, it certainly registers as being more significant than the physical relocation of decision-making bodies to Brussels.

Conclusion and future perspectives

This chapter opened by distinguishing between the committee structures of CFSP and other policy portfolios within the EU. It went on to argue that while many features were indeed distinct the question posed about EU committees ('What was the nature of governance?') remained germane. It is hoped that the preceding will have offered an answer to that question. Committees within the

CFSP were initially established to shield this policy process from any cross-infection deriving from the Community. Over time it was adduced that these structures were failing to establish a strong, credible and effective European voice on the world stage. In a series of ad hoc adjustments this committee structure was brought within the temple of the European Union and merged and/or redesigned upon existing Community models.

Crucially, however, this merger occurred through the Council and its Secretariat rather than through the Commission. That battle – over whether to focus the EU's international identity through the Commission or through the Council has, at this juncture, been resolved in favour of the Council. Nonetheless, there remains a process that perhaps distinguishes this realm of intergovernmental co-operation from arguments about the 're-nationalisation' of Community policy through committee structures. While the early socialisation of diplomats through EPC has been lost and/or diminished, the institutionalisation of CFSP through its committee structures has nonetheless contributed to the Europeanisation of national foreign policies. This process is characterised by a redefinition of so-called 'national interests' in a new European context. This goes beyond a Brusselisation of structures towards a shift in the identity of national foreign policy.

Through the changes wrought by the Amsterdam Treaty, the European Union's foreign policy capacity remains two-headed. The Commission has a strong, perhaps predominant role in what used to be known as the External Relations of the European Community while the Council and its Secretariat over the next few years will seek to sharpen the capacity of CFSP. At the same time the Council must seek to ensure co-ordination and coherence between the two policy realms based upon two substantively different decision-making models. It is to be expected that the continuing pressure for effectiveness, coherence and consistency will drive these two decision-making structures towards one another – just as it has driven their administrations and structures closer together.

Note

1   Not unil 1982 did the European Commission get its own COREU telex machine from which it received and could send out messages on the network. Until this point it was limited to receiving selected photocopies from the Belgian Government and sending rare messages by the same route (Nuttall, 1992).

ALBERT WEALE

9

Government by committee
Three principles of evaluation

European integration rests upon the Monnet method, 'integration by stealth' as it has been called (Hayward, 1996). According to this method, European integration is best achieved, indeed can only be achieved, by co-operation among national and international experts on technical matters related to mutual agreement on standards in specific areas. Attempts to confront explicitly the fundamental questions of constitutional principle that the construction of a new European political order involves should be postponed or avoided. To be sure, the Monnet method is not the only element in European integration. Intergovernmentalist bargains of various kinds have also been necessary, most notably in securing reforms to the Treaty of Rome in the Single European Act, the Treaty on European Union and the Treaty of Amsterdam. But the Monnet method is an essential element in the process, driving it relentlessly forward, so that in its absence, European integration would not have reached the point that it has today. As William Wallace (1996: 239) has noted, looking 'back on the era of post-war reconstruction, the central role played by rational administrators working within the permissive limits of political consensus is impressive'. If this account of the logic of integration is correct, it follows that government by committee is not an accidental or incidental feature of decision-making within the EU, but is rather a logical implication of the overall strategy that such integration entails. As Monnet rather nicely put it in his memoirs, his hope was that a few hundred European civil servants would be enough to set thousands of national experts to work (Monnet, 1978: 373).

Some argue that in the context of positive integration the Monnet method has run its course. However useful the method may have been in the past, it is argued, Europe is now at the stage where it needs a constitutional settlement akin to that formulated in Philadelphia in 1787 for the United States of America. If this is so, then it almost certainly has implications for the way in which the phenomenon of government by committee is conceived. Since government by

committee is an upshot of the Monnet method, an explicitly constitutional contract among leading European political actors might be expected to unpick
some fundamental features of the processes to which that method has given rise.
If we further assume that any such constitutional contract would imply further
moves in the democratisation of the Union, to the point where the European
Parliament plays the dominant, if not the exclusive, policy-making role, then
such an approach automatically implies shifting much of the locus of decision-
making authority in the setting of standards from the Commission, the Council and their committees – the representatives of the expert authority under a
series of intergovernmentalist bargains – to the European Parliament – the only
directly elected representatives of the citizens of Europe.

Yet, before we jump to drastic conclusions, there are various other considerations to be borne in mind. Even if we accepted that the Monnet method is no
longer the principal way in which European integration is to be carried forward,
we would still have to consider its legacy in the working arrangements of the EU
policy process. Moreover, the EU is a political system that is *sui generis*. In any
attempt to maintain its continuing legitimacy the position and standing of both
the representatives of EU citizens and the Member States as actors in their own
right will have to be acknowledged, and one way of securing the consent of the
latter may be to ensure that their expert representatives can participate in a continuing way in the setting of standards.

In any case, as Simon Hix points out in Chapter 3, judged in terms of comparative politics and policy, the politics of expertise in the European Union is
neither a novel nor a unique phenomenon. Political scientists have documented
the way in which in many countries rule-making has become a routinised
process of bargaining between state actors and interested parties within the
framework of the delegated authority for which legislation provides when it sets
out the broad principles of public policy for a specific sector. The by now extensive literature on policy networks is nothing other than a testimony to the extent
to which rule-making and implementation is a highly specialised process across
all developed political systems. Even in Germany, which for a variety of historical reasons is especially careful about securing parliamentary approval for the
implementation of technical regulations, it is clear that public officials in the relevant ministries spend a great deal of time with interested parties involved in
negotiation over detailed specifications, say over the setting of environmental
emission standards.

Behind these comparative trends there lies of course the character of the
policy issues that modern governments have to deal with. In part, the problem
arises because in a 'risk society' (Beck, 1992) modern production methods pose
problems of latent and diffuse risk that consumers and citizens are concerned
about. This being so, the familiar distinctions between policy formulation and
policy implementation or between legislated principles and executive administration, on which the classical separation of powers doctrine rests, become more
and more difficult to maintain. Detailing the implications of a policy, which is

necessary for the purposes of implementation, also becomes a way of formulating it more precisely.

How then should we evaluate the system of governance to which this collapse of the distinction between policy formation and policy implementation gives rise? In reviewing the evidence presented in the previous chapters, it is useful to have some definitions in mind. All of the contributors make it clear that the use of committees is extensive in EU decision-making, but that there is no single form that committees can take. However, we can distinguish comitology, the specific use of committees for the implementation of Council decisions under the formula decided in 1987, from the broader use of committees in COREPER, mandated bodies like the European Central Bank and other decision-making and advisory bodies. The broad phenomenon, including comitology itself, I shall call 'government by committee', and I shall reserve the term 'comitology' only for those bodies that are constituted according to the 1987 Council decision. Comitology is thus a species of the genus government by committee.

It makes a difference in this context that there has been a transposition of technical discussion and standard-setting from the level of the nation state to that of Europe, by virtue of the Monnet method. The effect here is to invert the usual logic of federalism. This logic rests on a bargain among component units of a given territorial area to protect its integrity from external threats (see Riker, 1964). Thus, it is no surprise that it is foreign and defence policies that are most usually associated with the highest level of government in federal systems. Of course, these policy sectors have their own technical dimensions, most obviously in matters of defence procurement, but they more typically involve intelligence gathering, analysis and strategic decision-making rather than the specification of detailed standards for products and processes within the economy. Under the Monnet method, by contrast, the technical tasks of devising the detailed specification of standards for goods and services traded in the economy is central.

To note the economic basis of European integration is to note also a latent tension that arises from the Monnet method, namely that between the stress on market liberalisation, essential so that barriers to trade and commerce can be broken down as the precondition for a wider social and political integration, and the demand for some political control over the conditions under which markets operate, so that European publics collectively are not simply the passive recipients of economic fate but also, to some degree at least, the shapers of their common future. This is of course the passage from negative integration to positive integration, as defined by Scharpf (1996). If this is a fundamental problem, the question of government by committee concerns what its role might be in a Europe that was pursuing positive integration.

An essential feature of the Monnet method is that it institutionalises a form of uncertainty. The environmental policy about which Flynn writes provides a good illustration of this point. Barely recognised before 1972, environmental policy rose from silence to salience in the subsequent twenty-five years (Weale,

1996). There was no provision made for environmental policy in the Treaty of Rome and early measures were taken either under single market provisions or under the 'catch-all' Article 235 provisions. In some ways, the Committee on Spatial Development, about which Faludi, Zonnefeld and Waterhout (Chapter 6) write and the designated task of which is to formulate the basic working perspective of European spatial planning policy, is an even more striking example, since it is impossible to find a rational basis for its growth in the existing competences of the European Union. But its emergence is consistent with the deeper logic of that Union, once we see that functional integration has an unpredictable quality to it.

Such an institutionalisation of uncertainty is not an aberrant feature of the Monnet method but is an essential ingredient in its success and it implies the rejection of the strategy of wholesale institutional redesign according to principles negotiated in a constitutional contract. This brings us to the point where we started: the legacy of the Monnet method for the evaluation of the EU's institutional performance. To say that government by committee is an essential feature of the process of European integration is not to say that there is no point in the evaluation of current institutional performance together with suggestions for reform. But it does mean that we should spend as much time on the specification of the standards for institutional reform as on the detailed prescriptions for redesign themselves.

For the remainder of this chapter, this is what I propose to do. Rather than seeking to move from a particular set of principles to institutional recommendation, I want to look at what standards we should be operating with. There is a further reason why I shall take this approach. Normative democratic theory tells us not to identify the principles of democracy with the specifics of institutional arrangements (Dryzek, 1996). The historical origins of democracy are in a form of government in which the ultimate source of political authority was to be found in an assembly of all citizens. When what Dahl (1989) calls the first transformation of democracy took place and the scale of politics shifted from the city state to the nation state, the form of democratic authority changed to emphasise the importance of representative assemblies and a constitutional system of checks and balances. Dahl's second transformation of democracy, from the nation state to the international order, promises to raise just as many questions about the appropriate institutional form that democratic accountability and representation should take. We should not assume that a democratic Europe would merely be a replication on the continental level of institutional patterns that are characteristic of nation states.

Standards of evaluation

In this section I set out three principles for the evaluation of government by committee: functional effectiveness, transparency and deliberative rationality.

In particular, I shall pursue the argument that the complexities of achieving functional effectiveness also require us to look at questions of transparency and deliberative rationality. The standard these principles imply are not intended to constitute a complete list of all the criteria for evaluation that may be relevant in assessing government by committee. No doubt others can think of yet more criteria. However, each element of the set I define often implies quite demanding tests taken on its own, and also each involves potential conflicts with various political values that we might think important. So it is not simply a question of listing the standards and principles but also a matter of seeing how they might be related to other political principles we think are important.

Functional effectiveness
The first and most obvious criterion for any system of decision-making is functional effectiveness. A decision-making system should produce satisfactory solutions to the problems that are presented to it. (A more demanding test of functional effectiveness would be that the solutions were optimal, but that seems to me to be aiming rather high for most decisions on public policy.) Of course, it is a long-standing claim of the functional approach to European integration that decision-making by experts, rather than by elected representatives, was more effective in the problem-solving sense. According to this view, government by committee has a higher probability of solving the problems that modern governments have to deal with. This was the view, in various forms, of Mitrany, Monnet and Hallstein, and more recently it has been vigorously advocated by Majone (see Majone, 1996: 284–301). In short, the claim is that if we want functional effectiveness in the making of public policy, government by committee is the way to get it. In the context of European integration, this message carries the added advantage, as I have already noted, of avoiding the need to confront the large constitutional questions that European integration inevitably raises.

From one point of view, the most elementary considerations of the division of labour in decision-making suggest that this view must be correct in some measure. When dealing with the details of product standards or the implementation of various regulations, there is no reason to believe that busy elected representatives, with limited attention spans and broad responsibilities, are likely to be able to make functionally effective decisions. As long as there is an attempt at positive integration, therefore, the resolution of policy problems will necessarily involve the practice of government by committee and the technical rationality on which it rests.

However, what from one point of view is unexceptionable raises from another point of view a difficulty. Sometimes the detailing of product standards, for example, is not a simple matter of defining a solution on which all producers can reasonably co-ordinate, but also involves the definition of acceptable risks for consumers and citizens – an aspect of the risk society to which I have already referred. Detailing the acceptable risks associated with pesticide levels in food, the release of genetically modified organisms into the environment or the procedures for dealing with BSE in cattle, whilst irreducibly involving technical issues, are never purely technical tasks. Approaches to such issues that rely exclusively on the skills of technical rationality might be perfectly satisfactory if the definition of acceptable risk could be conducted in terms of the quantitative specification of hazards, that is, in terms of the numerical likelihood of death or injury occurring given the specification of a standard. But study after study on the public acceptance of risk shows that the definition of acceptable risk is not simply a matter of the quantitative likelihood of an adverse event, but also involves assessments of how voluntary exposure to risk is, what the source of the risk might be and what the benefits might be from the risk-causing activity (for a recent balanced assessment, see Royal Commission on Environmental Pollution, 1998: Chapter 4). Functional effectiveness in solving this policy problem goes beyond functional effectiveness in solving the problem of how to estimate risks per se. The problem turns on the definition of the problem.

In this context it is noteworthy, as Brendan Flynn points out in Chapter 4, that environmental standard setting gives rise to an extensive use of committees. Since the reduction of risks from environmental hazards typically incurs rapidly diminishing marginal returns to investment past some point, the specification of a standard goes beyond technical issues of risk assessment to more intangible issues of the proportionality between cost and benefit. One point that follows from this is that the composition of committees becomes an important question. None of the studies cited in the present volume shows that much innovative thinking has gone into the question of how committees are appointed, what range of skills they might need or how they in turn conduct their own consultation both with wider groups of experts, including experts that would provide the committee with some multi-disciplinary insights, and with the public at large.

A further problem of functional effectiveness in relation to government by committee arises from the way in which committee mandates are written. Expertise is specific to particular fields so that care needs to be taken that the right issues are being discussed and dealt with by the right committee. Moreover, traditional constitutional principles of the separation of powers can be read as intended to prevent what may be called problem drift – the tendency for committees charged with responsibility for one matter to pursue other issues. Since the authority of a committee rests on its ability to perform the tasks that are assigned to it, problem drift means that their decision-making spills over into issues that should not concern the committee. The most obvious way to deal with this problem is to write a specific and narrow task-specification for the relevant committee.

The clearest example of such narrow mandate setting in the EU is to be found in the constitution of the European Central Bank, with its specific responsibility to set monetary policy for the purpose of maintaining price stability. The difficulty here, it has been argued, is that it is not helpful to measure the success of a central bank in terms of price stability when the main economic threat to Europe may be deficient demand (*Financial Times*, 1999). Yet to add the task of maintaining adequate aggregate demand to the mandate of the ECB would be to assign it two potentially conflicting goals – price stability and demand maintenance – the balancing of which is an inherently political responsibility. Unless we believe that functional effectiveness in the solving of one problem is always costless in terms of other problems, we have here an unavoidable difficulty.

Questions arising from the political accountability of committees have been important for those who wish to shift the locus of decision-making within the EU from the present structure of Council, Commission and appointed committees more towards the European Parliament. Simon Hix points out in his chapter that institutional proposals to make the EP more central and active in standard setting ignore the evidence from comparative political science on how to deal with the inherent asymmetries of information between a legislative principal and a delegated agent. These points are well taken, and they indicate how difficult it is to address problems of political accountability in the design of institutions for government by committee. Yet there is also a problem of functional effectiveness that arises from the very process of institutional reform itself, namely, the way in which the institutional struggle for competence and control can itself give rise to a failure to address problems effectively. The most common form this takes is delay in the passing of measures, for example directives on pesticides or land-fill, when the Parliament decides that the proposals that emerge from the comitology provide inadequate safeguards for the environment or public health.

Functional effectiveness, then, whilst an obviously desirable feature of any decision-making system is not easy to achieve. With no clear separation between the technical core of a problem and the broader issues of social, economic and political values to which any solution to the problem might give rise, as well as the difficulties of satisfactorily institutionalising expertise, we cannot take the functional effectiveness of government by committee for granted.

Transparency

If the principle of effectiveness says that the solution to a problem should satisfactorily address the problem, the principle of transparency means that it should be possible to see how a particular standard was adopted, and who was involved in the decision according to a certain set of standard operating procedures. In other words, whereas the principle of effectiveness is related to the substance of a decision, the principle of transparency is related to the process by which a decision was taken. The value of transparency in this sense lies is the notion of constitutional government under the rule of law: decision-making should be predictable and open to scrutiny by those affected, and this is only possible if the process by which decisions are taken is clear to all.

As far as comitology is concerned, one might be tempted to think that the

Council decision of 1987 had dealt with the issue of transparency. By that decision various procedures were laid down according to which particular issues would be routed through the decision-making process according to standard operating procedures. However, if we take the principle of transparency seriously, we can see that there are various ways in which that Council decision falls short of the full requirements of transparency.

In the first place, government by committee is more pervasive than the comitology regulated by the Council's decision. Whilst the implementation of standards may be regulated according to the common set of standards for the comitology issues, the same does not apply to the other sorts of committees, those working under COREPER for example, whose decisions may also be influential.

Second, there is the problem of how far it is really possible to keep clear watch on the way in which the remit of committees may drift over time. Particularly noteworthy in this context are the 'sleeping committees' to which Brendan Flynn (Chapter 4), citing Buitendijk and van Schendelen, draws attention. The existence of such sleeping committees means that it will not always be possible for those outside the decision-making process – interest groups, the attentive public and the like – to know how an issue is being dealt with and who has responsibility.

Third, it is clear from the history of the controversy between the Commission and the Parliament, as reported by Hix (Chapter 3), that even after the 1987 Council decision the degree of transparency attained was very limited. Under the Plumb–Delors agreement, the Parliament was given access to certain information about the operation of the comitology procedures, but the agreement was implemented in a way that excluded urgent or secret issues, that failed to detail the timetable for the adoption of decisions or that meant that the Commission did not have to take account of the Parliament's view on matters of implementation. After a running inter-institutional battle, the Parliament found that some of these issues were addressed in the so-called *Modus Vivendi* of 1994. Even so, it is clear from the Hix narrative that the earlier failure of transparency was in part the impetus pushing the Parliament towards a more interventionist stance on the whole question of the scrutiny of implementation, a stance which, if the logic of Hix's overall argument is correct, may well be counter-productive.

Finally, there is an intrinsic problem in assigning sectoral areas to specific types of procedure. These problems are well detailed by Dogan (Chapter 2). Despite the codification adopted in 1987 under the comitology decision, the Commission appears to have made little systematic effort to apply the measures to committees established prior to that date. Moreover, as Dogan rather nicely shows, it is not even possible to predict the favoured process of important actors from what is generally assumed to be their institutional preference. Although the Commission and the Parliament might be thought to favour procedures that strengthen EU control (essentially Procedures I, IIa and IVa) whilst the Council might be thought to favour procedures that facilitate its own involvement in implementation (Procedures IIb, IIIb and IVb), the pattern of allocation of different measures to different procedures does not seem to follow such a logic. The Commission includes Council dominated procedures in its proposals and the Council is often prepared to employ procedures that allow a high degree of executive autonomy. It is going too far to say that there is no rhyme or reason to the allocation, but it is certainly not one that is obviously transparent.

Deliberative rationality

It is one thing for measures to work or for the process by which they were arrived at to be clear. It is yet another thing for them to be the product of deliberative rationality, so that the decisions they embody rest on considerations that are genuinely relevant and pertinent to the issue at hand. In other words, the test of deliberative rationality for any measure is what its grounds for adoption were and why alternatives were rejected. A measure that meets the standards of deliberative rationality ought to be one for which it will always be possible to say that it falls into the category of what is reasonably eligible for choice – even when there are other measures that are also reasonably eligible for choice.

One barrier to deliberative rationality in this sense may be the social conditions under which a group makes its decisions and in particular the implicit tension between the need to maintain civilised social relationships in a small working committee and the need to ensure that awkward, discrepant or uncomfortable issues are not avoided. All this can be summarised in the need to avoid 'group-think', or the generation of premature consensus by virtue of the pattern of social relationships in the decision-making committee (Janis, 1982).

In this context, the club-like atmosphere of the Monetary Committee that Verdun describes may inhibit deliberative rationality. As Verdun describes the situation (Chapter 7), the club-like atmosphere is not simply a matter of cordial personal relations, but also extends to similarities of economic philosophy. We do not have to go as far as Sir Karl Popper (1972, p. 352) and say that if there were no Tower of Babel we should have to invent it. However, we should recognise that rationality in decision-making requires the embodiment of a critical capacity that may well be at odds with the social need to maintain good working relationships. Perhaps the problem was not serious in the case of the Monetary Committee, even if we consider the way in which the convergence criteria were set for economic and monetary union, since there was always a political override implicit in that process and in any case the standards that were set were the subject of considerable public discussion. On the other hand, one wonders whether there was ever any awkward voice on the committee inviting it to consider the process of evidence and reasoning by which it came to the recommendations that it did.

One problem with the test of deliberative rationality is of course that the setting of standards should not be expected to issue from a pure process of reasoning, but also involves consideration of the capacities of Member States to reach the targets that are required by the standards. Here the mixing of scientific rationality with negotiation referred to by Flynn (Chapter 4) is relevant. Flynn argues that one consequence is that hard decisions on risk may be shirked because they offend particular parties. Negotiation and the pressure to unanimity do not matter of course provided that the result that emerges is one of the elements in the set of decisions that deliberative rationality would have converged upon anyway. It does matter if it leads to decisions that evidence would otherwise indicate should have been rejected.

Conclusions

The case for government by committee in the context of the European Union is double-barrelled. It is not simply that the character of modern policy-making is such that it needs to deal with complex problems that only experts can handle. It is also that international co-operation and functional interdependence is fostered by delegating decisions to committees that are freed from the constraints of everyday political accountability.

Accepting that the EU is *sui generis* and that the demands of political accountability may be inappropriate for all the reasons I have discussed earlier does not mean, however, that we should not seek to evaluate how well the present system of government by committee is doing by standards that are relevant to a system of delegated political authority. In an ideal world, transparent procedures based on deliberative rationality ought to produce solutions to policy problems that are functionally effective in the general run of cases. The chapters in this volume show that, as far as the present performance of government by committee in the European Union is concerned, we are a long way from that ideal world.

BIBLIOGRAPHY

Agence Europe (1997a), Europe Daily Bulletins, No. 6961, 24 April.

Agence Europe (1997b), Editorial, Europe Daily Bulletins, No. 7012, 9 July.

Akademie für Raumforschung und Landesplanung (1996), *Europäische Raumentwicklungspolitik*; Rechtliche Verankerung im Vertrag über die Europäische Union, Arbeitsmaterial No. 233, Hannover, Verlag der ARL.

Allen, David (1998), 'Who Speaks for Europe: The Search for an Effective and Coherent External Policy', in John Peterson and Helene Sjursen (eds), *A Common Foreign Policy for Europe*, London, Routledge.

Andewig, R.B. and Irwin, G.A. (1993), *Dutch Government and Politics*, London, Macmillan.

Ansell, C.K., Parsons, C.A. and Darden, K.A. (1997), 'Dual Networks in European Regional Development Policy', *Journal of Common Market Studies*, 35:3, 347–75.

Austrian Presidency (1998), 'The Future of European Spatial Development Policy: CSD and ESDP after 1999', CSD seminar organised by the Federal Chancellery under the Austrian Presidency, 23–4 November, Vienna.

Bach, Maurizio (1992), 'Eine leise Revolution durch Verwaltungsverfahren. Bürokratische Integrationsprozesse in der Europäischen Gemeinschaft', *Zeitschrift für Soziologie*, 1, 16–30.

Bakker, Age F.P. (1995), *The Liberalisation of Capital Movements in Europe: The Monetary Committee and Financial Integration 1958–1994*, Boston, Dordrecht and London, Kluwer.

Bastrup-Birk, H. and Doucet P.H. (1997), 'European Spatial Planning from the Heart', in A. Faludi and W. Zonneveld (eds), *Built Environment: Special Issue: Shaping Europe: The European Spatial Development Perspective*, 23:4, 307–14.

Baylis, T.A. (1988), *Governing by Committee: Collegial Leadership in Advanced Societies*, New York, State University of New York Press.

Beck, U. (1992), *Risk Society: towards a New Modernity*, trans. M. Ritter, London, Thousand Oaks, New Delhi, Sage.

Beyers, J. and Dierckx, G. (1998) 'The Working Groups of the Council of the European Union: Supranational or Intergovernmental Negotiations', *Journal of Common Market Studies*, 36:3, 289–319.

Blin, O. (1998), 'L'Article 113 CE après Amsterdam', *Revue du Marché Commun et de l'Union Europeenne*, 420, 447–56.

Blumann, Claude (1996), Le Parlement européen et la comitologie: une complication pour la Conférence intergouvernementale, *Revue trimestrielle de droit européen*, 32, 1–24.

Bourgeois J. (1995), 'The EC in the WTO and Advisory opinion 1/94: and Echternach Procession', *Common Market Law Review*, 32, 763–87.

Bradley, Kieran St. Clair (1992), 'Comitology and the Law: through a Glass, Darkly', *Common Market Law Review*, 29, 693–721.

Bradley, Kieran St Clair (1997), 'The European Parliament and Comitology: on the Road to Nowhere?', *European Law Journal*, 3:3, 230–54.

Bradley, Kieran St Clair (1999), 'The GMO Committee on Transgenic Maize: Alien Corn, or the Transgenic Procedural Maze', in M.P.C.M. Van Schendelen (ed.), *EU Committees as Influential Policymakers*, London, Ashgate, pp. 207–23.

Buitendijk, G., and Van Schendelen, M.P.C.M (1995), 'Brussels Advisory Committees: A Channel for Influence?', *European Law Review*, 20:1, 37–56.

Bulmer, S. (1993), 'The Governance of the European Union: A New Institutionalist Approach', *Journal of Public Policy*, 13:4, 351–80.

Bulmer, S. (1998), 'The Territorial Dimension', in G. Smith, W.E. Paterson and P.H. Merkl (eds), *Developments in West German Politics*, London, Macmillan.

Bundesministerium für Raumordnung, Bauwesen und Städtebau (1995), *Principles for a European Spatial Development Policy*, Bonn: Bundesministerium für Raumordnung, Bauwesen und Städtebau.

Bundesministerium für Raumordnung, Bauwesen und Städtebau (no date) *Europäische Raumentwicklung: Beratungsergebnisse des informellen Raumordnungsministerrates in Leipzig am 21. und 22. September 1994*, Bonn: Bundesministerium für Raumordnung, Bauwesen und Städtebau.

Bundesverfassungsgericht (1993), 'Urteil über die Verfassungsbeschwerden gegen den Vertrag von Maastricht, Judgement of October 12 1993', in Andrew Oppenheimer (ed.), *The Relationship between European Community Law and National Law: The Cases*, Cambridge, Bundesverfassungsgericht, p. 190.

Burley, Anne-Marie and Mattli, Walter (1993), 'Europe Before the Court: A Political Theory of Legal Integration', *International Organisation*, 47:1, 41–76.

Burnham, J., and Maor, M. (1995), 'Converging Administrative Systems: Recruitment and Training in EU Member States', *Journal of European Public Policy*, 2:2, 185–204.

Cameron, D.R. (1995), 'Trans-national Relations and the Development of European Economic and Monetary Union', in T. Risse-Kappen (ed.), *Bringing Trans-national Relations Back In: Non-State Actors, Domestic Structures and International Institutions*, Cambridge, Cambridge University Press.

Cameron, Fraser (1998), 'Building a Common Foreign Policy: Do Institutions Matter?', in John Peterson and Helen Sjursen (eds), *A Common Foreign Policy for Europe?*, London, Routledge.

Caporaso, James (1996), 'The European Union and Forms of State: Westphalian, Regulatory or Post-Modern?', *Journal of Common Market Studies* 1, 29–52.

Carey, J. and Shugart, M. (1998), *Executive Decree Authority*, Cambridge, Cambridge University Press.

Cerny, Philip G. (1996), 'What Next for the State? ', in E. Kofman and G. Young (eds), *Globalisation: Theory and Practice*, London, Pinter Publishers.

Christiansen, T. (1996), 'Second Thoughts on Europe's Third Level: The European Union's Committee of the Regions', *Publius Journal of Federalism*, 26:1, 93–116.

Christiansen, T. (1997), 'Tensions of European Governance: Politicised Bureaucracy and Multiple Accountability in the European Commission', *Journal of European Public Policy*, 4:1, 73–90.

Commission of the European Communities (1990), *Communication from the Commission to the European Parliament pursuant to Article 149(2b) of the EEC Treaty: Common Position of the Council on a proposal for a Council Directive on nutrition labelling of foodstuffs*, SEC (90) 469 final – SYN 155, 8 March 1990, p. 4. EP Document, C3–74/90.

Commission of the European Communities (1991), 'Conferment of Implementing Powers on the Commission', *Communication from the Commission to the Council,* Brussels, 10 January 1991 – SEC(90)2589 final.

Commission of the European Communities (1991), *Europe 2000: Outlook for the Development of the Community's Territory,* Luxembourg: Office for Official Publications of the European Communities.

Commission of the European Communities (1991a), 'Common Commercial Policy, Draft Text', *Bulletin of the European Communities,* 2, 89–116.

Commission of the European Communities (1994), *Europe 2000+: Co-operation for European Territorial Development,* Luxembourg: Office for the Official Publications of the European Communities.

Commission of the European Communities (1996), 'Commission Opinion on Reinforcing Political Union and Preparing for Enlargement', Luxembourg, Office for Official Publications.

Commission of the European Communities (1997), 'Commission Decision of 23 January 1997 concerning the combined modification for insecticidal properties conferred by the Bt-endotoxin gene and increased tolerance to the herbicide glufosinate ammonium pursuant to Council Decision 90/220/EEC', OJ L 31, 1/2/97, p. 69.

Committee of Governors of Central Banks of Member States of the European Economic Community (CGCB) (1992), *Annual Report (July 1990–December 1991),* April.

Committee of Governors of Central Banks of Member States of the European Economic Community (CGCB) (1993), *Annual Report 1992,* ISSN 1021–3384.

Corbett, R. (1994), *Note for the Attention of the Members of the PES Group, Re: Comitology,* PE/GS/239/94, Brussels, Group of the Party of European Socialists.

Corbett, R., Jacobs, F. and Shackleton, M. (1995), *The European Parliament,* 3rd edn, London, Catermill.

Council of Europe (1985), *European Regional/Spatial Planning Charter,* Schriftenreihe Landes- und Stadtentwicklungsforschung des Landes Nordrhein-Westfalen, Sonderveröffentlichungen, Band 0.028, Dortmund: Institut für Landes- und Stadtentwicklungsforschung des Landes Nordrhein-Westfalen (ILS).

Council of the European Communities (1987a), 'Council Decision 87/373/EEC of 13 July 1987 laying down the procedures for the exercise of implementing powers conferred on the Commission', OJ L 197, 18/07/87, p. 33.

Council of the European Communities (1987b), 'Explanatory Memorandum', *Common Position adopted by the Council on 18/12/87 with a view to the adoption of a Council Directive on the inspection and verification of the organisational processes and conditions under which laboratory studies are planned, performed, recorded and reported for the non-clinical testing of chemicals (Good Laboratory Practice),* p. 3, EP Document C2–273/87.

Council of the European Communities (1989a), 'Second Council Directive 89/646/EEC of 15 December 1989 on the co-ordination of laws, regulations and administrative provisions relating to the taking up and pursuit of the business of credit institutions and amending Directive 77/780/EEC', OJ L 386, 30/12/89, p. 1.

Council of the European Communities (1989b), 'Council Directive 89/684/EEC of 21 December 1989 on vocational training for certain drivers of vehicles carrying dangerous goods by road', OJ L 398, 30/12/89, p. 33.

Council of the European Communities (1990a), 'Council Decision 90/220/EEC of 23 April 1990 on the deliberate release into the environment of genetically modified organisms', OJ L 117, 6/5/90, p. 15.

Council of the European Communities (1990b), 'The Council's Reasons', *Common Position adopted by the Council on 20 June 1990 with a view to adopting a Council Regulation on Community transit*, European Parliament Document C3–200/90, p. 8.

Council of the European Communities (1990c), 'Council Directive 90/377/EEC of 29 June 1990 concerning a community procedure to improve the transparency of gas and electricity prices charged to industrial end-users', OJ L 185, 17/7/90, p. 16.

Council of the European Communities (1990d), 'Council Directive 90/496/EEC of 24 September 1990 on nutrition labelling for foodstuffs', OJ L 276, 6/10/90, p. 40.

Council of the European Communities (1990e), 'The Council's Reasons', Common Position adopted by the Council on 20 December 1990 with a view to adopting a Council Regulation on the single administrative document, European Parliament Document C3–0009/91, p. 4.

Council of the European Communities (1991a), 'Council Regulation EEC/2092/91 of 24 June 1991 on organic production of agricultural products and indications referring thereto on agricultural products and foodstuffs', OJ L 198, 22/7/91, p. 1.

Council of the European Communities (1991b), 'Council Decision 91/394/EEC of 8 July 1991 adopting a specific research and technological development programme in the field of information technologies (1990 to 1994)', OJ L 218, 06/08/91, p. 22.

Council of the European Communities (1991c), 'Council Directive 91/504/EEC of 9 September 1991 adopting a specific programme of research and technological development and demonstration programme for the EEC in the field of agriculture and agro-industry including fisheries', OJ L 265, 21/9/91, p. 33.

Council of the European Communities (1991d), 'Council Directive 91/495/EEC of 27 November 1991 concerning public health and animal health problems affecting the production and placing on the market of rabbit meat and farmed game meat', OJ L 268, 24/9/91, p. 41.

Council of the European Communities (1991e), 'Council Directive 91/676/EEC of 12 December 1991 concerning the protection of waters against pollution caused by nitrates from agricultural sources', OJ L 375, 31/12/91, p. 1.

Council of the European Communities (1992a), 'Council Directive 92/50/EEC of 18 June 1992 relating to the co-ordination of procedures for the award of public service contracts', OJ L 209, 24/7/92, p. 1.

Council of the European Communities (1992b), 'Council Regulation 2082/92/EEC of 14 July 1992 on certificates of specific character for agricultural products and foodstuffs', OJ L 208, 24/7/92, p. 9.

Council of the European Communities (1993a), 'Council Regulation EEC/315/93 of 8 February 1993 laying down community procedures for contaminants in food', OJ L 37, 13/2/93, p. 1.

Council of the European Communities (1993b), 'Council Decision 93/246/EEC of 29 April 1993 adopting the second phase of the trans-European co-operation scheme for higher education (TEMPUS II) (1994–1996)', OJ L 112, 6/3/93, p. 34.

Council of the European Communities (1993c), 'Council Directive 93/40/EEC of 14 June 1993 amending directives 81/851/EEC and 81/852/EEC on the approximation of the laws of the member states relating to veterinary medicinal products', OJ L 214, 24/8/93, p. 31.

Council of the European Communities (1993d), 'Council Regulation 1836/93/EEC of 29 June 1993 allowing voluntary participation by companies in the industrial sector in a community eco-management and audit scheme', OJ L 168, 10/7/93, p. 1.

Council of the European Communities (1993e), 'Council Directive 93/65/EC 19 July on the definition and use of comparable technical specifications for the procurement of air-traffic management equipment and systems', OJ L 187, 29/7/93, p. 52.

Council of the European Communities (1993f), 'Council Directive 93/119/EC 22 December 1993 on the protection of animals at the time of slaughter or killing', OJ L 340, 31/12/93, p. 21.

Council of the European Communities (1994a), 'Council Regulation EC/517/94 of 7 March 1994 on common rules for imports of textile products from certain third countries not covered by bilateral agreements, protocols or other arrangements, or by other specific community import rules', OJ L 67, 10/3/94, p. 1.

Council of the European Communities (1994b), 'Council Regulation 1734/94/EEC of 11 July 1994 on financial and technical co-operation with the occupied territories', OJ L 182, 16/7/94, p. 4.

Dahl, R.A. (1989), *Democracy and Its Critics,* New Haven and London, Yale University Press.

Delbrück, Jost (1987), 'Internationale und Nationale Verwaltung-Inhaltliche und institutionelle Aspekte', in Kurt G.A. Jeserich *et al.* (eds), Deutsche Verwaltungsgeschichte, Vol. 5, Stuttgart, Deutsche Verlags-Austalt, pp. 386–403.

Demmke, C. (1997), 'National Officials and their Role in the Executive Process: "Comitology" and European Environmental Policy', in C. Demmke (ed.), *Managing European Environmental Policy: the Role of the Member States in the Policy Process,* Maastricht, EIPA, pp. 23–40.

De Schoutheete, Philippe (1986), *La Cooperation politique Européene,* 2nd edn, Editions Labor.

De Vries, J. and Van den Broeck, J. (1997), 'Benelux: A Microcosm of Planning Cultures', in W. Zonneveld and A. Faludi (eds), *Built Environment; Theme: Vanishing Borders: The Second Benelux Structural Outline,* 23:1, 58–69.

Docksey, C. and Williams, K. (1994), 'The Commission and the Execution of Community Policy', in G. Edwards and D. Spence (eds), *The European Commission,* London, Lagman, pp. 117–45.

Dogan, Rhys (1997), 'Comitology: Little Procedures with Big Implications', *West European Politics,* 20:3, 31–60.

Doucet, Ph. (1997), 'Can European Spatial Planning Learn from the Benelux', in W. Zonneveld and A. Faludi (eds), *Built Environment; Theme: Vanishing Borders: The Second Benelux Structural Outline,* 23:1, 75–81.

Drake, H., (1995) 'Political Leadership and European Integration: The Case of Jacques Delors', *West European Politics,* 18:1, 140–60.

Dryzek, J.S. (1996) *Democracy in Capitalist Times: Ideals, Limits and Struggles,* New York and Oxford, Oxford University Press.

Economic and Social Committee (1980), *Community Advisory Committees for the Representation of Socio-Economic Interests,* Wetmead, Farnborough, Saxon House.

Economist (1998), 'Federalism by Stealth' 24 Oct., p. 40.

Eeckhout P. (1994), 'The External Dimension of the Community's Commercial Policy', in M. Maresceau (ed.), *The European Community's Commercial Policy after 1992: The Legal Dimension,* Dordrecht, Martinus Nijhoff Publishers, pp. 79–104.

ENDS (1996–97) Various reports, as cited, London, Environmental Data Services.

Epstein, D. and O'Halloran, S. (1999), *Delegating Powers: A Transaction Cost Politics*

Approach to Policy Making Under Separate Powers, Cambridge, Cambridge University Press.

European Commission (1991), 'Common Commercial Policy, Draft Text', *Bulletin of the European Communities*, 2–1991, pp. 89–116   .

European Commission, (1996), 'Commission Opinion on Reinforcing Political Union and Preparing for Enlargement', Brussels, Commission.

European Commission (1997a), *European Spatial Development Perspective: First Official Draft*, presented at the Informal Meeting of Ministers Responsible for Spatial Planning of the Member States of the European Union, Noordwijk, 9–10 June 1997, Luxembourg, Office for Official Publications of the European Communities.

European Commission (1997b), *The EU Compendium of Spatial Planning Systems and Policies*, Regional development studies 28, Luxembourg, Office for Official Publications of the European Communities.

European Court of Justice (1994), 'Opinion 1/94', 15 November 1994, Press Release of the Court of Justice, Luxembourg.

European Court of Justice (1994), Rs. 1/94 (World Trade Organisation) Summary in *Proceedings of the Court of Justice and the Court of First Instance of the European Communities*, 30, pp. 7–14.

European Environment Bureau (1996), *Review of the 5th Action Programme*, Brussels, EEB.

European Parliament (1962), 'Resolution on the powers of implementation of the Commission', OJ 17/1/62, Rapporteur: Mr Stobel.

European Parliament (1984), *Report drawn up on behalf of the Legal Affairs Committee on Committees for the Adaptation of Directives to Technical and Scientific Progress*, Document No. 1–205/84 of 5 May 1984, Rapporteur: Mr. Alan R. Tyrrell.

European Parliament (1986), 'Resolution on the proposal for a Regulation laying down the procedures for the exercises of implementing powers conferred on the Commission', OJ C 297, 24/11/86, p. 94.

European Parliament (1990), 'Resolution on nutrition labelling for foodstuffs', OJ C 175, 16/07/90, p. 76.

European Parliament (1991a), 'Resolution on the executive powers of the Commission (comitology) and the role of the Commission in the Community's external relations', OJ C 19, 28/01/91, p. 274.

European Parliament (1991b), 'Resolution adopting a specific research and technological development programme in the filed of communications technology', OJ C 158, 17/06/91, p. 59.

European Parliament (1994), *Prospects for a Common Foreign and Security Policy: Preliminary Review*, Working Papers, W7, Directorate General for Research.

European Parliament (1996), 'Resolution on bio-safety and food security', OJ C 362, 2/12/96, p. 277.

European Parliament (1997), 'Resolution on genetically modified maize', OJ C 132, 27/4/97, p. 29.

Fabien, D. (1995), 'Comitologie: quel controle democratique sur les pouvoirs de regulation de la Commission?', masters thesis, Bruges, College of Europe.

Falke, Josef (1996), 'Comitology and Other Committees: A Preliminary Empirical Assesment', in R.H. Pedler and G.F. Schaefer (eds), *Shaping European Law and Policy: The Role of Committees and Comitology in the Political Process*, Maastricht, EIPA, pp. 117–65.

Faludi, A. (1996), 'Framing with Images', *Environment and Planning B: Planning and design*, Vol. 23, pp. 93–108.

Faludi, A. (1997), 'European Spatial Development Policy in 'Maastricht II', *European Planning Studies*, 5:4, 535–43.

Faludi, A. (1998), 'From Planning Theory Mark 1 to Planning Theory Mark 3', *Environment and Planning B: Planning and Design*, 25th Anniversary Issue, pp. 110–17.

Faludi, A. and Zonneveld, W. (1997), 'Introduction', in A. Faludi and W. Zonneveld (eds), *Built Environment: Special Issue: Shaping Europe: The European Spatial Development Perspective*, 23:4, 256–66.

Financial Times (1999) 'Heads in the Euro-Sand', Saturday 6 February, editorial.

Fit, J. and Kragt, R. (1994), 'The Long Road to European Spatial Planning: A Matter of Patience and Mission', *Tijdschrift voor economische en sociale geografie (TESG)*, 85:5, 461–5.

Flynn, B. (1998), 'Review Section: EU Environmental Policy at a Crossroads? Reconsidering Some Paradoxes in the Evolution of Policy Content', *Journal of European Public Policy*, 5:4, 691–6.

Frowein, J.A. (1986), 'Integration and the Federal Experience in Germany and Switzerland', in M. Cappelletti, M. Seccombe and J. Weiler (eds), *Integration through Law: European and the American Federal Experience, Volume 1: Methods, Tools and Institutions, Book 1: A Political Legal and Economic Overview*, Berlin, De Gruyter.

Garrett, G. (1995), 'From the Luxembourg Compromise to Co-decision: Decision Making in the European Union', *Electoral Studies*, 14:3, 289–308.

Goldstein, Judith (1989), 'The Impact of Ideas on Trade Policy: The Origins of U.S. Agricultural and Manufacturing Policies', *International Organisation*, 43:1, 31–71.

Goldstein, Judith (1993), *Ideas, Interests and American Trade Policy*, Ithaca and London, Cornell University Press.

Goldstein, Judith and Keohane, Robert O. (eds) (1993), *Ideas and Foreign Policy: Beliefs, Institutions and Political Change*, Ithaca and London, Cornell University Press.

Gourevitch, Peter (1986), *Politics in Hard Times: Comparative Responses to International Economic Crises*, Ithaca, Cornell University Press.

Gourevitch, Peter (1989a), 'Keynesian Politics: The Political Sources of Economic Policy Choices', in P. Hall (ed.), *The Political Power of Economic Ideas: Keynesianism across Nations*, Princeton, Princeton University Press.

Gourevitch, Peter (1989b), 'The Politics of Economic Policy Choice in the Post-War Era', in P. Guerrieri and P. Padoan (eds), *The Political Economy of European Integration*, London: Harvester Wheatsheaf, pp. 264–83.

Grams, Hartmut A. (1995), 'Komitologie im Gesetzgebungsprozeß der Europäischen Union', *Kritische Vierteljahresschrift für Gesetzgebung und Rechtswissenschaft*, Vol. 78, pp. 112–31.

Grieco, Joseph M. (1988), 'Anarchy and the Limits of Co-operation: A Realist Critique of the Newest Liberal Institutionalism', *International Organisation*, 42:3, 485–507.

Haas, Ernst B. (1968), *The Uniting of Europe: Political, Social and Economic Forces, 1950–1957*, Stanford, Stanford University Press.

Haas, Peter (1992), 'Introduction: Epistemic Communities and International Policy Co-ordination', *International Organisation*, 46:1, 1–35.

Haibach, G. (1997), 'Comitology: A Comparative Analysis of the Separation and Delegation of Legislative Powers', *Maastricht Journal of Comparative and European Law*, 4, 373–85.

Hall, Peter A. (1986), *Governing the Economy: The Politics of State Intervention in Britain and France*, New York, Oxford University Press.

Hall, Peter A. (ed.) (1989), *The Political Power of Economic Ideas: Keynesianism across Nations*, Princeton, Princeton University Press.

Hancher, Leigh and Moran, Michael (eds) (1989), *Capitalism, Culture and Economic Regulation*, Oxford, Clarendon Press.

Hanny, Birgit and Wessels, Wolfgang (1999), 'The Monetary Committee of the European Communities: A Significant Though Not Typical Case', in R. Van Schendelen (ed.), *Do EU Committees Matter? A Case Study Book*, Dartmouth/Aldershot: Robin Pedler.

Hayes, J.P. (1993), *Making Trade Policy in the European Community*, London, Macmillan.

Hayes-Renshaw, Fiona and Wallace, Helen (1996), *The Council of Ministers*, London, Macmillan.

Hayward, J. (1996), 'Has European Unification by Stealth a Future?' in J. Hayward (ed.) *Elitism, Populism, and European Politics*, Oxford, Clarendon Press, pp. 252–57.

Hesse, J.J. (1987), 'The Federal Republic of Germany: From Co-operative Federalism to Joint Policy-Making', *West European Politics*, 10:4, 70–87.

Hix, Simon (1994), 'The Study of the European Community: The Challenge to Comparative Politics', *West European Politics*, 17:1, 1–30.

Hooghe, L. and Marks, G. (1996), 'Europe with the Regions: Channels of Regional Representation in the European Union', *Publius Journal of Federalism*, 26:1, 73–92.

Horn, M. (1995), *The Political Economy of Public Administration: Institutional Choice in the Public Sector*, Cambridge, Cambridge University Press.

Houvenaghel, S. (1998), 'Recente ontwikkelingwn in verband met EROP en de conclusies van de ministerconferentie in Glasgow', *Planologisch Nieuws*, 18, 175–7.

Ikenberry, G. John (1988), 'Conclusion: An Institutional Approach to American Foreign Economic Policy', *International Organisation*, 42:1, 219–43.

Ikenberry, G. John, Lake, David A. and Mastandundo, Michael (1988), 'Introduction: Approaches to Explaining American Foreign Economic Policy', *International Organisation*, 42:1, 1–14.

Institute for European Affairs (1995), *The 1996 Intergovernmental Conference: Issues, Options, Implications*, Dublin, Institute for European Affairs, pp. 115–21.

Italianer, A. (1993), 'Mastering Maastricht: EMU Issues and How They Were Settled', in K. Greschmann (ed.), *Economic and Monetary Union: Implications for National Policy-makers*, Maastricht, European Institute of Public Administration, pp. 51–115.

Jachtenfuchs, Markus and Kohler-Koch, Beate (1996), 'Regieren im dynamischen Mehrebenensystem', in M. Jachtenfuchs and B. Kohler-Koch (eds), *Europäische Integration*, Opladen, Leske und Budrich, pp. 15–44.

Jacobsen, John Kurt (1995), 'Much Ado about Ideas: The Cognitive Factor in Economic Policy', *World Politics*, 47, 283–310.

Janis, I.L. (1982) *Groupthink*, 2nd edn, Boston, Houghton Mifflin.

Joerges, C. and Neyer, J. (1997a), 'From Intergovernmental Bargaining to Deliberative Political Processes: The Constitutionalisation of Comitology', *European Law Journal*, 3:3, 273–99.

Joerges, C. and Neyer, J. (1997b), 'Transforming Strategic Interaction into Deliberative Problem-Solving: European Comitology in the Foodstuffs Sector', *Journal of Euro-*

pean Public Policy, 4:4, 609–25.

Johnson, M. (1998), *The European Community and the Article 113 Committee*, London, Royal Institute of International Affairs.

Kees, A. (1987), 'The Monetary Committee of the European Community', *Kredit und Kapital*, 20:2, 258–67.

Kees, A. (1994), 'The Monetary Committee as a Promoter of European Integration', in A. Bakker, H. Boot, O. Sleipjen and W. Vanthoor (eds), *Monetary Stability through International Co-operation*, Boston, Dordrecht and London, Kluwer, pp. 127–45.

Kiewiet, D.R. and McCubbins, M.D. (1991), *The Logic of Delegation: Congressional Parties and the Appropriations Process*, Chicago, University of Chicago Press.

Kincaid, J. (1995), 'The Advisory Commission on Intergovernmental Affairs: Background and Performance', in R. Dehousse and T. Christiansen, Florence, European University Institute.

King, Sam and Lee, Sonya (1997) 'Austria Gives Brussels Food for Thought', *The European*, 18–24 September, p. 22.

Kirchner, E. and Schwaiger, K. (1981), *The Role of Interest Groups in the European Community*, Aldershot, Gower.

Klerkx, E. (1995), *Plannen voor Europa: Een historische analyse van de Nederlandse pleidooien voor Europees ruimtelijk beleid*; stagerapport, De blik gericht op Brussel: Rapport 2/Working Papers AME, Amsterdam, Amsterdam study centre for the Metropolitan Environment (AME).

Knaap, Peter van der (1996), 'Government by Committee: Legal Typology, Quantitative Assessment and Institutional Repercussions of Committees in the European Union', in R.H. Pedler and G.F. Schaefer (eds.), *Shaping European Law and Policy: The Role of Committees and Comitology in the Political Process*, Maastricht, European Institute of Public Administration (EIPA), pp. 83–116.

Kohler-Koch, Beate (1996), 'Catching up with Change: the Transformation of Governance in the European Union', *Journal of European Public Policy*, 3, 359–80, 371.

Kreher, A. (1997), 'Agencies in the European Community: A Step towards Administrative Integration in Europe?', *Journal of European Public Policy*, 4:2 225–450.

Kruse, D.C. (1980), *Monetary Integration in Western Europe: EMU, EMS and Beyond*, London and Boston, Butterworth.

Kuklinski, A. (1997), 'The New European Space (N.E.S.) – Experiences and Prospects: A Paper for Discussion', in A. Kuklinski (ed.), *European Space, Baltic Space, Polish Space – Part One (European 2010 Series)*, European Institute for Regional and Local Development, University of Warsaw, Warsaw, pp. 312–30.

Kunzmann, K.R. (1996), 'Euro-megalopolis or Themepark Europe? Scenarios for European Spatial Development', *International Planning Studies*, 1:2, 143–63.

Laver, M.J., Gallagher, M., Marsh, M., Singh, R. and Tonra, B. (1995), *Electing the President of the European Commission*, Trinity Blue Papers in Public Policy: 1, Dublin, Trinity College.

Lenaerts, K. (1991), 'Some Reflections on the Separation of Powers in the European Community', *Common Market Law Review*, 28:1, 11–35.

Ludlow, Peter (1991), 'The European Commission', in R.O. Keohane and S. Hoffman (eds), *The New European Community: Decisionmaking and Institutional Change*, Oxford, Westview Press, pp. 85–132.

MacCormick, N. (1993), 'Beyond the Sovereign State', *The Modern Law Review*, 56:1, 1–18.

MacLeod, I., Hendry, I.D. and Hyett, S. (1996), *The External Relations of the European Community*, Oxford, Clarendon Press.

Majone, G. (1993), 'The European Community: Between Social Policy and Social Regulation', *Journal of Common Market Studies*, 31:2, 153–70.

Majone, G. (1994), 'The Rise of the Regulatory State in Europe', *West European Politics*, 17:3, 77–102.

Majone, G. (1996), *Regulating Europe*, London, Routledge.

Marcussen, Martin (1997), 'The Role of "Ideas" in Dutch, Danish and Swedish Economic Policy in the 1980s and the Beginning of the 1990s', in P. Minkkinenen and H. Patomaki (eds), *The Politics of Economic and Monetary Union*, Boston, Dordrecht and London, Kluwer, pp. 75–103.

Maresceau M., (1994), 'The Concept "Common Commercial Policy" and the Difficult Road to Maastricht', in M. Maresceau (ed.), *The European Community's Commercial Policy after 1992: The Legal Dimension*, Dordrecht, Martinus Nijhoff Publishers, pp. 3–19.

Marks, Gary *et al.* (1996), 'European Integration from the 1980s: State-Centric v. Multilevel Governance', *Journal of Common Market Studies*, 34:3, 341–79.

Martin, D. and Ten Velden, H. (1997), 'Extra Options as Optional Extras: What Ideas are behind the ESDP?', *Built Environment: Special Issue: Shaping Europe: The European Spatial Development Perspective*, 23:4, 267–80.

Maurer, Andreas (1999), *What Next for the European Parliament?*, London, Kogan Page.

Maurer, Andreas (1999a), (Co-Governing after Maastricht: The European Parliament's Institutional Performance 1994–99, Working document (Political Series POLI 104), Luxembourg. (Also at http://www.europarl.eu.int/dg4/wkdocs/poli/en/default.htm(#104).

Mayntz, Renate (1982), 'Problemverarbeitung durch das politisch-administrative System: Zum Stand der Forschung', in J.J. Hesse (ed.), *Politikwissenschaft und Verwaltungswissenschaft*, PVS-Sonderheft 13, Opladen, pp. 75ff.

Mazey, Sonia and Richardson, Jeremy (1993), *Lobbying in the European Community*, Oxford, Oxford University Press.

McCarthy, R. (1997), The Committee of the Regions: Advisory Body's Tortuous Path to Influence', *Journal of European Public Policy*, 4:3, 439–54.

McCubbins, M.D. (1985), 'The Legislative Design of Regulatory Structure', *American Journal of Political Science*, 2:4, 721–48.

McCubbins, M.D. and Schwartz, T. (1984), 'Congressional Oversight Overlooked: Police Patrols versus Fire Alarms', *American Journal of Political Science*, 28:1, 165–79.

McCubbins, M.D., Noll, R. and Weingast, B. (1989), 'Structure and Process, Politics and Policy: Administrative Arrangements and the Political Control of Agencies', *Virginia Law Review*, 75:2, 431–82.

McGowan, Francis and Wallace, Helen (1996), 'Towards a European Regulatory State', *Journal of European Public Policy*, 3:4, 560–76.

McNamara, K.R. (1998), *The Currency of Ideas: Monetary Politics in the European Union*, Ithaca, Cornell University Press.

Meny, Yves, Muller, Pierre and Quermonne, Jean-Louis (1996), *Adjusting to Europe: The Impact of the European Union on National Institutions and Policies*, London, Routledge.

Miller, G. (1995), 'Post-Maastricht Legislative Procedures: Is the Council "Institutionally Challenged"?', paper prepared for the Fourth Biennial International ECSA Conference, Charleston, SC.

Minister of Housing, Physical Planning and the Environment (1991), *Urban Networks in Europe: Third Meeting of the Ministers of the EC Member States Responsible for Physical Planning and Regional Policy*, The Hague, National Physical Planning Agency.

Mitrany, David (1943), *A Working Peace System*, London, Royal Institute of International Affairs.

Moe, T. (1989), 'The Politics of Bureaucratic Structure', in J. Chubb and P. Peterson (eds), *Can Government Govern?*, Washington, DC, The Brookings Institution.

Monetary Committee of the European Communities (1959), *Premiere Rapport d'Activité de la Comité Monetaire*, Brussels, CEE.

Monetary Committee of the European Communities (1960), *Deuxième Rapport d'Activité de la Comité Monétaire*, Brussels, CEE.

Monetary Committee of the European Communities (1988), *Twenty-ninth Activity Report*, Luxembourg Office for the Official Publication of the EEC.

Monetary Committee of the European Communities (1994), 'Notes for the Chairman's Address on 26 January 1994 to the European Parliament's Subcommittee on Monetary Affairs', Brussels.

Monetary Committee of the European Communities (1995), *Compendium of Community Monetary Texts*, 1994 Luxembourg, Office for the Official Publications of the European Communities.

Monnet, J. (1978) *Memoirs*, trans. R. Mayne, with a Foreword by Rt Hon. Roy Jenkins, London, Collins.

Morgan, R. (1991), *The Consultative Function of the Economic and Social Committee of the European Community*, EUI Working Paper EPU, No. 91/11, Florence, European University Institute.

Müller, Wolfgang C. and Wright, Vincent (eds) (1994), 'Special Issue on the State in Western Europe: Retreat or Redefinition?' *West European Politics*, 17:3.

Murphy, A. (1990), *The European Community and the International Trading System: The European Community and the Uruguay Round*, Brussels, Centre for European Policy Studies.

Murphy, A. (1996a) 'The European Union and the Visegrad States: Governance, Order and Change', Ph.D. thesis, University College, Dublin.

Murphy A. (1996b), 'Regionalism and Multilateralism: Keeping up with the European Union', in T. Geiger and D. Kennedy (eds), *Regional Trade Blocs, Multilateralism and the GATT*, London, Cassell, pp. 79–94.

Neyer, Jürgen (1997), 'Administrative Supranationalität in der Verwaltung des Binnenmarktes: Zur Legitimität der Komitologie', *Integration*, Vol. 1, pp. 24–37.

Norton, P. (ed.) (1990), *Legislatures*, Oxford, Oxford University Press.

Nugent, N. (1999), *The Government and Politics of the European Union*, 4th edn, Basingstoke, Macmillan.

Nuttall S. (1992), *European Political Co-operation*, Oxford, Clarendon.

Ogul, M.S. (1997), 'Congressional Oversight: Structures and Incentives', in L.C. Dodd and B.I. Oppenheimer (eds), *Congress Reconsidered*, New York, Praeger.

Olsen, D. and Mezey, M.L. (eds) (1991), *Parliaments in the Policy Process: The Dilemmas of Economic Policy*, Cambridge, Cambridge University Press.

Page, E. and Wouters, L. (1994), 'Bureaucratic Politics and Political Leadership in Brussels', *Public Administration*, 72:3, 445–59.

Patterson G. (1983), 'The European Community as a Threat to the System', in W. Cline (ed.), *Trade Policy in the 1980s*, Washington DC, Institute for International Economics.

Pedler, Robin H. and Schaefer, Guenther F. (eds) (1996), *Shaping European Law and Policy: The Role of Committees and Comitology in the Political Process*, Maastricht, European Institute of Public Administration.

Pelkmans, J. and Murphy, A. (1992), 'Strategies for the Uruguay Round', in *Europe and North America in the 1990s*, Brussels, Centre for European Studies (CEPS), pp. 11–46.

Pentland, C. (1973), *International Theory and European Integration*, London, Faber and Faber.

Pollack, M.A. (1995), 'Creeping Competence: The Expanding Agenda of the European Community', *Journal of Public Policy*, 14:2, 95–145.

Pollack, M.A. (1997), 'Delegation, Agency and Agenda Setting in the European Community', *International Organisation*, 51:1, 99–134.

Popper, K.R. (1972), *Conjectures and Refutations*, 4th edn, London, Routledge.

Presidenza Consiglio dei Ministri, Dipartimento per il Coordinamento delle Politiche Comunitarie (1990), *Objectives and agenda for the Meeting of EEC Ministers, on new problems of territorial planning and balanced regional development connected with the implementation of the Single Market*, 23–4 November, Turin, Castello di Rivoli.

Putnam, R.D. (1988), 'Diplomacy and Domestic Politics: The Logic of Two-level Games', *International Organisation*, 42:3, 427–61.

Radaelli, Claudio, M. (1999), *Technology in the European Union*, London, Longman.

Rein, M. and Schön, D. (1986), 'Frame-reflective Policy Discourse', *Beleidsanalyse*, 15:4, 4–18.

Riker, W.H. (1964), *Federalism: Origin, Operation, Significance*, Boston and Toronto: Little Brown and Co.

Risse-Kappen, T. (1996), 'Exploring the Nature of the Beast: International Relations Theory and Comparative Policy Analysis Meets the European Union', *Journal of Common Market Studies*, 34:1, 53–80.

Rometsch, Dietrich and Wessels, Wolfgang (1996) (eds), *The European Union and Member States: Towards Institutional Fusion? Conclusion*, Manchester, Manchester University Press, pp. 328–65.

Rosenthal, G.G. (1975), *The Men Behind the Decisions: Cases in European Policy-Making*, Lexington, Mass., Toronto and London, Lexington Books, D.C. Heath.

Royal Commission on Environmental Pollution (1998), *Twenty-First Report: Setting Environmental Standards*, London, The Stationery Office, Cm 4053.

Rusca, R. (1998), 'The Development of a European Spatial Planning Policy: A Learning-by-Doing Experience in the Framework of Intergovernmental Co-operation', in C. Bengs and K. Böhme (eds), *The Progress of European Spatial Planning* (Nordregio report 1), Nordregio, Stockholm, pp. 35–47.

Sbragia, A. (1996), 'Environmental Policy', in H. Wallace and W. Wallace (eds), *Policy-making in the European Union*, Oxford, Oxford University Press.

Schaefer, Günther F. (1996), 'Committees in the EC Policy Process: A First step Towards Developing a Conceptual Framework', in R.H. Pedler and G.F. Schaefer (eds), *Shaping European Law and Policy: The Role of Committees and Comitology in the Political Process*, Maastricht, European Institute of Public Administration, pp. 3–38.

Scharpf, F.W. (1988), 'The Joint-Decision Trap: Lessons from German Federalism and European Integration', *Public Administration*, 66, 239–78.

Scharpf, F.W. (1991), 'Die Handlungsfähigkeit des Staates am Ende des zwanzigsten Jahrhunderts', *Politische Vierteljahresschrift*, 4, 621–34.

Scharpf, F.W. (1996), 'Negative and Positive Integration in the Political Economy of European Welfare States', in G. Marks *et al.* (eds), *Governance in the European Union*, London, Thousand Oaks, New Delhi, Sage Publications, pp. 15–39.

Schmidt, Vivien A. (1996), 'Loosening the Ties that Bind: The Impact of European Integration on French Government and its Relationship to Business', *Journal of Common Market Studies*, 34:2, 223–54.

Schmitter, P. (1992), 'Representation and the Future Euro-Polity', *Staatswissenschaften und Staatspraxis*, 2:3, 379–405.

Schmitter, P. (1996), 'Imagining the Future of the Euro-Polity with the Help of New Concepts', in G. Marks, F.W. Scharpf, P.C. Schmitter and W. Streeck (eds), *Governance in the European Union*, London, Sage, p. 132.

Schmitter, P. (1996), 'If the Nation-State Were to Wither Away in Europe What Might Replace it?' in S. Gustavsson and L. Lewin (eds), *The Future of the Nation-State*, Stockholm, Nereuins and Santerus, pp. 211–44.

Schneider, Heinrich (1994), 'Föderale Verfassungspolitik für eine Europäisch Union', in H. Schneider and W. Wessels (eds), *Föderale Union: Europas Zukunft? Analysen, Kontroversen, Perspektiven*, München, Beck, pp. 21–50.

Siedentopf, Heinrich and Ziller, Jacques (eds) (1988), *Making European Policies Work: The Implementation of Community Legislation*, London, Sage.

Smith, A. and Rollo, J. (1993), 'The political economy of Eastern European Trade with the European Community: Why So Sensitive?', *Economic Policy*, 16, 140–81.

Spinelli, Altiero (1966), *The Eurocrats, Conflict and Crisis in the European Community*, Baltimore, Johns Hopkins University Press.

Steunenberg, Bernard, Koboldt, Christian and Schmidtchen, Dieter, (1996), 'Beyond Comitology: A Comparative Analysis of Implementation Procedures with Parliamentary Involvement', *Network on Enlargement and new Membership of the European Union*, NEMEU Working Paper, No. 96–6, University of Twente, the Netherlands.

Strange, Susan (1996), *The Retreat of the State: The Diffusion of Power in the World Economy*, Cambridge, Cambridge University Press.

Streeck, Wolfgang and Schmitter, Philippe C. (1991), 'From National Corporatism to Transnational Pluralism: Organised Interests in the Single European Market', *Politics and Society*, Vol. 19, pp. 133–64.

Sun, Jeanne-May and Pelkmans, Jacques (1995), 'Regulatory Competition in the Single Market', *Journal of Common Market Studies*, 33:1, 67–89.

Swyngedouw, E.A. (1994), 'De produktie van de Europese maatschappelijke ruimte', in W. Zonneveld and F. D'hondt (eds), *Europese ruimtelijke ordening: Impressies en visies vanuit Vlaanderen en Nederland*, Vlaamse Federatie voor Planologie, Nederlands Instituut voor Ruimtelijke Ordening en Volkshuisvesting, Gent, Den Haag, pp. 47–58.

Toura, Ben (1996), 'Denmark, Ireland and The Netherlands in EPC/CFSP, 1970–1996', unpublished doctoral dissertation, Trinity College, University of Dublin.

Toura, Ben, (1997), 'The Impact of Political Cooperation', in Kund Erik Jorgensen (ed.), *Reflective Approaches to European Governance*, London, Macmillan.

Tranholm-Mikkelson, Jeppe (1991), 'Neo-Functionalism: Obstinate or Obsolete? A Reappraisal in the Light of the New Dynamism of the European Community', *Millen-*

nium: Journal of International Studies, 20:1, 1–22.

Tsebelis, G. and Money, J. (1997), *Bicameralism*, Cambridge, Cambridge University Press.

Turner, M. (1998), 'Shake-up Planned for Complex EU Committee System', *European Voice*, 28 May, p. 2.

Van den Broeck, J., (1997), 'The Spatial Development Perspective for the Benelux', in W. Zonneveld and A. Faludi (eds), *Built Environment: Theme: Vanishing Borders: The Second Benelux Structural Outline*, 23:1, 14–26.

Van der Knaap, P. (1996), 'Government by Committee: Legal Typology, Quantitative Assessment and Institutional Repercussions of Committees in the European Union', in R.H. Pedler and G.F. Schaefer (eds), *Shaping European Law and Policy: The Role of Committees and Comitology in the Political Process*, Maastricht, European Institute of Public Administration (EIPA), pp. 83–116.

Van Schendelen, M.P.C.M. (1996), 'EC Committees: Influence Counts More than Legal Powers', in R.H. Pedler and G.F. Schaefer (eds), *Shaping European Law and Policy: The Role of Committees and Comitology in the Political Process*, Maastricht, European Institute for Public Administration, pp. 25–37.

Verdun, Amy (1996), 'An "Asymmetrical" Economic and Monetary Union in the EU: Perceptions of Monetary Authorities and Social Partners', *Revue d'Integration Européenne/Journal of European Integration*, 20:1, 59–81.

Verdun, Amy (1998a), 'The Increased Influence of the EU Monetary Institutional Framework in Determining Monetary Policies: A Trans-national Monetary Elite at Work', in B. Reinalda and B. Verbeek (eds), *Autonomous Policymaking by International Organisations*, London, Routledge, pp. 178–94.

Verdun, Amy (1998b), 'The Institutional Design of EMU: A Democratic Deficit?' *Journal of Public Policy*, 18:2, 178–94.

Verdun, Amy (1999), 'The Role of the Delors Committee in the Creation of EMU: An Epistemic Community?', *Journal of European Public Policy*, 6:2, 308–28.

Verdun, Amy (2000), *European Responses to Globalization and Financial Market Integration: Perceptions of Economic and Monetary Union in Britain, France and Germany*, Houndsmills, Basingstoke: Macmillan/New York: St. Martin's Press.

Verdun, Amy and Christiansen, Thomas (2000), 'Policy-making, Institution-building and European Monetary Union: Dilemmas of Legitimacy', in C. Crouch (ed), *After the Euro: Shaping Institutions for Governance in the Wake of European Monetary Union*, Oxford, Oxford University Press.

Vos, Ellen (1997), 'The Rise of Committees', *European Law Journal*, 3:3, 210–29.

Wallace, W. (1996) 'Has Government by Committee Lost the Public's Confidence?' in J. Hayward (ed.), *Elitism, Populism and European Politics*, Oxford, Clarendon Press, pp. 238–51.

Wallace, W. and Smith, J. (1995), 'Democracy or Technocracy? European Integration and the Problem of Popular Consent', *West European Politics*, 18:3, 137–57.

Weale, A. (1996) 'Environmental Rules and Rule-Making in the European Union', *Journal of European Public Policy*, 3: 4, 594–611.

Weber, Max (1966), *Staatssoziologie*, Berlin, Duncker and Humblot.

Weingast, B. and Moran, M. (1983), 'Bureaucratic Discretion or Congressional Control? Regulatory Policymaking by the Federal Trade Commission', *Journal of Political Economy*, 91:4, 775–800.

Wessels, Wolfgang (1990), 'Administrative Interaction', in W. Wallace (ed.), *The Dynam-*

ics of European Integration, London, Pinter, pp. 229–41.

Wessels, Wolfgang (1992), 'Staat und (west-europäische) Integration, Die Fusionsthese', in M. Kreile (ed.), *Die Integration Europas*, PVS-Sonderheft 23, Opladen, pp. 36–61.

Wessels, Wolfgang (1996), 'Verwaltung im EG-Mehrebenensystem: Auf dem Weg in die Megabürokratie?', in M. Jachtenfuchs and B. Kohler-Koch (eds), *Europäische Integration*, Opladen, Leske und Budrich, pp. 165–92.

Wessels, Wolfgang (1997a), 'A Corporatist Mega-Bureaucracy or an Open City? Brussels and the Growth and Differentiation of Multi-level Networks', in H. Wallace and A.R.Young (eds), *Participation and Policy-making in the European Union*, Oxford, Clarendon Press.

Wessels, Wolfgang (1997b), 'An Ever Closer Fusion? A Dynamic Macropolitical View on Integration Processes', *Journal of Common Market Studies*, 35:2, 267–99.

Wessels, Wolfgang (1998), 'Comitology: Fusion in Action. Politico-administrative Trends in the EU system', *Journal of European Public Policy*, 5: 2, 209–34.

Wessels, Wolfgang and Rometsch, Dietrich (eds) (1996), *The European Union and Member States, Towards Institutional Fusion?*, Manchester, Manchester University Press.

Westlake, Martin (1995), *The Council of the European Union*, London, Cartermill.

Wheare, K.C. (1979), *Government by Committee*, London, Greenwood Press.

Wilks, Stephen (1996), 'Regulatory Compliance and Capitalist Diversity in Europe', *Journal of European Public Policy*, 3:4, 536–59.

Williams, R.H. (1996), *European Union Spatial Policy and Planning*, London, Paul Chapman Publishing.

Woolcock, S. and Hodges, M. (1996), 'EC policy in the Uruguay Round', in H. Wallace and W. Wallace (eds), *Policy-making in the European Union*, Oxford, Oxford University Press, pp. 301–24.

Woolley, J.T. (1992), 'Policy Credibility and European Monetary Institutions', in A.M. Sbragia (ed.), *Europolitics: Institutions and Policy-making in the 'New' European Community*, Washington, DC, Brookings Institution, pp. 157–90.

Wright, Vincent (1992), 'The Administrative System and Market Regulation in Western Europe: Continuities, Exceptionalism and Convergence', *Rivista trimestrale de diritto pubblico*, 4/1992, pp. 1026–41.

Wright, Vincent (1994), 'Reshaping the State: The Implications for Public Administration', *West European Politics*, 17:3, 102–37.

Yee, A. (1996), 'The Causal Effects of Ideas on Policies', *International Organisation*, 50:1, 69–108.

Zellentin, Gerda (1992), 'Der Funktionalismus: eine Strategie gesamteuropäischer Integration?', in M. Kreile (ed.), *Die Integration Europea*, PVS Sonderheft 23, Opladen, pp. 62–77.

Zonneveld, W. (1989), 'Conceptual Complexes and Shifts in Post-War Urban Planning in the Netherlands', in A. Faludi (ed.), *Built Environment: Special Issue: Keeping the Netherlands in Shape*, 15:1, 40–8.

Zonneveld, W. and Faludi, A. (1998), *Europese integratie en de Nederlandse ruimtelijke ordening (V102, Voorstudies en achtergronden)*, Wetenschappelijke Raad voor het Regeringsbeleid, Sdu uitgevers, Den Haag.

Zonneveld, W., Faludi, A. (1997), 'Vanishing Borders: The Second Benelux Structural Outline: Introduction', in W. Zonneveld and A. Faludi (eds), *Built Environment; Theme: Vanishing Borders: The Second Benelux Structural Outline*, 23:1, 5–13.

Environment Committee 80–3
epistemic communities 20, 87, 138–40
EURATOM 105
European Cartel Office 75
European Central Bank (ECB) 33, 75, 132, 136, 141, 163, 166–7
European Coal and Steel Community (ECSC) 13, 15, 34, 105
European Commission
  DG I 36
  DG IA 36, 157
  DG XI 81, 83–4, 85
  DG XVI 120–1, 123, 127, 128
  Legal Service 123
  rule making 62–4
European Court of Justice (ECJ) 103
European Environment Bureau (EEB) 85, 96
European Monetary Institute (EMI), 133
European Monetary System (EMS) 135, 138
European Monetary Union (EMU) 60, 133, 137, 141, 142
European Parliament
  comitology system 68–77
  demands 74–7
  oversight 63–5
  participation 93, 100, 106
European Political Cooperation (EPC) 99, 104, 145, 147, 148, 152–3
  Secretariat 154–5
  see also Common Foreign and Security Policy
European Regional Development Fund (ERDF) 118, 119–20
European Spatial Development Perspective (ESDP) 7, 116, 120, 122–3, 124–5, 126, 128–9
European Spatial Planning Observatory Network (ESPON) 127, 130
  see also Committee on Spatial Development
Exchange Rate Mechanism (ERM) 135, 138

functional cooperation 30, 31–2
functional effectiveness 165–7
fusion theory 33

General Affairs Council (GAC) 109, 154–5

General Agreement on Tarriffs and Trade (GATT) 98, 103, 105, 107, 108, 110–11, 112
  see also World Trade Organisation
Genetically Modified Organisms 88–90, 91–2, 95
  Directive 55
de Giovanni Report 72

Hass, E. 31
Helms–Burton Act 111

institutional vacuum 117–20
integration theories 27–9
International Labour Organisation (ILO) 105
Interreg programme 130

Justice and Home Affairs (JHA) 99

K3 committee 5

legislative framework 63
lobby groups 40
Luxembourg Report 149–52

Maastricht Treaty 6, 17, 42, 63, 71–2, 77, 99, 103, 104, 105, 149, 153, 161
Modus Vivendi agreement 72–3
Molitor Committee 85, 96
Monetary Committee 5, 6, 20, 133–8, 139, 140, 142, 143
monetary policy 20, 132–4
Monnet method 163–4
Monsanto 88, 89, 90
Monti, M. 84
multi-level governance 10–11, 23–6, 32–4

neo-functionalism 31–2
Non-Governmental Organisations (NGOs) 40, 85, 149
Noordwijk Council 116, 122, 125, 129
Novartis 89, 90, 91
Novel Foods Regulation 89

Packaging Waste Directive 80, 82–3
parliamentary oversight 65
  Germany 65–8, 76–7
  United States 65–8